CITYBOY

BEER AND LOATHING
IN THE SQUARE MILE

CITYBOY

BEER AND LOATHING IN THE SQUARE MILE

Geraint Anderson

headline

First published in 2008 by
HEADLINE PUBLISHING GROUP

5

Cataloguing in Publication Data is available from the British Library

Hardback ISBN 978 0 7553 4616 5
Trade paperback ISBN 978 0 7553 4617 2

Typeset in Scala by Avon DataSet Ltd, Bidford on Avon, Warwickshire

Printed and bound in the UK by
CPI Mackays, Chatham ME5 8TD

Headline's policy is to use papers that are natural, renewable and recyclable
products and made from wood grown in sustainable forests. The logging and
manufacturing processes are expected to conform to the environmental
regulations of the country of origin.

HEADLINE PUBLISHING GROUP
An Hachette Livre UK Company
338 Euston Road
London NW1 3BH

www.headline.co.uk
www.hachettelivre.co.uk

In loving memory of Andy.
He was the best of us.

WHO IS CITYBOY?

He's every brash, bespoke-suited, *FT*-carrying idiot who pushed past you on the tube. He's the egotistical buffoon who loudly brags about how much cash he's made on the market at otherwise pleasant dinner parties. He's the greedy, ruthless wanker whose actions are helping turn this world into the shit-hole it's rapidly becoming.

For one period in my life, he was me.

Disclaimer:

While this book is true in the sense of being an accurate depiction of a certain kind of career in the City, none of the characters or institutions portrayed are in any way based on real people or banks and any similarity is purely coincidental. Just as 'Steve Jones' is not me, so the characters in this book are made up – they are not any particular person, but are instead classic City types, and are hopefully recognisable as such. Although real people and places are referred to throughout the book, they are intermingled with the fictional people and events that make up the story.

So, it is not just that names and places have been changed to protect the innocent (or guilty), it is also that my target has never been any specific individual or institution, but rather the culture of the City as a whole.

PROLOGUE
(The Cokehead)

With hindsight, it was that fifth glass of absinthe that cost my bank £1.2 million. A few Sunday evening pints of Old Thumper at the Masons had somehow graduated into the kind of old-school booze-up a twenty-nine-year-old stockbroker should know better than to indulge in. While still at the pub some comedian had called up The Dealer and a couple of grams of Bolivia's finest had arrived by scooter. As I took my turn to trundle into the cubicle and press the crisp rolled twenty into my hungry nostrils I thanked God that the next day was a bank holiday Monday. Soon my three esteemed peers were talking nonsense like it was going out of fashion while I slouched in the pub's finest leather armchair in a content and familiar state of auto-pilot oblivion.

To this day, how we all ended up back at Sam's remains a mystery. All I know is that things were getting out of control big time even before that foul-tasting green liquid made an appearance. Sam was living up to his reputation of being the host with the most and my three jobless, loser pals were doing what they do best – hedonistic self-indulgence. By around 5 a.m. The

Dealer had graced us with his presence twice more and coherent speech was proving sporadic at best. Everyone seated around Sam's grandmother's ancient dinner table covered in the conventional detritus of a good old-fashioned knees-up had exhibited the usual mood swings that a serious gak session invariably provided. It was while I was in a somewhat edgy, tense dip that I decided to try and say something to remind my mates that I existed. I thought I'd start with something trite and move on from there.

'Boys, all I can say is thank fuck it's a bank holiday today!'

For some sick and paranoia-inducing reason my mates all immediately stopped their speedy banter, turned around and, as one, cracked up in my face like maniacal banshees. Dope dealer and 'artist' Jim was the first to get his insane cackling laughter under control and, with what seemed like a madman's gleeful delight, shouted out: 'You fucking idiot! That's next week!'

'Don't wind me up, you tart,' I said with a false nonchalance that I knew everyone in the room could see right though. My rictus grin and nervous eyes wouldn't have looked out of place on a guilty teenager talking to his parents while hiding a cigarette behind his back.

'No, mate, today is the eighteenth, and the bank holiday Monday is on the twenty-fifth,' said Nick – the third member of 'Losers Anonymous'. How the fuck he knew so much about this shit when he hadn't done an honest day's work since 1992 was beyond me. But there was something in his confident tone that couldn't just be explained by his hooter being filled with enough bugle to keep the Colombian army marching for two weeks.

'Oh fuck, I've got to be at work in one hour. The Genius is on holiday and I look like a smackhead.' I can't remember whether I thought that or said it. All I know is that within what seemed like seconds I was running the mile down the road towards my pad with my heart feeling like Mike Tyson had been giving me CPR for the last four hours. I struggled with the keys in my door, ran upstairs and jumped in the shower. With my hair still glistening wet I slipped on my Thomas Pink shirt and was still struggling to put my Gieves and Hawkes suit jacket on as I left the house.

During the seemingly endless journey on the Central Line I occasionally caught the reflection of my face in the dark windows of the train and even from this imperfect image I could tell I looked like shit warmed up. Reading the *Financial Times*, twitchy and nervous and taking in none of the words, I began to wonder whether I should have just taken a sicky. This beautiful thought only entered my drug-addled brain around Oxford Circus but by then I was already halfway to work. Only some strange, probably misplaced, loyalty to my team-mates prevented me leaping off the train and swapping platforms. Despite the film of cold sweat on my forehead I thought I could probably style it out after a couple of coffees provided there was fuck all going on in my sector. I entered my building, swiped my way through the security barriers, and took the lift to the fourth floor. I walked though the huge open-plan office to my desk at precisely 6.55 a.m. and did not falter despite a highly unamusing 'Good weekend, was it?' from a pathetic little shit of a colleague who clearly saw me for the gibbering wreck that I was. I had five minutes to check out the Reuters headlines in my sector but, in reality, these were just spent praying to the big man upstairs that NOTHING WAS GOING TO HAPPEN IN MY FUCKING SECTOR.

When I saw the red headlines appearing on one of my two head-level screens at exactly 7 a.m. informing me that a power station owned by Scottishpower had blown up in Utah I could feel the life drain out of me. Before long toxin-filled sweat was making my shirt damp under the arms and around the chest and I felt unable to breathe properly. Christ almighty, of all the fucking things to happen nothing could be worse. My colleague, The Genius, was away on holiday and I was looking after the companies he analysed in his absence. Scottishpower was one of his key Buy recommendations in the sector we covered and some serious shit had clearly happened in a state run by effing Mormons thousands of miles from my confused little brain.

Barely a minute passed before my phone rang. Before I even looked at the digital caller display I knew it would be my wide-boy trader Gary asking me how he should position himself for the market opening at 8 a.m. Like a rabbit in the headlights I just stared at the flashing phone for what seemed like hours and only when colleagues began to look up at me did I summon the courage to pick up the receiver. As a research analyst on the utilities sector, informing Gary how the shares he traded would respond to newsflow was a fundamental part of my role, so sitting there like a lemon was not really an option.

With a false confidence that impressed even me I told Gary in no uncertain terms: 'This is only a four- or five-pence event. It's a four-hundred-and-thirty megawatt generation unit that's going to be out of action for around five months. It's currently making about one million dollars a day so if we tax that at, let's say, thirty-five per cent that means Scottishpower's gonna be missing out on approximately a hundred and three million dollars, i.e. around sixty-seven million pounds sterling assuming a constant exchange rate of one point four five. If we divide that by one thousand, eight hundred and thirty million shares that equates to four pence a share.'

Gary clearly bought it and after putting the receiver down I let out a huge sigh of relief while giving myself a major metaphorical pat on the back.

Just when I thought things were beginning to calm down the phone trilled again and this time I saw James Smythe's name flash up. This posh buffoon was in charge of arranging the 7.20 a.m. morning meeting at which analysts informed traders and salesmen about the price-sensitive developments in their sector or the research notes they'd recently written.

'Steve, you'd better come down immediately and give us two minutes on the mike about this Scottishpower incident.' His slimy, cultured tones irritated the fuck out of me. I knew I couldn't argue and immediately got up and began marching to the lifts – the cocaine in my system ensuring that I looked twitchy and wired the whole time.

There are few things like the buzz on a major investment bank's trading floor on a Monday morning just before the market opens. In a huge open-plan floor the size of a football pitch, hundreds of traders, salesmen, market makers and sales traders all sit behind six screens desperate to hear or see something that could give them the edge over thousands of other competitors in banks across the world during that anxious half-hour. Some speak in frenzied tones into two different receivers while others shout across to each other a series of numbers and terms unintelligible to anyone not involved in this soul-destroying business. The all-powerful urge to make money permeates every action and every shouted instruction and is only matched by the fear of losing vast amounts of cash from an ill-thought-out decision. The tension is made even more extreme because everyone around you can see and sense everything you're doing. The 'market' is an uncontrollable bucking bronco and you are just another rider trying to hold on for dear life and make a quid or two while you're at it.

I rushed towards the lectern just as the analyst before me finished speaking and, white as a sheet, with my eyes popping out of my head and a soaking shirt, I steadied myself and began to speak in a slow, measured tone to the hundreds of busy bees surrounding me about what had just happened. As I did so I occasionally looked up to see my pale, nervous face magnified to three times its size on the screens that dropped down from the ceiling at regular intervals across the floor. Traders and salesmen at our offices in Frankfurt, Milan, Paris and Madrid would all be watching my performance and our colleagues in New York would watch a recording of my words of wisdom five hours from now.

It was when I got to the valuation implications of the accident that I suddenly noticed that the usual noise and buzz of the floor had dramatically declined. I saw salesmen nudging each other and pointing towards me, and before long everyone in the desks around me had stopped working and were simply staring in my direction. A couple of secretaries covered their mouths in an almost theatrical display of shock while some of the more laddish chaps were cracking up. WHAT THE FUCK WAS GOING ON? I began to have a near-out-of-body experience as the drugs mixed with the stress literally made me feel as if I was in a dream – or, to be more accurate, a bloody nightmare.

It was in this horrific, surreal state that I must have looked up at the suspended screen immediately in front of me. At almost the exact moment that I noticed the large stream of blood exiting my right nostril magnified to three times its size and played out across Europe I felt it drip on to my lower lip and then on to my shirt. In a spontaneous reaction I pinched my nostrils together with thumb and forefinger and ran towards the bogs, pushing James Smythe out of the way with my free hand and leaving the trading floor in a state of shock and bemusement.

After stuffing some bog roll up my nostril I tried to steady myself and walked slowly up to my floor. As I tried to non-chalantly walk back to my chair a standing ovation broke out amongst my colleagues seated immediately around me. Some wag shouted, 'Just back from Colombia, are you?' while another asked, 'Or were you hanging out with Keith Richards this week-end?' I gave a theatrical bow complete with fluttering hand movement but despite all my fake bravado I, and everyone else, knew that this was going to take a long time to recover from.

At exactly 8.05 a.m. shares in Scottishpower were down ten pence. Gary rang up and in his inimitable way shouted at me, 'You said this is a four-pence issue, right? We should have a few down at these levels, right?' Sticking by my own rule of feigning confidence no matter how much doubt I felt, I said, 'You're damn right. Fill your boots, mate.'

Twenty minutes later the shares were down twenty pence. A now extremely irate Gary called back.

'What the fuck is going on? I've bought five-point-two million shares and they're tanking. What do I do now, dick-splash?'

With my voice cracking and my legs nervously tapping underneath the desk I tried to bullshit him again: 'Hold steady, geezer, them buyers are gonna come in soon.' I was now absolutely covered in sweat and I was biting my bottom lip.

But this time I could sense that he could tell that I was fucked and all my confidence drained out of me. Like one of the living dead I began to call up my clients in a half-hearted attempt to convince them to buy the shares and so support the stock.

But the buyers never came. Although shares in Scottishpower ended the day down only eighteen pence, Gary had panicked and sold his entire holding at the lowest possible level, when they were twenty-three pence down. The Utah incident had made the market attribute a huge risk premium to Scottishpower's entire fleet of US power stations and this had destroyed the perceived value of the shares. That's why I lost my bank £1.2 million.

It was during my third half-arsed attempt to convince some dismissive client that the market had overreacted that my secretary's phone rang. And as I looked across at her like a punch-drunk boxer, I knew before she had even opened her mouth what she was about to say.

'The boss wants to see you *right now*.'

I mumbled some unintelligible reply and like a condemned man about to face the firing squad raised myself weakly from my chair and stumbled towards the big man's office. On the walk over I could feel all eyes were on me and though I held my head up high pretending everything was cool all I wanted to do was swerve to the right, to the lifts and from there to freedom. My head pounded, I was as white as a sheet, sweat beaded my forehead and I was unbelievably fucking exhausted. It took a gargantuan effort to hold back the tears from flooding my bloodshot eyes as I approached his glass office. When I saw the boss's puce angry face staring at me from within I knew this was going to be a really, really fucking long day . . .

Knowing what I know now about the hideous shit that would happen to me during the four years after this incident I just wish that corpulent corporate cocksucker had sacked me there and then. Hell, I wish those crazy Mormon fucks had accidentally blown up another power station and that I had proved equally useless and been given half an hour to pack a black bag and piss off. That way I wouldn't have done things that still make it hard for me to look at myself in the mirror. I wouldn't have become all-consumed by the meaningless shit that Cityboys live by and turned into someone my friends and family hardly recognised. I wouldn't have become part of a system that is irreversibly making your world a less pleasant place to live in. I wouldn't have lost my mind.

Still, sitting here listening to the gentle sound of waves lapping on the shore, with a glass of chai in one hand and a joint in another, I am comforted by the realisation that this is pay-back time. I'm going to break the code of silence that governs everyone in the Square Mile and reveal what really makes the City tick. I want to illuminate the murky underbelly of this tight-knit club that is solely dedicated to making its members as much money as humanly possible. I want to expose the City's many vices to 'civilians' who are purposefully kept in the dark so that greedy Cityboys can perpetuate their own privileged lifestyles.

CITYBOY

As for me, I gain strength from Nietzsche's adage 'that which does not kill you makes you stronger'. And after all the shit I went through in that ridiculous business I must be the strongest motherfucker in town.

1

THE GURU

Everybody sells their soul to the devil . . . I just decided that I'd get a damn good price for mine. On a warm July evening in 1996 I was walking down Bishopsgate steadying myself for a meeting with a man who would change my life. Just as Luke Skywalker needed Yoda and King Arthur needed Merlin, fate had decreed that I would meet and learn from David Flynn. Little did I know then, but this great man would show me the tricks needed to thrive in this dreadful business while also ensuring that my corrupt side was cultivated successfully. Admittedly, this second task was made relatively simple by my natural propensity for the principal vices available on this planet.

I had spent the previous day having my ludicrous ponytail cut off by the local barber. I had also ceremoniously removed my three hoop earrings and solemnly shaved off my preposterous bum-fluff goatee in a symbolic ritual of 'growing up'. After putting on a second-hand suit I'd bought for six pounds at a charity shop I almost passed for a young, lean stockbroker – albeit an extremely poor and unsuccessful one (not necessarily a good look). Even in my complete ignorance about what the hell I was letting myself in for I knew that any clues about my hippy background would not go down too well in a world of pinstripe suits and 'sensible' haircuts. Now, when I look back at all the positive and negative consequences of my fateful decision to become a stockbroker, I can say with my hand on my heart that the premature termination of a hairstyle that made me resemble a German exchange student circa 1987 was unequivocally a major positive. Although the deep psychological trauma I would suffer as a result of my career choice somewhat clouds my current perception of my City experience, this surely was an indisputable silver lining.

But this look was not a mere façade – I was a genuine hippy back then, and a left-wing one to boot. I was obsessed by films and quotes from films and had never really thought once about the world of finance. I remember that some acquaintances in my final year at Cambridge had mentioned visiting investment bank stalls during the 'milk round' (the annual recruitment fair held by major corporations designed to attract bright students), but I was too busy smoking puff on punts bound for Grantchester for such tedious nonsense. Also, my father had been a prominent member of the Labour Party and had encouraged me to get involved in grass-roots activism from an early age. Admittedly, my political militancy took a bit of a back seat after I spent my gap year losing my marbles smoking weed in Asia. At Cambridge I merely graduated on to pills and speed and got seriously involved in the local rave scene. After somehow leaving with a 2:1 degree in history I thought I'd avoid reality for another year and so went back to Asia for six more months of debauchery. Again, I lost the plot and this time became so deranged that I decided that I would spend the next five years selling Asian trinkets that I'd bought in Delhi across European street markets. When I'd arrived back at Heathrow with four huge bags of this crap to sell, my parents were understandably concerned – especially since I'd managed to lose three stone while gallivanting around the Himalayas.

Fortunately for my parents, and my poor, befuddled little brain, I had also decided to pursue a year-long MA studying revolutions at Sussex University in Brighton before setting off on my grand adventure. My twisted logic was that I needed to learn karate, Spanish and how to drive if I was to survive as a global traveller, and that university was the best place to achieve these noble ambitions. My fetid fantasies that impressionable undergraduate girls would fall at the feet of a worldly-wise traveller like me may also have had something to do with it. It is with the benefit of hindsight that I can now conclude it was that moody ponytail that ensured those fantasies remained largely unfulfilled.

It was during this rather confusing period that my brother called me and completely changed the direction my life was to take. I think we can safely say that my parents had cajoled him into sorting out his rebellious younger brother and to this day I'm not sure whether to thank him or beat the shit out of him for doing so. My brother had been working in the City for a few years as a fund manager and was so straight that our interaction was always like two worlds colliding. The conversation went something like this:

'Hi, Steve, it's John.'

'All right, mate, how's it going?'

'Fine. Listen, let's cut to the chase – you're not still pursuing that ridiculous plan to sell crap around the world, are you? I mean, what are you actually going to do with your life?'

'Good question. Dunno. Doing a course I'm not really into, failing to pull birds and unsure if my plan to "sell crap around the world", as you call it, really holds water.'

'I can get you an interview at an investment bank if you're interested.'

'Er . . . fuck it, why not? I'll give it a bash. What do investment banks do, anyway?'

'Don't worry about that. Come to London next Thursday and

I'll sort out an interview with a French bank called Banque Inutile.'

My brother was able to arrange this because he was a client of Banque Inutile. As I would later learn there is no better way of securing business as a stockbroker than providing employment for a client's sibling. Once you've done that their indebtedness means that you've really got them by the short and curlies. Unless John's sales contact at Banque Inutile had at least gone through the motions of securing an interview he could have jeopardised his relationship with my brother. Although things have changed somewhat now, getting your foot in the door then was all about who you knew and not what you knew . . . and thank fuck for that because at the time the closest I'd come to a banker was asking some clown behind the desk at Barclays for an increase to my overdraft limit.

Having said that, I didn't go into that interview totally blind. Oh no, on Wednesday evening my brother gave me a ten-minute crash course in investment banking. Here is a summary of his salient points:

1. The City is a huge market place where people who want to invest money for a return meet people who want money invested in their companies (I'm down with that . . . so far so good).
2. Shares go up and down simply as a result of supply and demand. If there are more buyers than sellers then they will go up and visa versa (cool, I'm still with you).
3. The value of a share reflects the future cash flow of that company discounted to today by the cost of capital divided by the number of shares (no, sorry, we were doing quite well there for a minute but you've really lost me now . . . however, since I don't want to look retarded in front of my older sibling I'm not going to say anything and instead nod sagely).

4. The two main metrics for valuing shares are the price-earnings ratio, or PE, which is calculated by dividing the share price by the net profits attributable to that share and the divided yield which is calculated by dividing the dividend by the share price (yeah, whatever).
5. Bonds are basically IOU notes (that Clint Eastwood movie's on in about five minutes).
6. Em . . . that's basically it (thank fuck for that).

I think that it was probably the way my eyes were glazing over that must have given him a clue that not only did I hardly understand what he was banging on about but I was also beginning to wonder why I'd come up to London in the first place. I was also regretting the whole forced image change that I had undergone and the three pints of lager that I would have to forego as a result of buying that appalling suit.

In a fit of despair, John said: 'Look, I'm going to look like a proper tool if you don't at least look like a vaguely plausible candidate. So when the going gets tough and David asks you about your thoughts on how you see financial analysis progressing, say pretty much exactly what I'm going to tell you now.'

'OK, mate.'

'I think that PE ratios are looking increasingly outdated. Earnings can be so easily manipulated by cunning finance directors that they are almost meaningless – as revealed in Terry Smith's recent book *Accounting for Growth*. I believe that until financial statements become more robust it will be movements in free cash flow that begin to dictate share-price performance.'

I nodded wisely and stroked my newly bald chin as if I had the slightest clue what he was rabbiting on about. All I knew was that *Magnum Force* had started two minutes ago and that Big Bad Clint waits for no man.

*

At precisely five minutes to 6 p.m. the next day, as I approached my destination on Bishopsgate, I began to question the rather unusual venue for this all-important interview. Admittedly, I didn't know much about City practices but some dreadful bar called The Moon Under Water certainly didn't strike me as the kind of place I could truly reveal my expertise in all matters financial. Surely this was some kind of piss-take, considering the tremendous amount of diligent hard work that I had put into preparing for this meeting? Were these comedians really serious about potentially offering me a high-powered job in the City? I dismissed these thoughts as silly, took a deep breath to calm my unexpectedly frantic heartbeat and stepped into the noisy, smoky bar.

The scene I beheld as I opened the doors was as alien to me as a nineteenth-century opium den. Hundreds of men in smart navy blue suits stood around shouting at each other. Nearly all of them were white and most were under forty. The vast majority were still wearing gaudy ties with big, thick Windsor knots although some of the more rakish chaps had taken theirs off. There were about seven women who, irrespective of looks, had groups of lecherous men surrounding them. Most stood out like sore thumbs because they had dared to wear outfits of a colour other than navy blue or black. There was a thick fog of cigarette and cigar smoke and a high proportion of the tables supported orange ice buckets containing champagne bottles. There didn't seem to be a single pair of trainers, combat trousers or tracksuit bottoms in the whole establishment. There were about three black people but two of them were behind the bar. The extraordinarily loud chatter seemed to somehow exude confidence in a way that was intimidating to the uninitiated. Every few seconds someone would laugh incredibly loudly – so loudly that it was as if they were putting it on. Heads rocked back with loud guffaws in a way that reflected a degree of self-satisfaction that I could only dream of. The student bar at Sussex University it most certainly was not. Nor, for that matter, was it a beach bar on Had Rin beach.

Ignoring an urge to immediately hightail it out of there I sought out Banque Inutile's head of equities, David Flynn. My brother had given me a simple description but one that served its purpose well: 'David looks like a tall, brunette version of Henry the Eighth after he's been on the all-pie diet' (a diet I would later find was surprisingly popular amongst brokers despite being notoriously unsuccessful). Soon enough I spied the great man holding court in the corner with a bunch of his underlings. As I nervously approached the raised table he stood at, taking in the sycophantic looks of his disciples, I marvelled at my brother's perspicacity. David did indeed look just like a large version of Henry the Eighth, albeit with dark hair and an even larger belly. But there was also something in his gait, his regal stance and mischievous eyes that almost convinced me that I was meeting, if not the gluttonous Tudor royal, then some kind of modern-day reincarnation. He was clearly a man of enormous appetites and extremely loose morals.

I sidled up to this latter-day king and waited for his head to swing round in my general direction. After what seemed like an eternity he languidly did so and as his eyes caught mine I pushed my hand towards him saying, 'Steve Jones – brother of John. Here for the interview.' He looked me up and down, making me incredibly self-conscious. He seemed to take in my entire personality in about four seconds and I couldn't help but feel that almost immediately he saw me for the chancer I was. Was it just me, or could he tell that upon my chin not twenty-four hours before rested a moody goatee, that in those ears had been three silver hoop earrings, and that upon those shoulders had lain a German exchange student-like ponytail? He could certainly tell that the suit I was wearing was more appropriate for a salesman at Burtons than an up-and-coming star of financial services, but then I think the chaps behind the bar had probably clocked that before I'd even entered the building.

'So, you want to be a research analyst, do you?' he said in his low, soft voice, almost laughing as he did so. His underlings seemed to be waiting to crack up at his every sentence, making me as edgy as a ginger kid in an orphanage.

'Oh yes, I've wanted to be an analyst since school. It's always been my ambition,' I said, desperately trying to keep a straight face.

'Really? How very sad for you. And what have you done to fulfil that ambition? Your CV suggests that you have been under the misapprehension that smoking dope on beaches in Asia was the quickest route to becoming a banker.' Despite his keeping a straight face, something his fan club failed to do, his eyes seemed to be mocking my every utterance.

'Well, firstly I have to say that I didn't indulge in any drug-taking while I was abroad.' At this point he subtly raised a quizzical eyebrow that in a single blow succeeded in making me blush, something I hadn't done since my schooldays.

'Secondly, I've done a lot of travelling since I felt that I should get it out of my system because once I've entered the Square Mile I know hard work will put paid to fun for a bit.'

'So, you don't think working under me will be fun?'

'Well, I imagine the first years of my life as an analyst will be more hard work than fun,' I spluttered.

This wasn't going well at all. I was almost ready to call it a day there and then but my pride made me stay and endure this gentle, unrelenting mockery. After a few more incisive piss-take questions about my motivation and plans I began to relax knowing that this whole experience was a complete waste of his and my time. I was on the point of apologising and making my excuses and leaving when suddenly, from nowhere, I heard those beautiful and strangely familiar words: 'And where do you see financial analysis progressing over the next few years?'

As he began to speak these words I willed out the sentence that I longed to hear. With an almost unnatural haste, and speaking in a somewhat monotone voice that could have given away the fact that I had a pre-prepared answer, I delivered my brother's spiel.

David paused, looked me up and down as if appraising me and said, 'Interesting . . . now let's stop this nonsense and have a few bevvies.'

My relief was palpable. Hell, even the dickheads surrounding David seemed impressed with the answer. Some of them even seemed to get into a discussion about it and, to my horror, one even asked my opinion about how best free cash flow should be calculated. I pretended to mishear him and at the same time sloped off to the gents'. During what can only be described as one of the most satisfying slashes I'd had in my twenty-four years up to that point I couldn't help but grin to myself as I looked down at the urinal. Indeed, I had such a big cheesy smile on my face that I think the chap next to me must have wondered what it was I held in my hand that had given me such tremendous happiness to behold.

The 'interview' only ended after David and I had consumed at least two bottles of champagne each. As I rolled back west on the tube having barely been able to walk the fifty yards to Liverpool Street station, his last words rang in my ears.

'If you want me to be honest with you, you had the job five minutes into the interview. We need sharp, cocky dickheads and you fit the bill nicely. Besides, I like you. You almost blew it with all that crap about PE ratios and free cash flow but I'll let you off this time. Never, ever bullshit a bullshitter – especially one as good as me.' With his wise words still reverberating around my inebriated brain I went to sleep happy in the knowledge that what he wanted was someone who could talk crap and drink – two things I'd been doing extremely proficiently pretty much all my life.

*

Before I set off on my City career there was the small matter of completing my Masters dissertation on the French riots of 1968. I wasn't sure how a 25,000-word essay entitled 'French Workers and Students in May 1968 – A Study of an Ambiguous Relationship' was going to improve my life, my career prospects or, indeed, get me laid, but some residue of guilt I felt towards my parents who had paid for the course made me complete it. I eventually sent my hastily written Magnus Opus to Sussex University on 8 August 1996 and, much to my amazement, found out a few months later that it had passed.

The day after I sent off my dissertation, I was trundling east along the Central Line at the ungodly time of 6.30 a.m. Although my fellow Cityboys and -girls on the tube who glanced up from their *Financial Times* and checked out my cheap and nasty Terylene suit may have assumed that I was heading for some branch of Burtons to take up my position as a junior salesman, I knew different. OH YES . . . I WAS GOING TO BE A GODDAM STOCKBROKER . . . whatever that was. I sleepily walked out of Bank tube station at 6.50 a.m. wondering what the hell awaited me and nervously headed towards the twelve-storey office block that housed the esteemed Banque Inutile. I passed venerable old buildings and imposing modern monoliths and tried to keep up with the clearly stressed-out suited City workers who were all rushing in to work. As I approached the menacing building with butterflies in my stomach partying like it was 1999 a corrupted song lyric played itself in my head on a continual loop: 'Hey diddly dee, a broker's life for me.'

This had the strange effect of calming me down and somehow made the whole experience more bearable. After picking up my security pass I made my way to the twelfth floor and, after a deep breath, entered what would be my home for the next two and a half years. I knew I would be relatively well received because my brother had given Banque Inutile a gargantuan order the day before I had joined as a sign of his gratitude. That was a very early lesson for me of just how the City works.

The main floor of Banque Inutile's investment banking division was split down the middle into two distinct open-plan sections. On one side sat the research analysts staring at Excel spreadsheets on one of the two screens in front of them. The other screen was usually occupied with either a research note they were working on to send to clients or a Reuters screen displaying the breaking news for their sector and the market as a whole. This side of the building was relatively quiet and had the air of a studious library. Although analysts in the mid-1990s did talk to clients, they did so much less than they do nowadays. Back then their main role was to produce money-making ideas for the salesmen and traders on the other side of the building to market. To this end they would tirelessly compose financial models of the publicly listed companies that they analysed with a view to deciding if their shares were expensive, and hence a 'Sell', or cheap, and hence a 'Buy'. I was informed that this would be where I would be sitting – surrounded by the other 'teenage scribblers', as Nigel Lawson had dismissed types like us a decade before. Within the bank itself we were referred to as the 'rocket scientists' and these were the people I was introduced to on my first day – a bunch of mainly Oxbridge-educated numerate geeks, most of whom seemed to have had a charisma bypass operation at birth. Great, I couldn't wait – it promised to be a right barrel of laughs.

On the other side of the building was the much rowdier trading floor. Even the trading floor of a relatively small house like Banque Inutile was humming with frenzied activity at 7.15 a.m. on a Monday morning. This anticipatory buzz strangely reminded me of the five minutes before the start at a football match . . . although since I support Queens Park Rangers that may not be saying much. Here, salesmen shouted down the phone at their clients about how the market and specific shares were likely to behave that morning. Behind the salesmen sat the traders and market makers whose job it was to offer to buy and sell shares at a specific price. These mainly obese Essex boys were a formidable unit. Seniority seemed to be decided by the size of their pot bellies and analysts would approach them with extreme caution. Although most of them lacked a university education their sharpness of thought (often inherited from barrow-boy market-trader fathers) meant you needed balls like water melons to take them on in a verbal joust. They hated condescending, arrogant analysts with a passion only equalled by their love of pies and making a fast buck. Very early on in my career I witnessed the public humiliation of an egotistical dick of a colleague which ensured I wouldn't make the same mistake myself.

I was talking to my trader, Tony, when we both overheard the analyst on the banks sector getting into some kind of contretemps with his own trader. God knows what it was about but it ended with the analyst posing the valid, but not necessarily very polite, question: 'Anyway, Daryl, why are you such a fat bastard?' Daryl slowly swung round in his chair and, with perfect comic timing, delivered the only possible response under the circumstances: 'Because every time I fuck your wife she gives me a biscuit.'

Daryl's answer may not have had the wit of Oscar Wilde or Noël Coward but all his fellow traders cracked up and that was all that mattered. The analyst spluttered some unheard response, blushed and then tried to laugh along in a nervous, half-hearted way. He knew that he'd just had his arse whipped publicly and left with his tail between his legs as soon as practically possible. I'd never liked this notorious James Blunt anyway and could barely stifle my own laughter. There were two important take-home points from this encounter:

1. Don't fuck with the traders.
2. Playground banter is one of the most important skills in investment banking.

I like to think that I have a natural propensity for taking the piss and not flapping when I'm having the piss taken out of me. It seemed that these two skills were more important than diligence or analytical ability in gaining the respect of the trading floor, which was vital if I was to be trusted and hence introduced to important clients. All this was music to my ears.

However, it was this analysis shit I was supposed to be doing that was a little more worrying. I hadn't studied maths since I was fifteen and it was clear that my ignorance would be exposed fairly soon. Although I didn't know much about maths I did know that spreadsheets and mathematical formulae were not as susceptible as human beings to the kind of blagging that I was reasonably proficient at.

Still, these issues were not a problem on that first day. A friendly graduate from the insurance sector's team showed me where the toilets and coffee machines were and introduced me to the forty or so other analysts on my part of the floor. I was told forty different names and didn't remember a single one. Despite the fact that I would work at Banque Inutile for over two years I would still only ever know around half the people's names on my side of the building (and even fewer on the trading floor) by the time I left. This was not only because of my Alzheimer-like ability to forget someone's name immediately on hearing it but because each sector team had little reason to interact with any other. Occasionally, we would talk to the oil team about their oil-price forecasts (which we'd generally ignore since they were consistently wrong) because they had implications for our electricity-price forecasts and occasionally the chemical or engineering teams might talk to us about our electricity-price estimates since energy was a significant part of their input costs, but that was about it.

At lunchtime I was taken to the local Pret A Manger which, due to the lack of office canteen, would become my primary source of nourishment. The amount of tuna baguettes and bacon, lettuce and tomato sandwiches that I'd consume during that period must have been of record-breaking proportions. Apart from that, it was simply a case of knuckling down and trying to find out what the hell it was that a research analyst actually did.

Fortunately, David assigned me to a team that included a maths Ph.D. graduate named Henry who helped me out when it came to grossing up dividends and discounting cash flow. Unfortunately, though I didn't know it at the time, I had been allocated a sector that was universally seen to be about as interesting as an accountants' tea party: European utilities. Even less amusingly, I was immediately given the task of covering the UK water subsector which makes the other parts of the utilities sector look veritably racy. It still amazes me to this day that an off-hand decision by the head of research would dictate the nonsense I babbled for almost twelve years. Interestingly, I now thank the Lord (that's the big man upstairs and not David Flynn) that I was allocated utilities, having seen the carnage that enveloped some of the 'sexier' sectors after the bursting of the tech bubble in 2000.

After a few months of composing spreadsheets, researching my sector (mainly through reading other banks' research notes that my colleagues had obtained from friendly clients) and generally getting pissed with colleagues every Thursday evening and every Friday lunchtime, I began to settle into this strange career. It was at about this stage that David came over to me and said in his nonchalant, relaxed manner, 'Let's have a drink after work.' Of course, I gladly accepted his offer. Since I'd joined we'd had a few chats but they'd been in group situations in the pub and hence fairly superficial. I'd grown to like and respect David enormously. There was something about him that made me want to impress him and seek his approval. I felt that I would be able to do both of these things that Thursday evening.

At around 5.30 p.m. David walked by my desk and I immediately stood up and followed him out the door. To avoid our colleagues we went to a rarely frequented pub on Shoreditch High Street and settled down over a couple of pints of Guinness.

David started proceedings: 'So how are things going?'

'Cool . . . I guess. It's a piece of piss, this broking lark!'

'Well, although I suspect you're joking, you're speaking more truth than you may realise. This evening I want to give you a few tips about how to succeed in this God-awful business and once we've got that horseshit over and done with we'll go and see my girlfriend.'

Over the next half-hour my Obi Wan, my Yoda, my Merlin told me the secrets of becoming a successful City analyst. What he said may not have been rocket science, but it stood me in good stead for over a decade. Below is a summary of his six key points:

1. 'Press the flesh': i.e. present to clients regularly and take them out for expensive meals as often as possible. The younger ones should be taken out on the lash and shown rugby games, pop concerts and so forth. My later success at this aspect of the job was aided by the fact that most of my competitors were deeply tedious individuals whose idea of a fun night out was marginally less enjoyable than sticking rusty pins in your eyes. Relative to most of those losers Steve Davis's lust for life resembled that of Iggy Pop.

2. 'Publish or perish': i.e. write research notes fairly often. Some analysts get bogged down in spreadsheets and numbers but we weren't here to sell 'truth' because there was no such thing. The vast majority of share-price drivers were things like changes in interest rates, GDP growth, the oil price etc., which were near-impossible to predict. All you needed to do was spin a vaguely plausible yarn that was difficult to disprove, write it down and the suckers would bite.

3. 'Blow your own trumpet': There's no place for shyness in this job. Office politics may be rife in any business but in the City it's endemic. This is because well-timed self-aggrandisement to the boss, perhaps combined with a subtle criticism of a colleague's performance, could mean £30,000 of his bonus coming your way. You know everyone is at it and so you've got to get involved. It is a given in this business that if someone can steal your thunder and take credit for your achievement then they will do so. It is, of course, around Christmas time when bonuses are decided that ethics, which are always on the critical list in the City anyway, begin to flat-line. Successful political manoeuvring can explain how two brokers of equal experience, diligence and talent covering the same sector at the same bank can earn vastly different salaries.

4. 'Cover your back': Bold statements like 'these shares will go up because . . .' make you a hostage to fortune. If you know what's good for you, bung in a few caveats. More importantly, use emails to ensure that verbal agreements with colleagues are worth more than the paper they're not written on. These emails usually begin 'As we discussed, you have agreed to . . .' This practice has saved my bacon on more than one occasion.

5. 'Ride on a successful analyst's coat tails': The best way to rapidly move up the ladder is to join an already successful team – ideally with a star analyst who will show you the ropes and introduce you to all his clients. Once you've learned everything you can from him, you should fuck off to form your own team, stealing his clients and ideas while you're at it.

6. 'None of this shit matters': 'Stress will kill you quicker than a rabbit gets fucked' were David's exact words. The moment you take this job seriously, the moment you give a shit that a share-price movement goes against your

recommendation or that a client doesn't like you, you're done for. Never forget this job is just about money-grabbing dickheads pointlessly pushing around bits of paper. It ain't curing cancer – it's just the best legal means of making vast amounts of cash as quickly possible. This was his most important lesson and I never forgot it, though as events will show I did not always adhere to it.

David was bemused, and somewhat disappointed, to see that I was actually taking notes during his half-hour diatribe. As soon as he finished he downed his pint, slammed it on the table, stood up and simply said, 'We're off to see Isabella, let's go.' I knew David was married and the fact he was willing to introduce me to his mistress made me feel part of his 'inner circle of trust' and that made me feel good.

After a very short taxi ride (one of David's mottos was 'Why walk when someone can drive you?') to where Shoreditch High Street forked we stopped outside what appeared to be a strip joint called Pinks. I thought it a little unusual that we were meeting his bit on the side at a strip joint but was happy to roll with it. After giving the two heavies outside our five-pound entrance fee we walked through the thick velvet curtains into a proper, old-school den of iniquity. Ostensibly Pinks was just a normal pub – the principal difference being that it had no windows and that the clientele were all men, mostly old men, who were generally not talking but rather staring towards us as we walked in. Oh yes . . . and the other difference was that there was a stage with a beautiful naked chick sporting a shaven raven who was upside down slowly slipping down a pole just to the right of where we'd come in from. It took a few seconds of confused self-consciousness for me to realise why all these old geezers were staring in my direction and I was pleased to find out that for once it wasn't my shite suit that was the source of all the attention. The clientele themselves were an amusing mix of local impoverished degenerates dressed in cheap clothes and drinking bitter and the odd Cityboy whose bespoke suit and £200 shoes stuck out a mile. There's an admirable equality about these kind of East End strip joints – disparities in wealth and employment are left at the door and we spectators are unified by our common 'pastime'. At Pinks we were not brokers or builders or binmen; we were simply admirers of the female form . . . or perverts, depending on your point of view.

We ordered two pints and settled on a couple of stools with our backs to the bar so that we could enjoy the show. After a deep, satisfying glug of lager I asked David when his missus was turning up. Without batting an eyelid or looking at me he simply said, 'She's already here. She's over there on the stage.' In front of me, the same beautiful, tanned, naked brunette who had been on the stage as we entered the building was now bending over with her back to the audience, parting her butt cheeks as she did so. I almost choked on my mouthful of lager and quickly tried my best to regain my composure. After a few awkward seconds I said one of the less convincing lies I've come out with over the last thirty-five years. 'She, er, looks like a nice girl.'

Choosing to ignore any possible irony David merely grunted an acknowledgement. After the loud R&B track ended, signalling that Isabella's dance was over, a fellow stripper came around with a pint mug into which everyone placed a one-pound coin. While I fumbled in my pockets trying to find one David put in two with an insouciance that reflected a lifetime of watching young ladies getting their kit off for cash at dodgy East End dives.

After a few minutes Isabella appeared looking infinitely more respectable in a neon-orange thong and matching peephole bra. She demurely kissed David on the cheek and took a seat next to us. She was about twenty-five, had the body of a swimwear model, and a face with bone structure that would have intimi-dated Audrey Hepburn. I had to make the painful admission that she was significantly more attractive than any girl I'd ever been with and yet here she was with a fat old degenerate. Two simple questions posed themselves immediately. Firstly, is there no justice in the world? . . . and much, much more importantly – how do I get a piece of this action?

After a few brief pleasantries David gave me an unintentional clue to that all-important second question. He reached into his pocket, took out a beautiful gold necklace and, as Isabella leaned forward, placed it gently around her neck. With hindsight my naïvety was extraordinary but what was even stranger was David's own self-delusion. As Isabella left to perform another 'dance' he turned round to me and, with a look that can only be compared to that of a besotted teenager in the grip of puppy love, said, 'I really think she loves me. You know, I think this might be the real thing.' I couldn't believe that a cynical old trooper like David could actually ignore the obvious reason for her affection. The only thing that was real about the reasons for her 'love' was the Brazilian Real that his sterling would be converted into as soon as she was forced back to Sao Paolo by the immigration boys.

I would witness randy old stockbrokers display this extra-ordinary self-delusion again and again over my City career. Watching corpulent buffoons wearing appalling sports jackets actually believing that the fit young totty they're chatting to at dreadful clubs in Soho were interested in anything other than their wedge would be humorous were it not so tragic. One of the many, many reasons I vowed I would leave the City before I was forty was my fear of seeing a fat gurning idiot leching over some nubile chick and then suddenly realising that it was my reflection in some seedy nightclub's mirrored walls.

After that memorable evening I settled into the working life of an analyst and one-on-one encounters with my guru were few and far between. I sat around and continued to try to understand what the hell my sector involved and what it was that a research analyst did. Apart from getting arseholed fairly regularly at the local bar the routine seemed to involve an endless cycle of publishing research notes, marketing those notes to clients via phone calls and presentations, and taking those same clients out for posh lunches and the odd sporting event. We had to keep our clients, the salesmen and the traders informed about share-price sensitive developments in the sector and, no matter what our level of knowledge, we had to always have 'a view' if we didn't want to appear pointless. It didn't seem particularly challenging and nothing about the job seemed to explain why the salaries on offer dwarfed those of lawyers, accountants, management consultants, etc. Still, that wasn't my problem. In fact, that was a problem that all those lawyers, accountants and management consultants should have been contemplating.

The only major learning experience that remained for me in 1996 was Banque Inutile's Christmas party – where to say I made a tit of myself would be to insult mammary glands across this planet. It was the first in a long line of office Christmas parties that, at best, would end with me falling asleep on the tube home and waking up somewhere like Morden (or Mordor, as amusing colleagues dubbed it) and, at worst, being hustled out by concerned colleagues. Banque Inutile's 1996 Christmas party could have prematurely ended my City career were it not for David's obvious enjoyment of my absurdity and his clear wish to witness it again and again. On this count, unlike most others, I would not disappoint him.

There was a buzz of expectation on the day of the office Christmas party. During December, no one in the City does much work and the Christmas party is often the culmination of some serious liver-destroying sessions in the pub. 'Tis truly the season to be jolly hungover. Although the UK water companies reported their half-year results in early December I was not yet experienced enough to be trusted to inform the sales force what they meant; that pleasure was still Henry's. So I was free to spend most afternoons on the lash with colleagues, friends and even a few lowly clients that I had been allocated. The party began at 6.30 p.m. but I had been knocking back lagers and Zambucas since 4.30 p.m. with some of the more roguish Banque Inutile boys. I was already off my canister by the time I arrived at the party and can't really remember what happened during the five hours prior to my kind-hearted workmates pulling me out, but witness accounts suggest I managed to achieve the following:

1. I almost got into a fight with an acquaintance at the bank by incessantly mocking his appalling dancing. Apparently, I very magnanimously walked away from this hulking titan of a man before things got physical. I imagine this rugby prop forward still thanks his lucky stars to this day that I had the good grace to let it lie.

2. I made it quite clear to two married colleagues whom I knew were having an illicit affair that I, and everyone else, was quite aware of their late-night dalliances in the photocopying room. The look that I received from the fuming lady suggested I would undoubtedly be removed from her Christmas card list.

3. I threw shapes on the dance floor like an ecstasy-addled teenager. Apparently, I also removed my shirt as if performing a mal-coordinated strip routine and then introduced bemused spectators to a dance move that was out of place when first revealed at university and was certainly not appropriate at a reasonably formal party surrounded by a wunch of bankers. Word on the street was that my innovative semi-naked backward press-up manoeuvre with suggestive pelvic thrusts did not go down too well with some of our senior visitors from Paris.

4. I ruffled David Flynn's hair and patted his ever-expanding

paunch. Of all the dreadful things I did this was the one I regretted most. Not only was it about as appropriate as patting the Queen's bum but this man would be deciding my bonuses for as long as both he and I were at Banque Inutile.

5. I made appalling clumsy moves on the pharmaceutical team's forty-two-year-old happily married secretary. This was not only inappropriate but also a source of continual mockery from my colleagues since she had the misfortune of possessing a face like a well-slapped arse. To have made a move on such a munter was bad enough, but to have been blanked really showed a distinct lack of class.

6. Finally, I ended up puking behind a food counter having been unable to reach the toilets. It was at this stage that a few workmates gently forced me out of the building. I woke up the next day fully suited on the floor next to my bed feeling and smelling like Richard Burton after a five-day bender – and I say that fully aware of the fact that by 1996 he had been dead for twelve years.

Christmas parties at any office are a potential minefield, but at investment banks, if you have any propensity to get 'overexcited', they are best avoided. A drunken slap on the arse of the wrong woman could result in you losing your six-figure salary job and never working in the City again – perhaps a blessing in disguise but nevertheless something you'd prefer to voluntarily choose rather than have imposed.

Equally, office Christmas parties can be a great place for attractive gold-digging secretaries to bag themselves a million-aire. I have heard that certain ambitious middle-class mothers with daughters who aren't the sharpest pencils in the box have been known to persuade them to become City secretaries with this potential outcome in mind. These mothers may themselves have learned that trick from their own parents who had sent them to an Oxbridge-based secretarial college thirty years before hoping that they would meet some nice, clever (and hopefully naïve) student with 'good prospects'. However, at that 1996 Banque Inutile Christmas party I can say with some confidence that even if I had possessed Bill Gates's billions and Brad Pitt's good looks there was not a girl in the room who was desperate enough to make a move on me, such was my obvious state of slobbering inebriation. Indeed, such was the appalling nature of my behaviour that even a tolerant boss like David felt obliged to give me a telling-off in his office when I finally rolled into work the next day – barely able to string a sentence together and feeling like a bear had shat in my head. At an uptight and 'professional' bank like Goldman Sachs such a performance would probably have ensured that my potentially glittering City career would have been stillborn. But Banque Inutile's research department under the stewardship of David Flynn prided itself on its tolerance of 'eccentrics' (or childish pissheads, as some may call them) and hence I was able to get away with these early mistakes.

The months rolled by and the learning curve proved extremely steep. Before too long, with the help of Henry, I had set up financial models on Excel for the five UK water companies and in May 1997 I published my first research note which essentially told clients that they should buy shares in most of the UK water companies because . . . they were going to go up, or some equally sophisticated argument. David had proved a fairly hands-off boss – mainly because he had better things to do with his time like watching Brazilian chicks remove their undergarments – but his cursory glance at my note had managed to remove some glaring errors. This note was my opening gambit at establishing a reputation in my sector and, truth be told, wasn't a complete disaster.

However, there were two irritating consequences of writing a note of this nature. Firstly, I was now officially Banque Inutile's

UK water analyst. This meant that I had the ultimate responsibility for communicating to the market my bank's views on UK water shares. This responsibility would also mean that I had the ever-so-tedious job of responding to the UK water companies' full-year financial results which would be reported in June. The second annoying outcome was that I was obliged to do my first marketing trip – although this would only be to UK-based clients since I wasn't senior enough yet to warrant a trip to Europe or America.

Talking on the mike to a hundred or so uninterested pinheads at 7.20 a.m. for two minutes, having just picked up a company's thirty-page financial results at 7 a.m. from Reuters was not a lot of fun the first time and never became so. The time constraints ensure that the opportunities to screw up are myriad and errors early on in a City career can take years to recover from. The whole experience is stressful, yet analysts must appear calmer than the Fonz on Mogadon or they lose authority and will not be taken seriously. I once heard of a female analyst breaking down in tears on the mike at a US firm and that is NEVER a good look at an investment bank where emotions other than anger and smug self-satisfaction are generally out of place. Word on the street is that soon after she left the City to became a nursery school teacher – which probably wasn't that much of a change, really. This inherent stress in City careers has long been cited as a justification for our absurdly huge salaries but I never bought this horseshit. It's always seemed to me that nurses' jobs were fairly stressful and people died if they screwed up. Funnily enough, when I'm chowing down at Le Gavroche, I rarely see medical orderlies at the table next to me.

My first round of presentations to clients was pretty interesting . . . for about two days. Again, it was fairly stressful, but after six hour-long meetings a day the routine of repeating the same spiel, complete with scripted 'ad-libs', became exceedingly dull. Spending an hour going through a PowerPoint presentation trying to convince experienced fund managers, some of whom had been in the business for decades, that a twenty-five-year-old buffoon wearing a cheap, ill-fitting suit could aid their fund's performance was a big ask. Many of the clients were clearly totally uninterested in my arguments and sat there hardly deigning to listen, occasionally looking at their watches to check when their waking nightmare would end. Others, usually the younger, competitive types, would spend the time trying to find fault in my arguments. Inevitably, when I went back to the office and checked on their fund's holdings, I would discover that their hostility resulted from them holding shares I'd advocated selling and vice versa. Having said that, some of these arseholes just wanted to try and humiliate a newcomer on the block and it took the patience of Mother Teresa not to just tell them to fuck right off. Thankfully, I restrained these somewhat hostile urges, which was no bad thing since such behaviour would probably not have been conducive to establishing a lasting broker-client relationship.

Throughout these early meetings I would often suffer from what I would later hear referred to as 'impostor syndrome'. Truth be told, it never left me throughout my City career no matter how successful I became. I would sit there spouting lyrical about the virtues of a particular share or the inherent problems of another, and suddenly I would fall victim to a heinous bout of self-doubt. On many occasions, I've assumed clients and colleagues alike would see me for the fake I was. How could I possibly continue to pull the wool over their eyes when I was simply a chancer who had got lucky – a dope-smoking hippy who had fallen into a completely inappropriate career?

For example, on about day three of my marketing I was presenting to a group of around eight fund managers at the Prudential when I suddenly became absolutely convinced that the bored-looking, middle-aged, bespectacled chap at the back of the room was going to interrupt my verbal diarrhoea mid-flow and say something like: 'Just wait a goddam minute, I've suddenly realised you're talking absolute gibberish. I'm simply not prepared to waste any more of my precious time listening to this incessant bullshit.'

Such was my conviction that they could see right through me that when one of them interrupted me to ask a question, I had to stop myself from pre-empting him and shouting: 'You're right. Guilty as charged. Not only could I not give two shits about the impending cash-flow crisis at United Utilities, but it also probably won't happen anyway. PLEASE DON'T TAKE ME SERIOUSLY.' Fortunately, this never actually happened.

Clearly, impostor syndrome affects people in many different careers but because the salaries in the City are so absurdly large I believe that it is particularly prevalent amongst us stockbrokers. How can we possibly be worth the cash these mugs are throwing at us? It is also clear that the City requires people to say things extremely confidently that they don't actually believe because unless you give the impression of being a professional broker who is confident in your convictions, no one will take you seriously. Hence, investment banks across the world are full of people espousing views extremely confidently that they don't necessarily think are true. I'm convinced that events like the tech stock market bubble that happened in 1999–2000 (when share prices of Internet companies reached absurdly ludicrous levels) occurred because analysts were so used to feigning confidence. Hence, stockbrokers could look fund managers straight in the eyes and tell them that clearly overvalued shares would keep going up. I'm pleased to say that after only a few years in this God-forsaken business I realised that pretty much everyone in the City was a professional blagger. All you needed to do was spin a yarn that's just a little bit more convincing than all the other bullshitters and everything would be just fine. With hindsight, I can't have been too bad at this fine art because no one ever found me out over my career, but that didn't make things any easier at the time.

So by July 1997, I had set up financial models for my companies, written a research note and presented to many of the major London-based fund managers. I was now officially a City analyst, which was confirmed when a journalist rang up one day and garnered a quote off me for the business pages of the *Daily Mail*. The next day I proudly showed it to my father, whose pleasure at seeing his son officially become a 'serious individual' was only tempered by my name appearing in a Tory rag. Theoretically, all was going well – I was earning £24,000 a year and was looking forward to my first bonus in six months' time. The problem was that I still wasn't convinced that this was the life for me. Telephone calls and emails from my friend Alex, who was living the life of Riley as an artist in India, continually reminded me of the alternative to this grey, bespoke-suited drudgery. I had promised myself at the tender age of fifteen that I would not wake up on my fortieth birthday and conclude that my life so far had been 'average'. Was I going to become another time waster sleepwalking my way to death?

I was still questioning what my long-term life plan was when I started becoming a good friend of my trader, Tony Player. David had taught me well about how to thrive in this hideous business but Tony would show me an even filthier side of this game and his sage-like wisdom and practical advice would prove just as important to my success.

2
THE TRADER

When God was handing out vices, he cast his eye on Tony Player and thought: 'Fuck it. I'll give him all of them.' Over time I would discover that he was actually a genuinely lovely man but he just hid it well. Really, really well. After I officially became Banque Inutile's analyst for the UK water sector I chatted with Tony regularly as he traded shares in my sector (as well as others) with fund managers and other traders day in, day out. If there was any news I would attempt to rapidly inform him of its share-price implications. Otherwise he might, for example, sell shares too cheaply to some other, better-informed trader which he would then have to later buy off someone else for a higher price. Our mutual banter during these chats soon led to me forming one of the few City friendships that meant anything to me.

Tony was only thirty years old but had been working in the City since he was eighteen and hence was considered an 'old hand'. He had witnessed the 1987 stock market crash and Black Wednesday in 1992 when the then Chancellor of the Exchequer, Norman Lamont, made a risible attempt to keep Britain in the EU's Exchange Rate Mechanism by pushing interest rates from ten per cent to fifteen per cent in a single day. Clever speculators like George Soros were quick to realise that politicians' attempts to bet against fundamental economic realities were as futile as my attempts to get laid sporting a *Miami Vice*-like ponytail and bum-fluff goatee. The actions of Soros and his ilk, who continually sold sterling on the money markets, forced a humiliating climb-down by the Government and Britain's exit from the ERM. It is estimated that this incident cost Britain around three and a half billion pounds – about sixty pounds for every man, woman and child. It was this event that convinced Tony more than any other that Margaret Thatcher's oft-quoted adage that 'you can't buck the market' was a truism of almost biblical significance.

This conviction in the all-powerful and occasionally irrational nature of 'the market' was one that was shared by most traders and had some amusing implications for my encounters with Tony. On most mornings I would walk over to his desk to have a chat about what was happening 'on the Street'. He would swing round in his chair, taking his eyes momentarily off the six screens in front of him which were constantly feeding him potentially price-sensitive information, and say something like: 'Steve, she feels fucking tetchy this morning. She's nervous and jumpy.' He was talking about 'the market' but it was as if he was referring to an uncontrollable wild animal or a raging fire. Although this was initially vaguely comical, experience would show me that his description was not so incongruous. The market is the product of thousands of people's emotions. The two main emotions brokers and investors feel are fear and greed which, when combined with a herd mentality, can result in somewhat extreme and irrational 'boom and bust' market movements.

At other times Tony would refer to the market as if he were in some dreadful B-movie Western. He'd say things like, 'It's quiet out there . . . too damn quiet for my liking', as if a bunch of Armani-clad Apaches were just about to ride over a hilltop and encircle our venerable bank. But it is this ability to sense upcoming market movements before they happen that differentiates a profitable trader from an incompetent one. It seemed to me that this ability could not be learned and was more likely to be found in a quick-witted son of an East End market trader (as Tony was) than in some overly analytical, Oxbridge-educated posh boy. My City experience never changed that opinion.

Tony exhibited all the traits that a stereotypical trader should possess. Although his belly had not quite reached the requisite proportions that being a head of trading necessitated it would only take a few more pies and pints of Stella to improve his promotion prospects. The sharpness of his thought processes and banter were only matched by his appetite for booze and strippers and the crudeness of his language. He seemed to take special pleasure in swearing incessantly in front of analysts from the smarter public schools – especially those who were in any way condescending to him. He would refer to these characters as 'boss' when talking to them, which although superficially a deferential term, was clearly a coded insult that he and his fellow traders understood.

My first proper knees-up with Tony happened one Thursday in September 1997. It was about 5 p.m. and we were chatting about the potential share-price implications of an upcoming regulatory announcement when he suddenly stopped me dead and said, 'Fuck this bollocks, I'm feeling as randy as a dog with two dicks. Mate, I need some action so badly I'd shag a warm sock. Why don't you and me head off to the Corney and Barrow in Broadgate Circle and bag ourselves a couple of Essex slappers?'

Having nothing better to do and feeling honoured to be invited to go on the pull with a reasonably senior trader I nodded my agreement. Thursday night was usually the night City colleagues go boozing together since weekends are generally earmarked for your real friends and the missus and kids.

According to Tony this fact had not gone unnoticed by legions of Essex girls who would congregate in their white stilettos and low-cut dresses in bars across the City hoping to ensnare a rich, drunken Cityboy and so secure their financial future. On the walk to the bar he explained to me: 'All you need to do to pull a doris at the Broadgate C and B is slap on the Armani and buy a few hundred-pound bottles of shampoo. Before you can say 'gold-digger' they'll be all over us like a bad rash. We'll be batting them off with a shitty stick, my son.'

The thought of hundred-pound bottles of champagne scared me but I didn't want to show that to my new-found buddy. The fact that I was still wearing a six-pound suit also made me query the likely success of our mission but I hoped the obvious quality of Tony's Savile Row bespoke suit, his £250 Oxford brogues and the £3000 Rolex he sported might make up for my obvious inadequacies. We climbed the steps to the long, circular bar at Broadgate Circle and immediately set about putting Tony's cunning plan into action.

We sat down at a table that could accommodate a couple of new pals and displayed the bottle of vintage Bollinger champagne prominently in a standing ice bucket with the label displayed clearly just in case these Essex girls really were as discerning as Tony had suggested. Tony dispensed with my attempts to make small talk immediately and instead focussed his sophisticated intellect on describing the many blondes around us and what he'd like to do with them. Within the space of about five minutes he had come out with a stream of crude observations that, given my politically correct upbringing, made me somewhat uncomfortable. Of course, I was careful not to show this for fear of being labelled a posh knob: 'Check out the boat race and chassis on her. Fuck me, I'd crawl over broken glass just to wank over her shadow.' 'Oh dear, my son, I don't like yours much. She's definitely built for comfort not speed, d'you know what I mean?' 'Blimey, check out the rack on that chick by the bar. Look at her nips – it's either cold, or she's smuggling peanuts.' 'Look at the gnashers on that one. She could eat an orange through a tennis racket . . . an apple through a letter box.' 'She's worth a squirt, innit?' 'Body from *Baywatch*, but face from *Crimewatch*, I'm afraid.' 'That one was good from afar, but far from good. Still, every hole's a goal, innit?' 'I'm no Fred Flintstone, but I'd make her bed rock.' 'She's no show pony but she'll do to ride around the house,' etc., etc.

This endless stream of sexist rantings seemed to go on for ever and I laughed along, keen to ingratiate myself with this funny, but admittedly morally dubious character.

Tony also indulged in a practice that I have found numerous Cityboys enjoy; he would discuss the surrounding ladies in terms usually reserved for our trade. So breasts were 'a lovely pair of assets I'd like to get my hands on' and an older lady was one that had 'gone ex-dividend'. When eventually we were approached by a couple of dolly birds, just before they arrived within earshot, he exclaimed, 'Oh, I can feel the market hardening already. There's some serious upside potential here.' I stifled my laugh so as not to put this encounter on a bad footing.

Heavily made-up and with orange spray-on tans, Sharon and Tracey looked like classic Essex gold-diggers on the make. However, Tony's first question, 'Where are you ladies from, then?' revealed they were actually from Shepherd's Bush. This information allowed Tony to get them giggling immediately by saying: 'You know what they say? A bird in the hand is worth two in Shepherd's Bush.' Because Sharon had the Einstein-like intellect required to get Tony's complicated gag he nudged me and winked: 'She's smarter than the average Dani Behr, this one, d'you know what I mean?' I actually didn't know what he meant. Anyway, it very quickly became apparent that Tony was going to do nearly all the talking and that he would focus his attention on the relatively attractive Sharon while I would have to make do with her pal who was, frankly, a bit of a minger.

As I struggled to make conversation with Tracey, Tony and Sharon giggled and laughed as if both of them had experience of this kind of encounter and understood the rules of the game. I clearly did not. When Tracey asked me what my star sign was I responded with an age-old gag but one that clearly went way over her head: 'I'm a Virgo, but like all Virgos I don't really believe in star signs.' While this used to raise a titter from the girls at Cambridge, Tracey simply looked at me and said, 'Yes, I have heard that about you Virgos.' I didn't know if she was joking or not so I emitted a half-hearted laugh that merely resulted in a perplexed look on her face.

Soon we were getting through the champagne at a rate of knots and I was beginning to feel totally bladdered. I was also becoming tired of my forced, awkward chat with Tracey and becoming increasingly worried about the size of the bill that awaited us. Fortunately, at about this point a very drunk Tony made one sexist comment too far and offended the quarry. Even Sharon was not receptive to Tony's observation that 'One night with me, darling, and you'll be walking like John Wayne for a week.' Either that or she felt that striding around like a bow-legged cowboy was not a price worth paying for a night of pleasure with a crude, fat, inebriated wide-boy. After this comment, Tony further blotted his copy book by responding to Tracey's revelation that she was 'bipolar' by jokingly claiming that he 'didn't give a fuck' where she came from. The two ladies soon stood up unsteadily and departed, probably to find more free champagne. Tony and I were left feeling, as he so sweetly put it, 'like two spare pricks at a wedding'. It was at this point that Tony drunkenly turned round to me and showed me that when he said he wanted sex he really meant business: 'Fuck this, Steve, let's head to a brothel I know in Soho and get this party started right. I'm paying. Why have an amateur, when you can have a professional, d'you know what I mean? The brasses there are proper hard-core.'

Now, this really was a bridge too far. Despite my wish to bond with the charismatic Tony, shagging some prostitute was too much of a good thing. Ignoring his drunken protestations, I declined his kind offer and we went our separate ways. I would later find that the use of prostitutes was reasonably common amongst a certain breed of Cityboy – perhaps because the macho City culture made it difficult to relate to women. Buying sex for money, be it at a strip joint or at a brothel, also went hand in hand with the City's ethos that every asset has a price. A lot of my peers had clearly not been listening when the Beatles sang that money can't buy you love.

On the tube home I smiled to myself about the night's comical moments. Thankfully, Tony had refused my half-hearted attempts to share the £450 bill with a dismissive wave of the hand. Senior better-paid colleagues paying for all the drinks was something of a City tradition which was clearly a bonus at this stage in my career but a bit of a bugger later on. In reality, for most brokers, it was less of an act of generosity than an assertion of one's superior status and wealth – something Cityboys seemingly never grew tired of.

But Tony's role in my City education was not limited to the etiquette of pulling dodgy birds in hideous bars. After this first night out we became regular drinking partners and over these sessions he would bestow upon me lessons that I would never forget and that would help me thrive in the Square Mile. If David Flynn had shown me the theory behind career success, Tony gave me hands-on practical tips about how to win clients and, more importantly, maximise my earning potential. If David had been my Karl Marx, Tony was my Lenin. However, at this stage I wasn't sure which historical figure I would become . . . perhaps the ruthless, ultimately successful Stalin or maybe the ineffective Trotsky complete with ice pick in my head.

The first lesson Tony taught me was that clients who think

they are your friends are the best kind of clients. Over a pint or two of Stella Artois, which he touchingly referred to as 'wife-beater', he explained to me: 'Look, Steve, a client who thinks you're his mate is gonna feel really disloyal if he doesn't send a shedload of comm (commission) your way. Do what you have to do to con these suckers into thinking they're your pal and then you've got them by the balls. And as the septics [i.e. septic tanks – Yanks] always say, "If you've got them by the balls, their hearts and minds will follow", d'you know what I mean?'

Tony may not have realised when he gave this counsel that he was actually echoing one of the old-school City gents who had helped launch modern investment banking. One of the legendary Warburgs had famously said decades before: 'Become his friend; then his banker.' Tony's promotion of this strategy was probably one of the best pieces of career advice I ever received and one that, while fairly obvious, was not put into practice by most of my competitors who thought writing long, detailed research notes and having extended, tedious telephone conversations about 'industry developments' was going to win them friends and influence people. The problem with this conventional strategy is that the City is massively overbroked and since most clients covered more than one sector they would receive hundreds of telephone calls, research notes, emails and messages via Bloomberg (a screen-based investment tool) every day. Hence, it was difficult to differentiate oneself from one's diligent peers through these conventional means of 'establishing relationships'.

I decided fairly soon that my unique selling point would be that I would take my clients to parties, bars, nightclubs and music concerts and get them totally rat-arsed. The whole idea was that when it came round to the major clients voting in their firms' internal surveys for who was the best analyst, something which determined the amount of commission our bank should receive, they would feel terribly guilty if my name wasn't at the top of the list. The other reason for me favouring this career 'strategy' was even more compelling. I was, and always have been, a lazy, hedonistic degenerate who always found discussing the dynamics of the utilities sector to be marginally less interesting than drinking and chatting women up . . . or watching paint dry, for that matter. While this may not surprise most right-thinking individuals, these are pretty radical thoughts in a world populated by anally retentive, spreadsheet-obsessed spods. For a Goldman Sachs robot to even voice such an opinion is probably a sackable offence.

My task in forming a group of clients who felt a loyalty to me because of our partying was made easier by the fact that the European utilities sector in the second half of the 1990s was not particularly large (around five per cent of the overall market). It was also deemed not to be especially complicated because it was highly regulated. Consequently, the sector was often allocated to young, inexperienced clients (most of whom were men) who would be handed a sexier sector once they'd garnered some experience. This provided me with a rich hunting ground of chaps who were 'young, dumb and full of come' and whom I could influence due to being slightly older having 'wasted' a couple of years travelling the world before entering the City. While this strategy soon proved itself to be very effective over the years my poor liver and nostrils would suffer terribly. Meanwhile, my competitors' conventional computer-based strategies only resulted in short-sightedness and repetitive strain syndrome in their hands – something their other favourite pastime may have been the cause of anyway.

The only thing better than a client who thinks he's your mate is one who thinks you could get him in a lot of trouble if you so desired. Once, when I was dancing in Space in Ibiza like the bastard son of Prince and Michael Jackson (or at least I believed so at the time) and I spied a married client snogging a hot teenage Italian girl, I thought it was Christmas, Hanukkah and

Eid all rolled into one. Although he tried desperately to avoid eye contact I knew, even in my pilled-up state, that this was an opportunity I simply couldn't miss. I approached him with a smirk on my face and a slightly raised eyebrow that couldn't have been lost on the poor chap.

'Er, hi, Steve. Er . . . this is Sylvie . . . a friend of mine,' he spluttered, looking about as comfortable as George W. Bush at a Mensa convention.

'Hi, James,' I said, extending a hand to both him and his bit on the side. After a few drinks and some awkward pleasantries I left to refind my pals but not before I had asked him a few calculated questions about how his wife and kids were after Sylvie had popped off to the toilets to 'powder her nose'. When I was back at the office I made sure he was one of my first calls. Cynics may suggest that the dramatic increase in the amount of commission James handed over to my bank had little to do with a sudden improvement in his perception of the quality of my research.

Still, my bosses didn't care how I brought in the wonga (provided it was legal) – they simply subscribed to the view that numbers talked and bullshit walked. Admittedly, my methods may not have been hugely conventional but that was always the beauty of being a research analyst. Each sector team was essentially a self-employed entity. We were given an office, computers and an expense budget by our bank and told to go forth and make some cash – but how we did it was, to some extent, our business. The mix between publishing notes, calling and presenting to clients and client entertainment was in our hands. If what we did resulted in a healthy profit and loss account then management would not interfere, but if the numbers didn't stack up there could be trouble. If a bit of subtle blackmail helped avoid that scenario then what's not to like?

Although my meeting at Space proved lucrative there were also some major downsides to meeting clients at parties and festivals. In the good old days of my early City career I could feel fairly relaxed that my attendance of rave parties and festivals such as Glastonbury would not be tarnished by an unexpected encounter with one of my clients. The summer 'season' for City types used to begin with the indescribably tedious Chelsea Flower Show and proceed with equally dreary events like Royal Ascot and the Henley Regatta. I would never attend these types of events unless on a professional basis. But by the end of the twentieth century the world had changed. I suddenly began to see City clients at Glastonbury or the V Festival roaming around wearing green wellies and Barbours that they'd probably borrowed off Daddy, quaffing champagne and staying in expensively rented yurts.

Once, a few years later, I was at a twenty-four-hour fancy-dress party held in the grounds of a friend's stately home called Winstanley Hall. According to the *Daily Mail*, and they've really got their finger on the pulse so it must be true, this party represented the start of the 'alternative summer season'. On the way to having a slash I had the horror of bumping into a rather important hedge fund client of mine furtively exiting the toilets with a suspicious sprinkling of white powder under his hooter. The clearly embarrassed client quickly decided that discussing business was the best way to pretend everything was normal. I think I can safely say that this world has witnessed few things more ridiculous than an Egyptian Pharaoh discussing the impact of rising interest rates with a Russian Cossack outside a portaloo, with fireworks lighting up the sky and nosebleed techno in the background. Despite the dull subject matter my client was, for some peculiar reason, extremely enthusiastic and I wasted twenty precious partying minutes trying to extricate myself from the buffoon.

The only thing worse than meeting a client at a party who insists on talking shop is meeting one who continues to expect to be treated as a client despite the informal nature of the encounter. At the same party where I met the gibbering Pharaoh I bumped into another client, this time dressed as Julius Caesar. We sat down and it very quickly became apparent that despite the change of scene I was his bitch – or more appropriately, considering his outfit, his slave. Constant arse-kissing from brokers desperate to win business means certain misguided clients actually begin to believe that the sun really does shine out of their arse. This is one of the biggest causes of the arrogance which blights the City client base. Within minutes of meeting Mr Caesar he demanded I get him a drink, just as if we were having a formal client drink at the Coq d'Argent. Despite the potential negative ramifications for commission levels I smiled sweetly, said I'd be back in a minute, and ran away into the darkness. No client relationship has ever been important enough to screw up my Saturday night for.

Apart from teaching me about schmoozing (and blackmailing) clients, Tony gave me some far more important lessons about office politics that were aimed at surviving downturns and maximising bonuses. Because I was absolutely convinced that at any moment I would be found out and chucked out of this lucrative club I had from the word go decided to always opt for short-term salary maximisation over long-term career strategy.

With hindsight, I can say that the lessons Tony provided on these subjects helped ensure that my City career was perhaps a third more profitable than it might otherwise have been: 'Listen, Steve, these fuckers will pay you as little as they can get away with. They're all sweetness and light when it's the good times but as soon as the bad times arrive, and they will, they'll drop you quicker than an English wicket keeper. They show you no loyalty and you shouldn't show them none neither. Keep 'em on their toes by subtly making sure they know you'll leave for more pay at the drop of a hat. Word should get out if you go to a few interviews – especially if it's around bonus time. Oh, and for

God's sake never appear satisfied no matter how big your bonus is. That is a mug's game if ever there was one.'

This last pearl of wisdom is absolutely central to any City career and was particularly propitious because it was coming up to January 1998 which is when bonus day, or 'B day', as it was referred to, occurred at Banque Inutile. This was to be my first bonus since I had only been at Banque Inutile for a few months in 1996 and hence had not warranted one in January 1997.

B Day at any bank is always a highly amusing affair and one that requires the acting skills of De Niro. No one gets any work done and there is an air of nervous excitement similar to when you get your exam results at university. However, the difference is that everyone about to receive the news is sitting next to each other in a huge open-plan office checking out their colleagues' every facial expression. B Day is hence generally about pretending to those around you that you are feeling the exact opposite of your actual emotions. Since bonuses for research analysts can range from zero (which is a less-than-subtle way of the bank telling you that you should seek employment elsewhere) to ten times your salary or more (i.e. well over a million pounds), the stakes are fairly high.

On the morning of B Day the best vibe to give out is one of nonchalant calm despite the fact that another poor bonus may mean that your wife can forget about sending little Tarquin to Harrow. However, you must not appear too relaxed or everyone may assume that you are lucky enough to have a guaranteed bonus and that can cause resentment. Over my City career I managed to ensure that half of my bonuses were guaranteed through either moving to another bank and demanding one or two as part of my package or threatening to move and requiring a guaranteed bonus to ensure that I stay. I am not alone in this and used to enjoy not facing the same butterflies as my colleagues during the tense run up to bonus time.

However, I would point out to any aspiring Cityboy (God help you) that if you do ever receive a promise of a guaranteed minimum bonus, do not expect your boss to surprise you by giving you more than the minimum. The chances of that happening are somewhere between slim and none, and as far as I can see slim left town a long time ago.

The second acting requirement is that of total disappointment bordering on psychotic rage when it's your turn to trundle into the little room and receive 'the letter' from your boss. No matter what figure your boss mentions you should act as if he has just asked you to vigorously rub your genitals with a cheese grater for the next four hours. Any indication that you actually believe your bonus is satisfactory will be interpreted to mean that you're delirious with joy, which will be duly noted ensuring that next year's bonus is not increased dramatically. I'm afraid to say that I completely failed to follow Tony's advice in January 1998 when David gave me a £14,000 bonus and increased my salary to £30,000. I could not help the corners of my mouth immediately turning up and as soon as I left David's office I went to the bathroom and literally punched the air with glee. How could I be irritated when my remuneration for my first full year in the City almost matched that of my father who had been a successful public servant for over thirty years? Little did I know then that I would grow to view a paltry £14,000 as small change and go on to receive bonuses almost fifty times that amount.

The third element of acting on B day is that which you must exhibit as you leave the room. As you make the 'walk of shame' back to your desk all eyes will follow you and you must reveal absolutely no emotion. Showing anger will just suggest to everyone that you have been shafted. This could result in snide comments which may eventually reach the ears of other banks and headhunters and suggest you're not the appreciated big swinging dick you pretend to be. An overt expression of joy, however, will merely irritate those around you and openly contradict the act you just gave your boss.

The final acting required for colleagues is that which you display when in the bar for the inevitable B Day after-work drinks. There is a strict rule in the City that the size of bonuses is never discussed since it can be such a source of divisive resentment. I grew to learn that the correct demeanour at the B Day drinks is one of understated smugness. I tended to buy a few bottles of champers while pretending to be mildly annoyed. I did not want senior colleagues to feel I was satisfied while also wishing my peers to know that things weren't too bad. While this seemingly contradictory façade would test the acting skills of Larry Olivier it soon became second nature to me after a few years in my career.

While this may be the final act of the performance to colleagues of the stage play that is B Day there is usually one more act – that to 'her indoors', as Tony referred to his wife. If it's the kind of bonus that would embarrass an African dictator then being honest about its size merely ensures that half of it will be spent on Jimmy Choo shoes and kitchen improvements. However, underestimating the bonus if your partner has any gold-digger tendencies may lessen her respect for you and mean that her wandering eye moves on to Hugo or Rupert whose bonus resulted in the purchase of yet another Ferrari. I always found that pulling the wool over colleagues' eyes was infinitely simpler than performing the same trick for my various lady-friends but, then again, some of them were so perceptive that even dear Larry would have struggled.

Tony's invaluable hints about B Day were extremely helpful when the good times rolled, as they did in the late 1990s, but equally important was his advice about how to survive the bad times, which I and my peers would have to endure between 2000 and 2003. Obviously, being perceived as an important revenue generator with a solid bunch of clients is the best way to ensure survival, but there are a few tricks that he disclosed that, while extreme, could be utilised should it look like the axe was about to fall. While I never needed to use the tricks he taught me, my hedonistic, unethical behaviour (and that of many of my colleagues) and most banks' theoretically strict compliance procedures ensured that on most days I committed at least one sackable offence.

At every investment bank all stockbrokers' telephone calls are recorded and emails are randomly monitored. Hence, any hint of giving clients' inside information, front-running (when an analyst promotes a stock just prior to publishing a report doing the same) or selective disclosure (when only certain clients are told share-price sensitive information) can all end in you losing your job. Combine these regulations with a whole raft of rules designed to ensure that any contact with colleagues deemed to be racist or sexist can end your City career and it's a miracle that anyone survives more than about ten minutes – especially considering the City's macho, drink-fuelled culture. The main reason slapdash degenerates like me survive is because compliance departments often turn a blind eye, especially to the activities of profitable employees. Even taking this into account, I still made sure that I never forgot Tony's 'Seven Rules to Avoid the Sack' in case things got desperate:

1. 'The Breakdown Ruse': This classic trick requires pretending you've had some form of breakdown and hence devolving yourself of responsibility for the errant behaviour that got you into trouble. It can be hard to pull off if you displayed few symptoms prior to your indiscretion but it should get the HR department on your side and make dismissal unlikely. Tony said that Blackadder's trick of putting pencils up your nostrils and underpants on your head may be overplaying your hand.

2. 'The AA Play': If you're in trouble for a drink- or drugs-related issue then make sure the HR department know before your meeting with them that you're seeking

treatment. This should ensure that you are miraculously transformed from being a disruptive pisshead or junkie into a victim of a 'disease'. Tony was also sure to inform me that while exonerating yourself from having been caught smoking weed by claiming to have recently converted to Rastafarianism may work, no mainstream religion extols the virtues of 'snorting gak in the bogs'.

3. 'The Bereavement Act': Trying to get the sympathy vote and explain your unacceptable action by mentioning family bereavement, divorce or perhaps your football club's relegation may work for minor misdemeanours. However, losing too many relatives over a short period of time may raise suspicions that you're the Fred West of the Square Mile.

4. 'The Whistleblower Trick': Lodging a separate complaint regarding some unconnected misdeed you witnessed at the bank should ensure that your employer can't fire you until your allegation has been thoroughly investigated, which can take an extremely long time. Tony warned me that this move 'would make you about as popular as a pork chop at a bar mitzvah' and so should only be used if you don't value your colleagues' friendship.

5. 'The Closet Gambit': A P45 for someone who has just come out of the closet has got to have lawsuit written all over it. I remember thinking that Morgan Grenfell's rogue fund manager Peter Young had tried this trick when he went to court dressed in women's clothing in 1999. However, when I found out that he had mutilated his genitals too I thought that was probably over and above the call of duty. Tony kindly reminded me that while one shouldn't inform too many people that it's a scam because you could be rumbled, 'it's probably worth mentioning to the doris and your folks that you're not really a buftie'.

6. 'The Race/Sex Manoeuvre': A simple mention that you

have been the recipient of racial or sexual abuse in the workplace should definitely make any employer reassess the validity of their case. Tony's perceptive observation that I was a white male made this trick somewhat irrelevant.

7. 'The Pregnancy Scam': Claiming to be pregnant just before your meeting with HR will make any boss think twice about sacking you since the potential legal action could cost them a packet. Again, the relevance of this move to me was tenuous at best.

Apart from these tricks Tony also mentioned in passing blackmailing the boss as 'worth a bash'. He even claimed that once, during a disciplinary chat, he had subtly brought up the time his head of trading had spent a few hours in the VIP section of Crazy Horse in Las Vegas with a couple of charming ladies called Cherry and Simone. Apparently, Tony reminded his boss of this unseemly encounter while holding up a picture of the man's delightful wife and kids and enquiring as to the well being of 'little Tobias and Camilla'. Needless to say the matter was quickly forgotten about. In reality, banks hate being taken to court and all the associated negative publicity so legal threats and threats to inform the press can also reap dividends. Fortunately, I never needed to stoop so low but that was more the result of luck rather than sound judgement.

The final, and most important, piece of advice that Tony gave me was one that would help ensure that I was paid more than many of my contemporaries. Tony told me how to handle interviews at other banks and how to time them so that my own bank would feel that I was an extremely sought-after commodity and so be sure to pay me well. Because most job interviews happened in the November to February period, since banks wanted to take on new employees immediately after their bonuses are paid so as to get value for money, timing interviews for just before bonuses are decided was not a difficult thing to do.

It was then simply a case of subtly mentioning to a big-mouthed colleague that you were 'looking around' and word would soon get out. If the boss did find out and seemed a little peeved you can always use the age-old excuse that you were merely 'putting the feelers out' in order to assess your 'market value'. This was usually deemed a reasonable thing to do.

City types generally believe in the efficiency of the market – be it the stock market or the job market. Hence, maximising your pay is not just motivated by avarice but by deeper psychological drives. If you are paid less than a colleague and the market correctly assesses your and his worth then you must be a less 'valuable' person. This suggests that you are less intelligent and worthwhile, which in the hideously competitive environment of the City is simply an unacceptable thought. Not only did the size of your salary seem to me to be an extremely loose foundation upon which to build your confidence, but the whole theory also always seemed like a complete load of horseshit. This was because greed, luck and having the morals of a hyena were clearly the principal determinants of one's financial success. Fortunately, or not, I grew to possess these three 'virtues' over and above those of intelligence and drive that my peers foolishly deemed vital to climbing the greasy pole.

The main thrust of Tony's advice regarding interview technique was simple, as he explained to me: 'Make it clear that you're pretty happy where you are and that you'll be doing them a favour by joining them. Turn the interview around so that you're asking them why you should deign to join their bank. But most importantly, when asked why you want the job, make it clear that there's one reason and it's the same thing that makes the world go round: M.O.N.E.Y. At this early stage in your career it's gotta be double bubble or nuffink.'

The City is one of the few places where 'making more money' is the correct answer to any potential future employer's enquiry as to the interest you have in joining his outfit. This is not just because City types appreciate people who share the same interests as them and who possess a disarming honesty. It's also because anyone who receives a big bonus generally does so because they have made their bank lots of cash. Hence, the bank's and employee's fortunes are entwined in some appalling Faustian pact based upon maximising profits. Woe betide some idiot talking about 'intellectual pursuit' or some other claptrap in the interview as they simply condemn themselves to being royally shafted come bonus time. Likewise, if I hear my interviewer talking about 'long-term prospects' or 'great potential' I will make my excuses and leave there and then. The City catchphrase that 'a long-term investment is a short-term bet gone wrong' applies to the job market as much as a share recommendation. And besides, throughout my career I knew that it was only a matter of time before I was going to be found out as a chancer or before I decided to leave, and so talk of 'jam tomorrow' was never going to interest me.

The beauty of Tony's deep-rooted cynicism was that it chimed so well with my own and contrasted so profoundly with the nonsense that our bank's management insisted on talking. This was brought home to me most clearly when Banque Inutile held its first major off-site conference for nearly all its research analysts, salesmen and traders at a posh resort in the Dordogne in the summer of 1998. Like excited schoolchildren off on a camping holiday, we all took flights from City airport drinking steadily for the whole journey. On the aeroplane I had the pleasure of sitting next to David Flynn who, despite being part of management, shared my and Tony's doubts about the usefulness of this trip. Interestingly, we were to be joined by our Paris-based colleagues who we in London generally tried to avoid like the plague. We would also witness the continuing power struggle between Banque Inutile's London-based management and their French peers, which was also a source of tremendous amusement. There was even talk that the overall head of investment banking, '*le grand fromage*', as certain humorous wags had dubbed him, would be presenting. Predictably, the London–Paris power struggle would eventually be won by our French brethren but not before the conflict had ensured that Banque Inutile's ambitions of becoming a major investment bank had been pissed away like so much cheap French wine.

The off-site was predictable in two main ways. It was incredibly extravagant and it was a total waste of everyone's time. For the two nights that we were there we must have consumed restaurant meals that cost at least £150 a head involving lobster, caviar, foie gras and every other possible luxury. We drank incredible bottles of wine, some of which were older than me, and we were all given a bottle of Sauternes dessert wine which I was reliably informed by the resident wine-bore were worth over a hundred pounds each. Combine these expenses, the immensely tedious wine-tasting trip, the flights and the rooms at the five-star hotel, and I think we can safely conclude that the whole event cost well over £300,000. Combine that expense with the two days out of the office that a couple of hundred overpaid jokers enjoyed and the bill reaches over half a million pounds. I have no doubt that the shareholders of Banque Inutile would be chuffed to know that some of their profits had been spent getting a bunch of childish idiots so drunk each night that they could barely keep their eyes open during the completely pointless presentations the next day. Our French colleagues generally looked on in disgust as the British contingent got so arseholed that we could barely speak and then went on to nightclubs to try and pull French chicks. To say that this event failed to improve Anglo-French relations at our bank would be like saying that the Cuban Missile Crisis did not succeed in enhancing Soviet-US relations.

Of course, the most amusing parts of the whole shebang were the presentations made by the French head of investment banking and his immediate underling in London. Some comedian from the trading floor had carefully composed various sheets of 'management speak' terminology that was sometimes referred to as 'consultantese'. This language is generally spoken by the senior management of investment banks and, while sounding like English, actually has no meaning at all. The idea was that each of us would have around ten different, but commonly used, words or phrases of 'consultantese' on a piece of paper. As each phrase was utilised by the presenters we would tick them off and the winner, who got twenty pounds from all the other participants, was the one who first crossed off all his words. The game has since become known as 'bullshit bingo'.

As the presentation from the head of London operations began I looked down at my piece of paper – feeling confident that the meaningless words on it would be voiced soon. Amongst the words I needed to tick off were: 'right-sizing' (i.e. down-sizing), 'team player', 'cross-departmental synergies', 'belt and braces', 'core competencies' and 'leveraging'. Such was my concentration on winning the game that the message that was actually being put across was completely lost on me. To this day, I still have no idea what either of my erstwhile leaders actually said but I do feel confident that my life would not have been in any way improved had I listened. All I know is that, somewhat suspiciously, the same trader who composed the sheets won the game and earned himself a rather handy £200. Apparently, he almost jumped for joy, rather than overtly scratching his head, which was the agreed signal for having completed his 'bullshit bingo', when our English boss concluded that 'there was no I in team'. I was a bit narked off with this coincidence but less so when at the airport on the way back the victorious trader did the decent thing and used his winnings to buy everyone who participated in the game several drinks.

The Dordogne debacle was the first, but sadly not the last, of the many management chats that I received over the course of my City career – each one more pointless than the previous one. We stockbrokers are by nature a bunch of opinionated egotists convinced of our own brilliance. We have to be to do our job properly because we are constantly telling anyone who listens that we know better than everyone else. Hence, a eunuch has a higher chance of being tea-bagged than a manager has of changing a stockbroker's working habits. The City expression which best sums up this phenomenon is the 'herding cats syndrome'. Still, managers want to feel like they're being useful and hence continue to waste their time boring the pants off their employees with tired cliché after cliché.

Despite all this fun with Tony, one of my final episodes with him would show me a darker side to the City and Tony himself and leave a sour taste in my mouth. I was on the trading floor pretending to be enthused about some utility company or other with one of the salesmen. Since this particular individual had all the charm of Donald Rumsfeld after a serious crack session and was constantly trying to find fault in my arguments, I was relieved to spy Tony frantically beckoning me over. I quickly took the opportunity to remove myself from the repellent salesman and walk up to Tony's desk. With an overly surreptitious manner he handed me a cheaply manufactured white card just slightly larger than a business card with some large typed writing on one side: 'An invitation to a Gentlemen's Evening'. The smaller font writing below showed the price for this evening to be twenty-five pounds, the timing to be the upcoming Thursday and the venue to be a basement on a road I knew to be off Oxford Street.

'What's this all about then?' I asked innocently, but already aware that it was bound to be dodgy by the manner in which it was handed to me and, more importantly, because of who was doing the handing over.

'This, my son, will be a proper giggle. You ain't lived till you've seen this sort of caper. Just hand over your dosh and come over. There're a few of us going. You can trust Uncle Tony.'

All this was said with a leer on his face that Sid James would have been proud of. Without further ado I gave him the cash and walked off curious as to what fate had in store for me. Since my days of travelling I had always welcomed new and weird experiences and this looked likely to be one of those. Anyway, that's my excuse for attending this particular 'jaunt' and I'm sticking with it.

On Thursday after work I went for an early drink at a local bar with eight other Banque Inutile colleagues including, I was pleased to see, David Flynn. They were all men and none of them appeared to be particularly salubrious characters. There was a nervous air of anticipation and my questions as to what we were about to experience were batted off with knowing grins. By now I knew that this was definitely not going to be an evening listening to Shakespearean sonnets in a church hall. After about three pints we crammed into a few pre-booked black cabs and headed off towards Oxford Street.

We stopped behind a well-known department store and got out. The only visible door was a nondescript emergency exit. David Flynn knocked on the door and a huge man dressed in a cheap tuxedo opened it and let us in. After showing our tickets, we were led down some stairs to a reasonably large room, bare but for around fifty grey plastic school chairs arranged in a semi-circle around a square piece of lino by the wall. There were already about thirty suited men sitting down chatting to each other. Nearly all of them wore suits and most of them were clearly City types. The front row was mainly empty and this is where I ended up, sitting next to Tony. I noticed David had sloped off to one of the seats towards the back. Another man in a tuxedo came around with some bottles of cheap lager and some glasses of warm Chardonnay. Soon all the chairs were filled with braying Cityboys, not a single woman in sight.

After about fifteen minutes the door opened and two women entered the room dressed only in bra and panties. One was a reasonably attractive black woman with an athletic body and wearing what appeared to be a wig. The other lady was white and had the thin frame and sunken features of someone whose principal relationship was with the needle. They brought with them a ghetto blaster and an ominous-looking black sports bag. There was a spontaneous round of applause and all conversation stopped. The black woman plugged in the stereo and began playing a tape of some cheesy house music. By now I was beginning to have an inkling about what I was about to see.

The 'show' began with the ladies peeling each other's underwear off and kissing and licking each other's bodies. Then the black lady removed a cucumber from the bag and, after placing a condom on it, used it to pleasure the smackhead. All this was done on the lino under bright industrial-strength lights. I was slightly horrified and found the sheer biological openness of their actions really disconcerting. I had seen ping-pong balls fly across the room at sex shows at clubs in Patpong, Bangkok, but to see this kind of thing just off the most famous shopping road in London surrounded by suited men on a Thursday evening made the whole experience weird and somewhat disturbing. My deeply religious upbringing combined with some semblance of political correctness made me feel genuinely uncomfortable. The image of fifty suited men staring at two women abusing themselves did not sit well even with my admittedly ever-loosening ethical boundaries. As I write this now I wonder why I didn't get up and leave there and then and can only put it down to the clear embarrassment that this would have caused me, Tony and David. Again, that's my excuse and I'm sticking with it.

Things went from bad to worse when the black lady approached men in the front row, handed them the cucumber and bent over backwards while they took it in turns to feed it into her gaping maw. At the same moment Tony was approached by her 'colleague'. She expertly removed his trousers and pants, placed a condom on his already erect penis and promptly sat on it, moving herself up and down. As this was happening Tony looked over at me with a cheesy grin and winked. I hoped and prayed she would not try to hand me a similar treatment and thanked the Lord that she moved clockwise away from me to her next victim. I now knew why David, who possessed an element of discretion, had made sure he had not sat in the front row – as well as why Tony had made sure that he and I had sat right at the front. This performance went on for about an hour and as soon as it had finished I pretended I needed to go to the toilet and left the building. I felt slightly sick and seriously uneasy. I wanted to take a steaming hot bath and remove the guilt I felt about what I had just witnessed. What I had seen was the most horrific side of City life – suited men using cash to make women debase themselves for their own animal desires. In many ways, I think, that experience sums up what the City does so expertly across the world; using its own cash or the promise of cash to rape natural resources – be it coffee plantations in Brazil, oil reserves in Iraq or any other sellable commodity.

I never discussed the sleazy show that I witnessed in that Oxford Street basement with either David or Tony. They were both lovable rogues but they were still rogues and at that stage in my career I retained a few ethics. I was also never invited to another 'gentlemen's evening', having blotted my copy book by leaving early. Perhaps my actions had made both of my colleagues reflect on the morality of such spectacles, though I seriously doubt it. More likely, they just thought I was not as much 'fun' as they'd hoped. In fact, my relationship with both these formative characters suffered somewhat and during late 1998 the lingering doubts I had about whether this bullshit career really was for me resurfaced. As winter closed in and I walked to the tube station in drizzly darkness every morning and left the office in the same depressing conditions, I contemplated quitting the City. I often thought of my friend Alex gallivanting in the Goan sunshine, poor but happy, and wondered if I'd made the right life choice.

It would take a chance encounter with the biggest cocksucker this side of Bethnal Green to convince me that I had a moral duty to show these narrow-minded motherfuckers I could whup their collective ass.

3

THE NEMESIS

Hugo Bentley is the kind of self-obsessed, arrogant prick who clearly relishes the smell of his own farts. Foolish people who carelessly follow him into a lift are invariably taking a risk with their olfactory well being. I first had the misfortune of coming across him on a corporate jolly in Scotland but his reputation for being an egotistical arsehole preceded him. It has been said that a man's ego is often in direct inverse proportion to his intelligence and never was that more true than with Hugo. Although I never had the displeasure to find out, I can also say with little doubt that it wasn't the only thing that was negatively correlated with his enormous ego. If ever a man was hung like a baby shrew, it was surely Hugo Bentley.

Hugo had short dark hair and was tall with thin arms and legs. He had a smug smile perpetually on his face which had the extraordinary effect of irritating everyone within a ten-foot radius and he had the kind of weak chin that only centuries of inbreeding could account for. His stiff bearing betrayed a military background while his insurmountable ego reflected the superficial confidence that the top public schools tend to instil in their pupils. Time would reveal to me that he had all the modesty of Simon Cowell after a four-day coke bender while having a lack of consideration for others unmatched since Pol Pot strutted his funky stuff in Cambodia. This was not just my opinion but also the view of all the members of the team that he led from Mighty Yankbank (as well as anyone who spent more than four seconds in his company). It was the worst-kept secret in the Square Mile that his team hated him with a passion but knew that he was vital to their success because of his corporate contacts and smarmy ability to schmooze clients. Such was the contempt he inspired, that a member of his own team once openly disclosed to me and other utilities analysts that the joke on the trading floor at Mighty Yankbank was that Hugo's only friends were Ronald McDonald and Colonel Sanders. A cursory assessment of his greasy complexion and his personality defects meant no one amongst us questioned this rumour's validity.

Unfortunately, Hugo was not just a total and utter cocksucker. He was a total and utter cocksucker who happened to be the City's number-one-rated utilities analyst. Twice a year surveys are sent out to clients at all the major fund management institutions across the world that we analysts provide a service to. These characters rank us sector analysts from one to four in order of preference and these votes are then weighted according to the size of the institution and collated. Twice a year the results of these polls from two different companies, Extel and Institutional Investor, are announced and we analysts wait with bated breath to hear our ranking.

There was a time when obtaining votes meant speaking to a few fund managers at the major institutions. However, over time the businesses that invest your pension, ISAs, unit trusts, etc. (i.e. our clients) have merged and grown and so has the number of people that they employ to invest your money. In the 1980s the biggest contact between the sell-side (i.e. those of us at investment banks) and the buy-side (i.e. fund management institutions, our clients) involved salesmen talking to fund managers. Salesmen are essentially spivs who broke (sell) shares in any and all of the companies in the market while fund managers are also generalists who run funds that invest in shares across the board.

However, as the ever-expanding fund management institutions began to employ more buy-side analysts in order to have a more sophisticated assessment of the companies that they should invest in, the investment banks had to keep up or risk being less knowledgeable about stocks than the clients they were theoretically advising. The absurdity of this situation was that sector teams at banks grew larger and larger and, because the number of listed companies was not growing as rapidly, this resulted in ever-increasing specialisation. So, while a team covering the European pharmaceutical sector in the 1980s may have comprised three people at best, by the late 1990s there could be ten people covering the same number of stocks. A vicious circle developed with banks competing to have the biggest teams even though there was insufficient commission to justify their existence. The perception that lucrative corporate work (i.e. mergers, acquisitions and bringing companies to market) would be offered to banks with highly ranked teams meant money was thrown at expanding sell-side analysis despite a distinct lack of available commission. This process not only helped result in a massive job bonanza in the City but also meant there was not sufficient commission to go round. This, in turn, helps explain why the cost-income ratio of investment banks sometimes went over a hundred per cent, revealing the time-honoured truth behind the old adage that investment banking is a great business . . . if you're an investment banker.

The other impact of these ever-expanding teams was that our clients had the misfortune of being bombarded every day by hundreds of telephone calls, emails and messages on their Bloomberg terminals from ambitious analysts desperate to make their mark in an increasingly competitive world. It was these same poor clients who voted in the Extel and Institutional Investor surveys that were sent out in March and October respectively. The results of these surveys were published in big books in June and February with the Extel survey holding an awards ceremony that was dubbed 'the Oscars of the City'. While there were some similarities, I suspect the attendees of Hollywood's Oscar ceremony were a little more glamorous and charismatic than us analysts – although I imagine the egos of those attending each ceremony were on a par.

These surveys split the market into around thirty pan-European sectors, i.e. oil companies, banks, utilities, etc. Theoretically, the fund managers and buy-side analysts vote for the analysts they believe provide them with the best service, have the most in-depth knowledge of their sector, and make the most profitable stock recommendations. In reality, of course, things are a little more complex than that. As Tony had informed me early in my career, the best client is one that thinks you're his mate because they would feel guilty about not voting for you. This would be the key to my success and was central to Hugo's strategy too. Hugo was generally about as reasonable as Naomi Campbell in the grips of a serious bout of PMT when it came to his own team or competitors. However, he could charm the pants off clients in a way that seemed so unbelievably transparent to me but clearly paid dividends.

From the word go I had decided that the principal way of persuading clients to vote for me was through 'entertaining' them. I have no doubt that restaurant owners across the City witness a somewhat confusing increase in their revenues over the March and October voting periods as analysts like me and Hugo give our expense allowances a real hammering in order to bribe our clients into voting for us. This, of course, has not gone unnoticed by some of the smarter clients but even then you can make the whole procedure into a kind of ironic, self-aware joke that still ultimately has the desired effect of winning votes. This joke might not be quite as amusing if we analysed the fact that each glug of champers and mouthful of lobster is factored into the 0.2 per cent commission that we banks generally charge the buy-side whenever we buy and sell shares for them. In other words, my greedy lust for recognition ultimately meant that Mrs Miggins might have to sometimes forego her annual trip to Bognor Regis because her pension was less than she was hoping for. Dwelling on such a thought might make each mouthful of lobster Thermidor slightly less palatable for the average analyst . . . well, for about three seconds, anyway.

Everyone in the City pretends that these external surveys mean nothing – funnily enough especially those who don't feature in the top ten. They are dismissed as unrepresentative, easily abused and, for want of a better word, 'silly'. In reality, these surveys play an extremely important role in dictating how much we get paid, which, in the City, is akin to saying they are as important as life itself. These surveys are the most publicly accessible assessment of the effectiveness of an analyst as perceived by his clients and, hence, they are the first port of call when headhunters are given a mandate to fill a particular post. The fact that I may have garnered a vote by taking some bloke from Fidelity to L'Escargot the day before the voting form arrived on his desk is deemed irrelevant because the assumption is that everyone else has tried the same trick and yet he still voted for me. That's as maybe but in reality some analysts, like me, are much more open to buying votes through entertainment. Also, some of my competitors are so repellent that clients would probably prefer to share a four-day-old kebab with some pissheads on the street than be taken out by them for a £1000 nosh-up at Petrus – even if the other guests around the table were the Swedish female under-twenty-one beach volleyball team.

These surveys are also the most obviously quantifiable gauge of our success because other measures, such as the commission our bank makes in the sector, are either secret to external parties or not necessarily a true reflection of a team's ability. For example, sector rotation and market movements can have a far bigger impact on commission levels in a specific sector than the effectiveness of the sector team. Amusingly, I heard about one rival bank in 2000 that, despite having no utilities team in place for most of the year, produced record levels of commission in the sector. This was simply because all the investors had been piling into cheap, high-yielding utility shares after the dramatic end of the tech boom in March 2000 since they were more 'defensive', i.e. more likely to outperform in weak markets. Strangely enough, analysts don't like these facts to be publicised too much because they call into question the usefulness of having analysts at all.

So, the conclusion I made at a very early stage in my career was that if I wanted to make big bucks I needed to do everything possible to become highly ranked. Although commission (and corporate work, at least before regulatory changes in 2002–3) theoretically dictated my pay, a bank would only ever pay me as 'little' as they could get away with. Since banks knew that their competitors generally poached highly ranked analysts it was those in the top-ranked teams that they had to keep sweet. This, in turn, led to the absurd, yet completely logical, conclusion that I would prefer to be highly ranked than bring commission to my bank and make its shareholders some profits. I have, on several occasions, when asked by a client if I would prefer to be rewarded for my efforts through commission or votes, opted for the latter, knowing that it would have a greater impact on my bonus than actually making my bank money. This is one of the reasons why the interests of a bank's shareholders and those of an analyst who works for it are not necessarily aligned as they theoretically should be.

So, despite his extraordinary lack of redeeming features, Hugo at least could hold his head up high because he knew that all we other sell-side analysts envied his success. What was already an ego of almost biblical proportions was hence fed by the publicly acknowledged fact that he was the number-one-rated utilities analyst. The invincible demeanour that this status afforded Hugo somewhat reminded me of that held by the first kid in our school to lose his virginity. Just as the freshly deflowered thirteen-year-old Charles Scott could win any argument in 1985 by simply reminding the class that you were a virgin and he wasn't, so Hugo could in 1998 subtly ensure that you never forgot that he was number one and you weren't. Hence, any verbal battles that he might lose could never detract from the fact that he had already won the war – at least until the next survey was out. This, of course, made an unbearably irritating individual even more annoying . . . especially to a competitive joker like me with a chip on his shoulder big enough to feed the Chinese army.

I was on the pavement outside the Balmoral hotel in Edinburgh just about to climb the steps when I first saw Hugo. It was a Monday afternoon in late 1998, and I and all my fellow water analysts had been invited by Edinburgh Water on a corporate jolly. This was my first proper junket and the schedule looked to contain a pleasingly small amount of actual work and lots of 'fun' things like golf and a dinner at the Balmoral's Michelin-starred restaurant. The management of Edinburgh Water were clearly just as happy to try and bribe us analysts as we were our clients. Even at the early stage in my career it was clear that the whole business world ran on people schmoozing other people and generally using shareholders' cash for the privilege.

Edinburgh Water's management ultimately hoped that by letting me play a bit of golf or giving me a free spa treatment I would tell all my clients to buy the company's shares and so push up the share price. I would love to believe that the management of the companies that do this do so because of their magnanimous wish to increase the wealth of their shareholders. Indeed, it almost brings a tear to my eye to think that Edinburgh Water's management were striving to put a few extra quid in the pockets of the 'SIDs' who became part of the Thatcher revolution and invested their hard-earned cash in UK water stocks in December 1989. However, cynics may argue that, if this happens, it is simply a fortunate by-product of management's true motive which is to increase their own wealth since they are generally major shareholders and holders of stock options in their own company. Indeed, some deeply suspicious types have pointed out that these corporate jollies aimed at boosting share prices sometimes coincide somewhat remarkably with the date that management stock options vest . . . though, of course, I would never cast such aspersions.

What company directors don't understand is that we analysts are generally a sceptical bunch who have an attitude to management presentations similar to that which legendarily aggressive interviewer Jeremy Paxman has to politicians. He has been quoted as saying that when interrogating politicians the overriding thought he maintains is 'Why is this bastard lying to me?' What is even worse is that we analysts tend to view luxurious corporate trips as an example of poor cost control, which, in a highly regulated sector like UK water, is deemed a particularly bad show. In other words, lots of shareholders' cash is spent entertaining analysts in the hope of boosting a company's share price in order to make said company's management even richer when in fact it has the opposite effect. It is, without doubt, a funny old world.

Anyway, as I was about to enter the Balmoral, struggling with my golf clubs and somewhat tired after the five-hour train journey from London, I heard the unmistakable deep growl of a Ferrari's engine. I turned around to see a bright yellow Ferrari Testarossa pull up outside. The passenger's window whirred down and a bony hand reached out and beckoned the kilt-wearing doorman over to the car. The doorman paused for just long enough to show his irritation with the self-satisfied driver who hadn't even deigned to lean across the passenger seat so as to facilitate conversation. Hugo had actually managed to irritate someone within a second of being twenty feet from them and without uttering a single word, which I thought at the time must be some kind of a record. At a later period, when I was discussing Hugo with some of my more amenable competitors, one asked the question, 'Why do people take an instant dislike to Hugo Bentley?' The conclusion from everyone was quite simply 'because it saves time'.

I watched with a horrified fascination as Hugo aggressively demanded that the doorman park his precious car 'somewhere safe'. He was apparently 'knackered from two days' grouse shooting on Lord Clydesdale's estate'. Hugo's abrupt manner and posh English voice were clearly angering the doorman to an extraordinary degree. The doorman's face was turning puce and it was clearly only the thought that he would lose his job which prevented him from taking the little knife (the sgian dubh) from his long green sock and plunging it directly into Hugo's gaunt neck. With some bemusement I entered the hotel already aware that I had just experienced my first encounter with the legend that was Hugo Bentley.

In my hotel room I ruminated on the City tendency to flaunt wealth through flash cars, bespoke suits and Rolex watches. I had been brought up by devoutly religious left-wing parents who thought that consumerism and materialism were not only wrong but virtually sinful. I had been consistently told that discussing money was gauche and that worldly riches do not bring happiness and are, in fact, an impediment to the long-term goal of reaching Heaven. 'Here have we no abiding city' was an oft-quoted Bible passage, as was the well known 'It is easier for a camel to go through the eye of a needle than for a rich man to enter the kingdom of God'. Indeed, my mother would remind me whenever I came over for dinner of Timothy, chapter six, verse ten: 'The love of money is the root of all evil.' Meanwhile, my father would remind me of the sociologist Max Weber's view that 'a man should wear his possessions lightly as a cloak, but for us they have become an iron cage'. While I had not necessarily taken on board the religious element of my mother's views I certainly believed that how much money you had did not correlate to how happy you were – quite the opposite. Meeting numerous rich but oft-divorced, unfit, alcoholic, miserable men in the City only ever confirmed this opinion.

However, these 'hippy' attitudes to wealth were, somewhat unsurprisingly, the exception in the City, while Hugo's obvious wish to flash his cash was the norm. Oscar Wilde famously defined cynics as people 'who know the price of everything but the value of nothing', but he could just as easily have been referring to Cityboys. This is partly because we are, almost by definition, money-obsessed cynics whose job it is to put a price on assets without ever confusing the process with silly things like emotions, morals or artistic concerns. Since material goods are the most obvious signifier of financial success which, in turn, is what many Cityboys deem to be the gauge of how brilliant they are, Ferrari dealers and Rolex salesmen alike can lick their greasy lips as long as the good times roll in the Square Mile. This pathetic urge to one-up our peers ensures that Satan will be selling ice creams long before the consumerist restraint that this world is so clearly crying out for materialises; that is, so long as Cityboys sit at the top of the economic tree.

With these thoughts rebounding around my head I unpacked my bag and put on a golf kit I'd hastily assembled while half asleep early that morning. My classy ensemble consisted of a pink collared Lacoste T-shirt, a moth-eaten overly tight Aran jumper, a peculiar woolly bobble hat my gran had knitted me ten years before when clearly in the grips of senile dementia, and an appalling pair of thick purple cords that were about three sizes too big. To say I looked sartorially challenged would be akin to saying Mike Tyson looked like he could handle himself in a fight. As I nervously checked myself out in the cupboard mirror I cursed my ill-thought-out choice of attire but, as usual, decided that I could just about get away with it. After a brief hesitation about whether it was wise to present myself to my competitors looking like Terry Wogan on acid, my keenness to play on what was supposed to be one of the finest golf courses in Scotland helped me ignore my concerns. And, besides, my fellow players would be dressed in golfing clothes and no one, apart perhaps from Samuel L. Jackson, ever looks cool on the golf course. So, I bounded down the stairs to the lobby desperate not to miss the minivan taking myself and the others who selected the golfing option to the Royal Musselburgh golf course. However, there was no one in the lobby and after waiting around for a few minutes I asked at reception if they knew where the Edinburgh Water group was. The attractive receptionist looked up, clocked my threads and, with a disconcerting bemused expression on her face, pointed me in the direction of the main bar to the left of the reception desk.

On entering the noisy bar I immediately realised what a truly horrific error I had made. There was a group of mainly young men to the side of the bar and I recognised a few of my fellow water analysts amongst them. EVERY SINGLE FUCKING ONE OF THEM WAS EITHER WEARING A DARK SUIT OR 'SMART CASUAL' ATTIRE. I stopped dead as if I'd just walked straight into a sheet of plate glass, my shoes squeaking on the polished floor as I did so. Like a startled rabbit I stared at my fellow analysts and in a millisecond came to the simple conclusion that the only possible course of action was to remove myself from this potentially humiliating experience ASA fucking P. Just as I was about to slowly turn around and execute my escape plan one of the men glanced in my direction. By some sick twist of fate it was Edinburgh Water's investor relations manager. He was one of the few people who would definitely recognise me because we'd recently met at his company's full-year results presentation. I tried to avoid eye contact and actually found myself raising my hands in front of me as if I were trying to ask someone not to attack me. But it was too late. I had recently downgraded Edinburgh Water from a Hold to a Sell recommendation and now it was payback time. The clearly amused IR man wasn't about to miss this opportunity to make me feel like the prick that I resembled.

'Steve, come and join us,' he said, beckoning me towards the group, unable to disguise his joy at my embarrassment.

Like a small child gingerly approaching a blackboard having been asked by the teacher to spell a word he had never heard of, I slowly walked towards the group, dragging my feet while my face turned redder and redder. By the time I reached my fellow sensibly dressed water analysts every one of them was staring at me and some were actually cracking up. Feigning confidence in this situation was a big ask but I'd done this kind of thing before and if no one said anything too harsh I might just be able to style it out. It was then that Hugo chose to break the unnatural silence: 'Christ almighty, no one told me it was fancy dress. What's this chap come as? A vagrant Womble?'

Pretty much everyone in the group burst into raucous laughter. It was only the sole female analyst who stifled her snigger but somehow her pity made things even worse.

Come on, Steve, I thought, you can deal with this situation . . . you can show these arseholes that they don't intimidate you. I needed to think of something funny and any hesitation would prove fatal.

'What have you come as? A . . .' I stuttered.

I was about to say 'a posh fuckwit?' but realised just in time that such an insult would be way in excess of the level of aggression that had so far been exhibited. To have said such a humourless and blatant insult would have just led to an awkward silence for the whole group. In these kind of pseudo-friendly events aggressive one-upmanship was not only tolerated but was actually the norm; however, only within certain parameters. Hostile put-downs and catty comments were *de rigueur*, but only if done subtly and with a smile on the face.

Unfortunately for me, the alternative to actually voicing my unsubtle insult was to not finish my sentence at all and to keep everyone hanging waiting for a response, which was frankly almost as appalling. Hugo generously broke the silence: 'A what? Pray tell.'

He had me on the ropes and he knew it. He was relishing every second of my humiliation.

Finally, I managed to splutter, 'A . . . a . . . very nice young man.' While the forced laughs my comment received were only of the polite kind, the relief from those around me – who clearly found the whole experience excruciatingly painful – was palpable.

I think few would dispute that my first experience of corporate hospitality could have had a more auspicious start. Having failed to read the schedule properly and subsequently missing the formal 'welcome drinks' was a calamitous oversight. Unfortunately for me, things were about to get even worse.

When the IR man took out the piece of paper detailing who was going on which activity (spa, golf or shopping trip around the Royal Mile), there was a certain inevitability that Hugo had opted for the golf option. Even before our names were read out, I knew who I would be playing against.

'The harder I practise the luckier I get,' retorted Hugo smugly after he struck a near-perfect five-iron at the eighteenth hole and the ball had landed about five foot from the pin. Admittedly, I had had absolutely no right to exclaim 'lucky bastard' under my breath but my competitive nature was getting the better of me. All I could think, as I steadied myself to tee off on this tricky

212-yard par three, was that if he kept up his cocky nonsense he'd be damn lucky to be in full possession of his teeth by the time we reached the clubhouse. Such was the man's unbearable self-satisfaction that only a driver wrapped around his head would be sufficient to wipe that conceited grin off his stupid, smug face. For practically the whole duration of the game I had been considering which club to start my career as an amateur dentist with. I briefly thought that a three-wood could do the job but soon decided that no club lower than a driver would possibly do.

Up to that point my golf had been patchy at best but we were playing match play and, more by luck than skill, we were level on the final hole. Whoever won this hole would win the game. Despite looking immaculate in handmade tweed plus fours and with a set of the latest Calloway golf clubs that probably cost more than my car, Hugo was not as brilliant as he believed – something that I suspect may have been the case with several other aspects of his life. He claimed to play off fifteen, the same as me, but that was optimistic at best. While most golfers are 'bandits' who like to underestimate their handicap so as to increase their chances of victory, such was Hugo's vast ego that he did the opposite. If there was any justice in this sick and twisted world I should have been beating him but I was riled and edgy. The hideous experience at the Balmoral was still playing over and over in my little brain. Even worse, I was on one of the poshest golf clubs in Scotland and I still resembled a hand-me-down kid whose parents frequented charity shops. Hugo had also upped the ante by placing a hundred-pound wager on this final hole – a carefully chosen sum which clearly meant nothing to him but, being only a few years out of university, still felt like a lot of money to me.

As with all golf matches the game had begun long before we had even put our spikes on. Hugo knew he had a massive psychological advantage having already publicly humiliated me but he sensed blood and, like a vicious shark circling an injured baby seal, he wanted more. As soon as he had heard he was playing me he said loudly, so that I and everyone else could hear, 'Oh, this is going to be a lot of fun.' One–nil Hugo. In the mini-van over to the course he took one dismissive look at my clubs and, to a round of amused giggles, sneered, 'Where did you get those from? Woolworths?' Two–nil Hugo. Finally, as the eight of us began a tedious conversation about the merits of Essex Water he asked me directly what the previous chief executive's name was, pretending that he had momentarily forgotten. The current CEO had been in place for just over two years and so I, of course, had no idea who the hell he was referring to. This was no accident – Hugo knew that my relatively recent introduction to the ever-exciting world of UK water would ensure that I would not know the chap's name. As I struggled nervously to explain my ignorance in front of my peers, Hugo hastily interrupted me and blurted out, 'Oh, I remember now, it was William Caldeshott – how could I possibly forget, one of the most famous water executives of the early nineties.' Three–nil Hugo.

The terrible thing was that Hugo wasn't just publicly humiliating a fresh-faced newcomer to the world of finance in order to win a game of golf. He wasn't merely making sure that I realised who was the king of the jungle and that I should thank my lucky stars just to be breathing the same air as he was. He wasn't merely making sure that I knew that any thoughts of challenging his supremacy in the future were futile. What he was doing was even crueller than that. He was showing me up in front of my peers. I knew even at that early stage of my career that these guys around me were my potential employers or colleagues in the merry-go-round that is the City job market. I also knew that analyst communities were small and that battered reputations could take years to rebuild. Hugo wasn't merely making me feel like a twat, he was helping reduce my future earnings potential. There are a lot of things that we in the City may forgive people for but reducing our material wealth is certainly not one of them.

I pulled out my six-iron, carefully placed the tee in the ground, and threw some loose grass in the air to assess the speed and direction of the wind. There was no way I was going to let this tosser's mind games put me off. I had to be strong. I had to forget everything around me, swing the club as I had done a thousand times before, and hit through the ball. After one practice swing I stepped up to the tee, swung the club back and . . . bang, I completely fluffed it. I hooked the ball nastily and it was heading for the trees to the left of the green. Such was my desperation to take this wank-stain down a peg or two that I let out an extended 'FUCK' so loudly that a couple of coffin-dodgers on a completely separate fairway looked around in complete horror. My knowledge of golfing regulations has somewhat deteriorated but, even now, I seem to remember that paragraph four, sub-clause seven of the standard golf rules states quite clearly that shouting obscenities loud enough to give nearby pensioners a cardiac is generally frowned upon (apart, apparently, from certain clubs in the Liverpool area where such behaviour is actively encouraged).

As I watched the ball flying off towards a particularly large tree my heart sank as I realised that Hugo was going to win the match. Then a miracle happened. The ball struck the tree and bounced off perfectly to land on the green. Amazingly, it came to rest about six feet from the hole, just slightly behind Hugo's ball. Clearly the big man upstairs had been listening to my prayers. My agonising despair switched immediately into unfathomable ecstasy. Those same pensioners whom I had offended seconds before now witnessed me jumping up and down in triumphant delight. I swear if I had snuffed it there and then they would have needed to build me a special coffin just to accommodate my enormous grin. The glum look on Hugo's face only heightened my joy and I actually wagged my finger at him just as I remember Dennis Taylor doing when he beat Steve Davis in the Snooker World Cup final of 1985. It was not a particularly magnanimous or understated display of emotions, but by this stage my competitiveness had gone into overdrive and I would have been willing to pledge my soul to the devil in return for beating this arse-wipe. Frankly, at that particular stage of that particular game against that particular twat I would have been willing to pledge my soul and all the souls of my nearest and dearest just to whup his sorry ass. Mephistopheles would have been so excited at the sudden influx of condemned souls into his fiery pit that he would have shut up shop, taken the rest of the day off and gone home to give Mrs Mephistopheles a damn good seeing to.

Reading that last paragraph again, I realise that the reader may have come to the conclusion that I have a somewhat competitive personality. Well, you'd be wrong. I'm not just competitive, I was one of the most competitive people ever to work in the Square Mile, which is akin to claiming to be the biggest nutter in Baghdad or the fattest man in Florida. I had entered the City with a fairly competitive streak but had steadily become more so, being surrounded by ruthless buffoons who continually judged their success relative to their peers. This disease was catching and I had the requisite psychological make-up to bite. Even by this early stage of my career, I completely concurred with Gore Vidal's famous proposition that it is not enough to succeed; others must fail. I couldn't have agreed more with Richard Nixon's sentiment when he said, 'Show me a good loser and I'll show you a loser.' Having two older brothers meant I had no choice but to compete about anything and everything. It's not something I'm particularly proud of. It just is, and the City made it much worse – which is something that happens to many of those who enter its hallowed gates. I am painfully aware that anyone who is truly comfortable in their own skin would not feel the need to constantly remind every poor sucker within earshot how much smarter or richer they are. I can't really picture the notoriously chilled Dalai Lama sitting at his pad in Dharamsala telling every joker who turns up to see him how superfly he is. He leaves that sort of horseshit to insecure buffoons like Simon Cowell or Kanye West. Sadly, it seems pretty clear to me that the genius who wrote 'every external boast is the manifestation of an inner doubt' knew exactly what he was talking about.

My 'disease' is prevalent in the Square Mile, which both welcomes those with it and demands that those without it soon contract it. When I am asked what common feature most encapsulates us stockbrokers, people generally assume that I'll say something obvious like a psychopathic selfishness that would scare Hannibal Lecter or an inconsiderate ruthlessness when exploiting the world that Genghis Khan would deem excessive. While both of these are, of course, completely valid, the true common feature that unites practically all stockbrokers is a competitiveness that would shock champion cyclist Lance 'pain is temporary but quitting lasts for ever' Armstrong. We brokers will compete over everything: a game of squash, our intellectual ability, or the size of our bank balance or sexual equipment – with this last element, of course, underlying all the others. Indeed, I would argue that betting and investing, which is essentially all that happens in the City, are merely the perfect blend of intellectual one-upmanship and financial reward, which is why it appeals so wonderfully to us deluded Cityboys. When we invest in a company we are saying that we know better than everyone else about that company's prospects and that time will show us to be right and all those other suckers out there who mispriced the asset to be wrong. Such is our competitiveness that most Cityboys would rather forego a threesome with Kate Moss and Giselle Bundchen if it meant they could make such a declaration publicly and then be proved right by the share-price movement.

If my theory is correct that this competitiveness is endemic in the City and that it is the product of feelings of inadequacy, then I think it's safe to conclude that insecurity is the main force that drives the City (as well as insatiable greed of course). This helps explain why the vast majority of the Square Mile's front-office employees are young wannabe alpha males who have all the testosterone and self-doubt necessary to participate in a continual cockfight with their peers. Fortunately for our employers this competitive intellectual masturbation comes naturally to most graduate trainees. That's because they've generally just spent the last decade of their automaton lives trying to one-up their peers at school and university where such behaviour is wholeheartedly encouraged by those in charge. Only this carefully nurtured and desperate will to win catalysed by deep feelings of insecurity can explain why City workers are willing to get up at 5.30 a.m. every day and work seventy-plus-hour weeks when life is short and clearly not a dress rehearsal. Content, secure people just wouldn't have the drive to put themselves through that kind of nonsense.

Interestingly, this underlying competitiveness is actively encouraged by employers at investment banks. I once even heard a rumour (probably apocryphal) that, when selecting graduate trainees, those nice people at Goldman Sucks have a preference for those who were 'probably bullied' at school. Psychologists have allegedly informed the Human Resources department that the people most likely to be willing to work until 4 a.m. and utilise their weekends finalising the small print on some tedious corporate deal are those who are desperate to prove themselves, having been objects of derision when at school. They know that every bullied geek's dream of revenge is to earn enough cash to get the girl and buy the Ferrari and then make sure their former tormentors know about it. They know that the average spoddy loser is desperate to drive an open-top sports car around his old adversaries' council estate with a blonde next to him shouting: 'YOU SEE THIS, YOU MOTHERFUCKERS? I'M SOMEBODY

NOW! I'M A WINNER! I'M RICH!' Unfortunately, while this last assertion may be factually correct, they are, of course, still the same pathetic idiots inside and, deep down, they know that they always will be.

The other way that the City encourages competitiveness is by having surveys and league tables to cover every conceivable aspect of City work. Not only are there the aforementioned Extel and Institutional Investor surveys which publicly reveal how well regarded we analysts are by our client-base and by the companies we research. Surveys and league tables also exist for bonds, derivatives, corporate work, institutional funds' performance, hedge funds and so forth. The Thomson Financial survey of mergers and acquisition rankings is especially competitive since banks believe that they are more likely to win further corporate work if they have proven their worth by having undertaken lots of previous deals. The logic is that the more deals you've done and the bigger the deals you've organised the more deals you're likely to do. So, in theory, these surveys play their role in ensuring the existence of an efficient market by objectively revealing the best banks for mergers and acquisitions or the best hedge funds to invest in and so forth. That's as maybe, but what they really do is ensure that insecure competitive characters in the City (as I became), who have some pathetic desperation to prove themselves, have clear publicly visible goals to drive towards. In that sense, these dreadful surveys are part of a psychological trap designed to make sure that we throw away the best years of our life in pursuit of 'success'. The cunning bastards who thought up this dreadful ruse need to have their testicles removed and shoved down their throats for crimes against humanity.

Back on the golf course, Hugo regained his composure and quickly reverted to annoying mode. 'That, I believe, is what is called "an OJ Simpson" . . . in that you got away with it.' He had been making these kinds of comments throughout the game and while superficially they were light-hearted attempts to amuse, they were, of course, all part of his gamesmanship. A ball I had hit that had hardly risen more than ten feet above the fairway and then rolled along the ground but still managed to travel over 120 yards was 'a Sally Gunnell' ('ugly, but it gets there'). A rather awkward yet reasonably short putt I faced was 'a Dennis Wise' ('a nasty five footer'). When my ball went into a sand trap it was 'an Adolf Hitler' ('a shot in the bunker'), and after his ball joined mine it was 'an Eva Braun' ('two shots in the bunker'). Although some of these were almost amusing I refused to even break a smile, knowing that this would be playing into his little psychological mantrap.

On the green it was me to putt first since my ball was further away from the hole. I nervously pulled my putter out the bag. As I approached the ball I could feel the adrenaline coursing through my body. I had to beat this cluster-fuck if it was the last thing I ever did. I actually felt like I was in *Goldfinger* playing golf at Stoke Poges. But who was I – the ever-suave 007 and ultimate winner of the gladiatorial contest, or his defeated arch-enemy? Only the next shot would decide. The game's importance had assumed mythical proportions way beyond putting little balls in slightly bigger holes. This shot was going to produce a binary conclusion: I was a winner who had wiped the grin off the most repellent man I'd ever met or I was a pointless dickhead who would never amount to anything in the City or, for that matter, in life. It may sound extreme but at that particular moment this shot meant absolutely everything to me. Whether that little ball dropped in the hole would reveal to me whether my life was going to be a rich, fulfilling one during which I achieved my goals, or whether it was doomed to being a complete waste of time in which I never amounted to anything.

I knelt down to assess the lie of the land. The hole was about three inches above my ball and on a slight left-to-right slope.

I needed to aim for the left lip of the hole and hit it slightly harder than on the flat. After a single nervy practice shot I placed the club head next to the ball with its toe slightly raised. I took a deep breath and swung the club back. Just as the club head reached the pinnacle of its back swing I heard an almost imperceptible cough. It was Hugo's last gambit. He had timed it absolutely perfectly. It was too late to start the putt again as I had already started the downward swing. My club struck the ball. Time seemed to stand still as I watched it approach the hole. It looked like it was going to be all right. It looked like Hugo's trick hadn't worked.

It may have looked like a lot of things but what it didn't do was actually go in the fucking hole. It just didn't quite have the legs and came to rest about an inch from the mouth. I didn't know what to do. I wanted to shout. I wanted to cry. I wanted to shove a divot remover into Hugo's eyeball. There were a lot of things I wanted to do but I just kept quiet, placed a marker where my ball had come to rest, retreated five yards and stood there praying that Hugo would fuck up. Even Hugo's tiresome comment that 'if you're not up, you're not in, dear boy' failed to raise a response.

Of course, he punched his ball straight in the hole and with a nonchalance that suggested that there was never any doubt that he was going to win said, 'Hard cheese, old bean. You almost gave me a run for my money. Better luck next time, eh?' I shook his hand with a reluctance that would have been less extreme had he been a leprous Ebola victim and walked slowly towards the clubhouse like a punch-drunk boxer. My tail was so firmly between my legs that I found it rather hard to walk. My wounds were so severe that I didn't even want to lick them; these were mortal blows and all I really wanted to do was curl up and die. I can't really remember Hugo's smug witterings on the way back. I can't even remember handing him his ill-gotten gains. All I can remember is that I lost.

*

One of the classic City texts that I and many of my peers were told to read on becoming stockbrokers was *The Art of War* written by the Chinese warlord Sun Tzu in the sixth century BC. I had ignored this advice having always considered the book to be macho nonsense with few relevant lessons for a twentieth-century boy like me. While that may well be the case one of its key messages would really have helped me out on that fateful day: 'Fight only the battles you can win.' I had failed to do this and I had paid the price. I also wished I'd listened to Dirty Harry's equally wise advice on the fateful night just before I had started this appalling career: a man's got to know his limitations. I was beginning to find out mine, but in a way that couldn't have been more painful. Everything seemed pointless.

Back at the hotel, Hugo wasted no time in telling anyone and everyone within earshot that he had 'opened a can of whupass' and ensured that the 'uppity pipsqueak knew who was boss'. As I trudged up the stairs to my room I heard his braying voice say with mock sympathy, 'Well, he tried his best, God bless him.' I opened my door, slumped on the bed, and actually had to turn the television on just to drown out the endless 'what ifs' that were playing over and over in my head. After a long bath, I got dressed in my six-pound suit and walked down to the pre-dinner drinks being held in the same bar where all this pain had first begun.

The evening followed a routine that I am now horribly familiar with, having been to hundreds of these appalling events. The analysts around the dinner table generally begin dinner exhibiting a false friendliness towards each other. Soon, however, once the booze has been flowing for a few hours, deeply held rivalries and long-standing conflicts rear their ugly heads. Suddenly, thinly veiled insults are being traded across the dining table and belligerent tossers are reminding their competitors in front of everyone about recommendations that they have got badly wrong in the past. Sometimes senior company managers find themselves acting like boxing referees desperate to placate the petty squabbles of these overindulged idiots. I have only heard of one occasion when fisticuffs actually broke out between two analysts on a corporate jolly but the underlying aggression that would, in more honest venues like an East End pub or frankly anywhere else, break out in to a fight, is ever present. It just doesn't actually kick off because we nice middle-class Oxbridge boys have got just enough restraint to avoid glassing each other because of a disagreement over something as abstract and invisible as a share price. This is no bad thing since suited fuckwits who couldn't fight their way out of a paper bag going at each other with fluted champagne glasses in a Michelin-starred restaurant is rarely a good look.

Of course, these events are also wonderful opportunities to embarrass competitors who have said nasty things about the host company. And woe betide anyone who has just downgraded their recommendation on the company's stock recently because this is sure to be raised by a competitor keen to ensure that your bank never gets any corporate work off the host. I, of course, fell into this category and with a tiresome inevitability, dear Hugo loudly asked me across the table to explain my negative argument to the finance director. While I would have been happy to take on Hugo, confident that I would be able to whip his flabby arse in any intellectual debate, taking on a man who probably knew more about his specific company than any other was like challenging Diego Maradona to a game of keepy-uppy. Through gritted teeth, I politely declined saying, 'I don't think this is the time or place, Hugo', spitting out his name with purposeful venom. I then swiftly moved the conversation on to what the agenda was for the next day. I just about got away with this move but could tell the FD wasn't finished with me.

The problem with company managements is that they always take Sell recommendations so goddam personally. It's almost as if my view that a company's shares are expensive is akin to buying a full-page advert in the *Financial Times* stating in big, bold letters that Edinburgh Water's management team are 'INCOMPETENT TWATS WHO COULDN'T ORGANISE A PISS-UP IN A BREWERY'. Admittedly, this is something I've thought about doing many times about many different management teams but as things stand I have not actually done. In reality, the quality of a management team is only a very small part of the calculation as to whether a company is worth investing in (especially a utility where strategic options are limited). The prospects for the sector the company works in, movements in interest rates, the oil price and so forth, and where the shares happen to trade relative to my long-term fundamental valuation, were always far more important determinants to my recommendation. But companies' management's pride (or just possibly their concerns about their stock options) means that they are like the Mafia in that they may forgive you but they never, ever forget.

Having said that, certain companies don't just refuse to forgive you, they also don't let you or anyone forget about their less-than-charitable feelings towards you. In theory, company directors should be helpful to all analysts in equal measure no matter what their viewpoint. To be more pleasant and informative to fans of your company would be a clear breach of the regulatory principle relating to the equal and fair dissemination of 'material information' to the market. To do so would make a management guilty of 'selective disclosure' and if it is 'share-price sensitive information' that is being disclosed then it is clearly unfair as it results in one set of analysts or investors having a massive information advantage over another. This could result in a better-informed fan of the company knowing something which results in them trading shares in said company with the less well-informed detractor and, in so doing, making a profit and denying the critical investor a profit. In my opinion, this is tantamount to robbery with the naughty finance director effectively holding the victim down while his analyst mate riffles through his pockets. There is no doubt that this happens all the time. Not only is it human nature to benefit people you see as 'friends', company managements also want positive analysts to be well regarded by the market so that their opinions are taken more seriously than those of their negative peers. One way of achieving this is by making sure supporters are given more information more quickly. On numerous occasions I have noticed a remarkable change in the companies I have covered when I have switched recommendation on a share. Formerly pleasant managements whom I have down-graded have turned frosty and unhelpful and vice versa. This is just another reason why it is so logical for sell-side analysts to generally be positive on the companies they analyse – once again making a mockery of our supposed objectivity.

The other reason not to irritate management through unsupportive recommendations is that some of them can act like spoiled, petulant children whose sweeties you've just stolen. Some may bad-mouth you to their investors (i.e. your clients) and try and discredit your research by going through it with a fine-tooth comb to find minor factual errors that they can publicise. Others will publicly embarrass you at results meetings through nasty, cynical asides if you dare ask a question. One large French utility did not invite our French analyst to an investor away day that all the other analysts had been invited to because he rated them a Sell. The chief executive of a large UK utility once threatened my bank's overall head of investment banking that he would take our firm to court unless we had a two-hour meeting with him during which he would, through sheer force of personality, persuade us of his brilliance and that of his company. He claimed that the Sell note that we had emailed his company's investor relations department a few days prior to publication contained factual errors, but this was just a ruse to ensure the meeting happened. We had a fun-filled rendezvous, completely ignored his piss-poor arguments, and went ahead and published our Sell note. Within a year the stock was down over twenty per cent. I have heard since that if you look up the word 'cocksucker' in certain dictionaries a picture of this gentleman's face appears. This particular clown was the most extreme of aggressive executives but people like him certainly help make timid, easily intimated analysts choose an easy life and be positive.

Just before the stock market 'correction' that began in March 2000, around eighty per cent of US analysts had positive recommendations on the stocks they covered. Not only does this reveal how pointless these people were, it also reflects the overriding incentives that exist to have Buy or Overweight recommendations. Firstly, the management will give you information quickly and proactively, knowing that you are a supportive pal. Secondly, your bank is more likely to be offered corporate work (i.e. mergers and acquisitions, rights issues, etc.) if you are Buyers, which bodes well for the analyst's bonus. Thirdly, positive recommendations are known to result in more commission than Sell recommendations as funds have generally been growing as wealth grows. This naturally makes potential investments of greater interest than advice to sell down already-owned stock. Finally, 'friendly' banks are much more likely to be allocated investor lunches and corporate road-shows with company management teams, which are a great way of getting clients on your side. So, despite the fact that recommendations are generally relative (i.e. a Buy recommendation means the share will outperform the market), the absurd situation emerged in 2000 and many other times where the vast majority of shares are predicted to outperform their peers in the market – something that is, of course, mathematically impossible.

But, I hear you cry, surely the valuation of a share price is a very transparent and mathematical process that throws out a specific share-price target? Well, I'm afraid to say analysts often think of the number they want to reach and then work backwards to achieve it. A classic strategy would be to have a reasonably positive view of a company, acknowledge that it's logical to be supportive of its management for all the above reasons, and select a price target about ten to twenty per cent above where it's trading. Enough to interest a fund manager but not enough to really put your balls on the line and risk making you look like a tosspot if the share price falls. All the analyst then needs to do is manipulate his discount rate or his long-term growth forecasts in his discounted cash-flow model by perhaps half a per cent and you come up with the number you first thought of. To say this whole exercise is about as useful as nipples on a man would be an overstatement.

All this helps explain the extraordinary arse-kissing that Edinburgh Water's senior management received that night at the Balmoral. However, there was one man to whom the analysts were even more sycophantic. Never has there been such a contrast than the hostility that we analysts meted out to each other and the kowtowing this particular character received. He was a major investor in Edinburgh Water and was the sole client who had bothered to turn up. Despite the fact that his lack of charm would, in all other circumstances, make him go down about as well as a French kiss at a family reunion, the analysts were all over him like a cheap suit. Ironically, despite the fact that I was the only one wearing a cheap suit, I was one of the few people who refused to get on my metaphorical hands and knees and give this joker a metaphorical blow-job. Still, just watching my competitors take it in turn to encompass his engorged member was enough to make me gag. What was even worse was that this unpleasant, nasty individual clearly believed that he was well liked, for probably the first time in his sorry life. He failed to recognise that even if he had been the bastard son of Charles Manson and Rose West, we analysts would have licked his arse, such was our thirst for commission and votes. It is amazing how even the smartest of us can delude ourselves so completely.

One other incident that was worthy of note that fateful evening was a conversation I overheard between Hugo and a middle manager who organised the quality testing of shit or some other equally salubrious task. At one point I overheard this clearly intimidated individual make the terrible mistake of asking Hugo, 'What exactly is it that you do?' Hugo leaned back in his chair with an ever-widening smug smile on his face and proceeded to begin a five-minute spiel, braying loudly and loving the sound of his own voice. I listened to his explanation and hardly understood what he said myself – and even at that stage I had a vague idea what it was we did. Instead of saying quite simply that we analyse companies and explain to investors whether we believe the company's shares are going to go up or down, he went into a long, convoluted load of nonsense using every conceivable specialist terminology possible. His little speech went something like this:

'Enterprise value, blah, blah, blah, return on equity etc., etc., etc., earnings before interest, tax, depreciation and amortisation . . . economic value added . . . cash-flow return on investment and so forth.'

For all his poor victim knew Hugo was sitting there talking about the merits of duck spring rolls versus their vegetarian rivals . . . in Cantonese . . . backwards. I watched the middle manager's eyes flit around trying to make sense of this strange language. It sounded like English but had no discernible meaning. His darting, nervous eyes betrayed a deep fear that his ignorance was going to be exposed and so he chose to just sit there nodding. This whole experience made me reflect on how we in the City use arcane language and peculiar terminology to confuse those who don't earn as much as us (i.e. pretty much everyone). It makes us sound like we're doing something extraordinarily complicated and technically unfathomable and keeps our potential detractors in the dark. We are a much harder target if the 'common man' feels intimidated by our complex world and doesn't even understand what we do. We push around bits of paper. That's what we do. That's all we do.

Anyway, at about this stage the two vodka and tonics, the four glasses of champagne, the three glasses of white wine, the four glasses of red wine, the dessert wine and the single malt whisky (twenty pounds a shot) were beginning to make me feel a tad light-headed. My traumatic day and my nerves had clearly made me drink fast and furious and I suddenly realised that the whole room was spinning in a most disconcerting fashion. I must have gone deathly white because Hugo loudly asked with mock concern: 'Are you all right there, old boy? You look a bit queasy.' I mumbled something. I think it was 'fnngdngn'. I tried to stand up, grabbing the table to stop me falling backwards. I stumbled past the finance director and wished him goodnight. Or at least I thought I did. He may have heard something that sounded more like 'grrfgghhnnaggt'. Desperately trying not to knock anything over and appear sober but walking like a zombie on ketamine, I staggered towards the three shimmering doors in front of me. I cunningly chose the one in the middle, struggled with the handle for a few seconds and finally opened it. On finding out it was a broom cupboard and, feeling all eyes on me, I turned around. Thankfully, I found myself being ushered out by a concerned-looking waiter who led me to the exit. As soon as I turned the corner out of the restaurant I heaved a huge sigh of relief. I finally found my bedroom after about seven wrong turns and, without switching the light off or removing my suit, I passed out face-down on my bed. My last thought before I lost consciousness was, 'Another career-enhancing performance, you little fanny fart.' My self-destructive streak really was pulling out all the stops in an attempt to stifle any chance I had of succeeding in this God-awful business.

When I awoke the next day it soon became very clear that

some nasty bastard had actually removed the top of my cranium at some point during the night, extracted my brain and then kneaded it like so much soft dough for an hour or two before clumsily replacing it – probably dropping some as he did so. While he was doing that, his mate had slit open my stomach and poured battery acid into it. The third member of this unholy trinity had occupied himself rubbing sandpaper on my eyeballs and throat (though that could have been the after-dinner cigar) while hitting various parts of my body with a steak tenderiser. He had done this quite gently so as not to leave bruises but he didn't spare a single inch of my skin. I don't know what kind of agenda these little fuckers have got against me but I have found that pretty much every time I have a quiet drink they find me, wait until I pass out and then perform their cruel little routine. It's either that or I lack self-control and can't handle my drink which, let's face it, seems highly improbable.

I blinked. Then I blinked again. Where the hell was I? What the fuck had happened last night? The telephone let out another shrill ring. That's why I was awake. Answer it now. Crawling across the huge bed on my stomach and forearms, as if doing an army assault course under barbed wire, I finally reached the phone. After the four-foot journey I actually felt like I had just completed an SAS assault course though, at the time, I thought my achievement was significantly more impressive. I struggled with the receiver and eventually put it to my ear. It was Edinburgh Water's investor relations man.

'Good morning, Steve. I do hope you're OK. Just to say that the coach to Seafield sewerage works is leaving in five minutes. We *do* hope you can make it.' Even in my dreadful state, I could sense him relishing my appalling predicament.

'I'll be right down,' I mumbled, though it probably sounded more like 'Ahhhlll beeee riiiiite daaaaaan' as my dulled brain, gummy lips and tattered throat conspired to make the task of talking incredibly demanding. Had I had my wits about me I probably would have called down sick but if there's one thing that I didn't have about me it was my wits, which at that point were enjoying a game of hide and seek somewhere – along with my dignity and self-respect.

Slowly gathering my shit together and trying to remember who I was, required a Herculean effort. There was no time for a shower so all I could manage was a quick splash of water on my face. Unfortunately for me that job necessitated me looking into the bathroom mirror and what I saw then was something that will haunt me to my deathbed.

The face in that mirror resembled that of a putrefying zombie who'd been up for a couple of months partying really hard. Frankly, if zombies existed and read that last sentence and had seen my countenance that morning I have little doubt that they would find a zombie lawyer and take out a class action against me for libellous defamation. I didn't just look (and feel) like the living dead; I looked liked the dead dead. My mottled skin was deathly white, my bloodshot eyes were sunken with huge black rings below them and my lips were cracked with dehydration and discoloured by red wine. I didn't really resemble a human being at all but rather some hastily constructed approximation of one. Instinctively, I immediately sought out my sunglasses in my jacket pocket. There could be women or children in the lobby and in situations like this you have to think about the traumatic impact seeing eyes like mine could have on unsuspecting kids. Unless they had nerves of steel, they'd have nightmares for years to come.

Of course, my catatonic body had somehow managed to roll over at some point in the night and broken both arms off my Ray-Ban Wayfarers. I stared at the pieces of broken tortoiseshell plastic in my hand and despaired. The concept of hiding behind my trusty old Ray-Ban's had been the last remaining thought that was giving me any solace. I would now have to face my adversaries, the predictably bright, low-hanging winter sun and several million gallons of Edinburgh's finest shit as naked as the day I was born.

As I walked down the long curving stairway into the lobby, my head pounding and my stomach feeling like it could evacuate its contents at any moment, I heard a now familiar voice: 'Oh, look what the cat dragged in!' said a chortling Hugo, loudly enough to ensure that all the other analysts in the lobby looked up at me. I flushed crimson, managed a weak smile and shuffled off towards reception to check out. On looking up at my face, the receptionist could barely contain her giggles. I'd had some appalling hangovers in some appalling situations in my time, but this wiped the floor with all previous competition.

The half-hour coach journey was mainly spent trying not to be sick. Each bend of the road almost led to the head of the poor chap in front of me being covered in the previous evening's rich, creamy food. I lay back in my seat, eyes closed, praying for this nightmare to end. But it was only just beginning.

Seafield was the first sewerage works that I had ever visited. Of course, over the last ten years I have had the pleasure of checking out how shit is treated from Philadelphia all the way to Paris and, let me tell you, it just gets more and more exciting each time. To hear impassioned waste treatment professionals wax lyrical about 'vermiculture' (where tiny worms are used to break down faeces) or ultra-violet waste treatment never gets dull. I reminded myself that morning, and during many other sewerage site visits over the next decade, that the next time I saw David Flynn I should gratefully shake him by the hand and thank him for not giving me a tedious sector like media or technology to cover. The off-hand decision that David made in late 1996 that I should be a UK water analyst had the enormously pleasant upshot that I would spend numerous days in my twenties and thirties staring at the contents of millions of different people's bowels across Europe. To think I could have been wasting my time analysing the technological innovations that were transforming our world, for example, made me thank my lucky stars each and every single day. What an absolute, unqualified result.

While walking around Seafield sewerage works in our hard hats, fluorescent gilets and protective glasses, all my scrambled brain could focus on was the dreadful smell. The commentary that our friendly plant manager was giving in an almost indecipherable Glaswegian burr just blended with the industrial noises to become a meaningless buzzing sound. No matter how they tried to hide it, it just felt like we'd entered an enormous toilet which, feeling the way I was feeling, seemed strangely appropriate.

What was almost worse was that whenever we met genuine plant workers my fellow analysts crowded around them like David Bellamy would on unearthing some strange arachnid. Here were people with 'real jobs' who did 'real things' with their hands. Since most of us had never done anything with our hands other than swing a golf club or click a mouse my colleagues seemed to find these types genuinely fascinating. Condescending questions were asked as if my esteemed peers were meeting an alien race for the first time. Even in my hideous state I could sense the annoyance these poor drones felt being confronted by a gaggle of posh, effete English fools who, despite generally being half their age, earned more in a month than they did in a year. Surely, only the presence of their plant manager restrained them from throwing some of the more obnoxious ones into the seething pools of shit.

The plant manager, however, was also an object of fascination for my esteemed peers but for different reasons. Meeting some poor bugger halfway down the food chain of Edinburgh Water was an opportunity for my delightful competitors to catch someone out. Hugo and his peers competed with each other to ask nasty questions that they hoped would contradict the senior executives' party line and unearth some titbit of information to bore their clients with when they returned to London.

'Are you running at full capacity at the moment?' Hugo innocently enquired of Donald, our pleasant guide to all things shit.

'Aye, that's right,' responded Donald, not realising that he had fallen into Hugo's carefully sprung trap.

'But we were informed over dinner last night that Seafield could handle a twenty per cent increase in volumes if that were to prove necessary.'

Donald looked up to see Edinburgh Water's scowling finance director. Seeing his boss staring at him clearly put him off kilter and he began to stutter a response. Eventually, the FD interrupted and explained that the confusion 'quite simply' related to definitional differences. All Hugo had succeeded in doing was embarrassing the plant manager and possibly reducing his promotion prospects. Oh, as well as have his needy ego stroked again.

While all this was going on I was beginning to feel absolutely terrible. The chamber we had just emerged from had been particularly fetid and I knew it was a question of when, not if, the content of my own heaving stomach would join forces with the product of the recently evacuated alimentary canals of thousands of Edinburghians. With a decisiveness that still impresses me now I casually backed out of the group, calmly walked around the corner to a large gantry overlooking a particularly foul pool of swill, and put my fingers down my throat. The resultant projectile vomit sprayed over the crap and I almost fell to the floor, such was the effort my action required. Feeling a little better I rejoined the group. Only a slightly raised eyebrow from Hugo suggested I hadn't entirely got away with it.

The rest of the day is a bit of a blur. At some point we had a traditional Scottish lunch of 'haggis, tatties and neeps' at a beautiful castle in the middle of nowhere and I seem to remember some tedious presentations extolling the virtues of Edinburgh Water's management and business plan back at the Balmoral. I managed not to make a total cock of myself during these latter parts of the trip but, in reality, to have done so again after the performance I had already given would have been a truly extraordinary achievement. Making even more of an idiot of myself would have meant an already legendary first performance at a company jolly would surely have entered the annals of corporate history. There was supposed to be a final cream tea to see us on our way but I sneaked out and got an earlier train than my peers to avoid the ignominy of sharing a five-hour journey with a bunch of fuckwits who probably believed they had just witnessed the premature termination of the shortest analyst career in history.

On the train home one thought and one thought only occupied my aching brain: I MUST BEAT THAT PUTRID ARSEHOLE AND MAKE HIM WISH HIS PATHETIC LIFE HAD NEVER BEGUN. Henceforth, my life would be dedicated to showing Hugo and all the other Hugos out there in the Square Mile that I was not intimidated by their cultivated arrogance. I would do whatever was necessary to beat these pricks and make them rue the day that they humiliated me.

I knew almost immediately that the only way to hurt a smug tosser like Hugo was to beat his team into second place in the rankings. My tiny, battered brain envisaged me attending the Extel awards ceremony at the City of London's Guildhall and hearing those sweet words: 'And the number-one-rated team in the utilities sector is . . . Banque Inutile.' But even at my most optimistic I knew that I'd never attain that goal at the second-rate bank I was at. Despite my loyalty to David and Tony I needed to join an investment bank that had the resources and reputation required to beat Hugo's brutally efficient team. Remembering David's wise words, I knew that the most important thing I needed to find was a star analyst who would join me on my quest. If I was going to set off on this odyssey I needed a genius to show me the way – someone to complement my expertise at bullshit. To do this I needed to meet someone special – someone really, really special.

4

THE GENIUS

To call Michael Brent a genius is to understate his intelligence to an almost libellous degree. As soon as I met him I knew he was the star analyst whose coat tails I should grab hold of with every ounce of my strength so that I could fulfil my God-given mission. My understanding of my own intellectual limitations made me fully aware that I needed someone like Michael Brent on my team if I was going to show that dick-splash Hugo Bentley who the daddy was. He would provide the brains and I would serve up the bullshit.

It was February 1999 and I had just received my second bonus when the headhunter called me up. Three weeks before, David Flynn had taken me into a little room, handed me an envelope and told me that my bonus in respect of the previous year was £50,000 and that my salary was being increased to £45,000 plus a £6000-a-year car allowance – which, seeing as I didn't have a car at the time, seemed rather generous. Unlike the previous occasion I knew that I had to pretend to be hideously offended despite the fact that I couldn't believe that these mugs were paying me so much cash for bowling around getting toffs drunk and spouting meaningless nonsense about a pointless sector. I had left the room with a petulant slam of the door looking mortally offended, as if David had just asked me if my girlfriend would be willing to perform the rusty trombone for him. After I left, I like to imagine that David had smiled to himself knowing that his student was beginning to learn how to play the game. Later that morning, when I had called my father to tell him what these clowns were paying me he had almost wept with joy – his left-wing misgivings about my City career being overshadowed by a working-class pride in his son's financial success. I was beginning to dig this gravy train; now I wanted a first-class ticket.

'Hi, this is James Cassock – a recruitment consultant. Can you talk?'

Nearly all City-based headhunters begin telephone conversations like this. They are aware that every single front-office telephone call at investment banks is recorded and that all the recordings are kept for at least five years. This is mainly done to prevent insider trading but it is also done just in case clients dispute telephone orders they have made and they require verification. 'Recruitment consultants' were also aware that we generally needed to keep conversations with them secret from our colleagues. Unless you purposefully want to appear sought-after near bonus time, blatant discussions about moving bank would show a disloyalty to one's team that would be frowned upon, even in investment banking circles. James Cassock knew that my colleagues around me would soon grow suspicious if I started speaking in hushed tones about 'guaranteed bonuses' and so forth, hence his question. Up to this point in my career I'd been rung by a couple of these leeches but nothing serious had materialised.

'Probably not, actually,' I said nonchalantly, knowing how the next part of the conversation would go.

'I understand. How about you give me your mobile number and I'll give you a call this evening.'

I did so and then forgot about it.

Even in the few words I exchanged, I couldn't really hide my contempt for the odious Mr Cassock. The thing is that I've always felt that headhunters make traffic wardens, estate agents and even Manchester United supporters seem relatively acceptable human beings. They are essentially parasites living in the bloated stomach of capitalism. I know that they are just doing a job but it is the way that they do it that offends my sensibilities. Just like football agents who have a self-interest in promoting as many transfers as possible, headhunters will tell you whatever lies are required to encourage you to switch banks. If I had £10,000 for every time a headhunter told me that my bank was falling apart and that all my colleagues were constantly calling him up desperate to move shop I'd be almost as rich as I actually am. You may think that estate agents getting two per cent of the value of your house just for finding a buyer is a complete piss-take but headhunters often receive between thirty and forty per cent of a new recruit's first year's compensation. When you're dealing with City types, who are sometimes earning seven-figure salaries, that can be a disgustingly huge amount for essentially doing bugger all. I've also noticed that these spongers often ring up to get your details just so they can pretend to be involved in a specific job placement even if they have diddly squat to do with it. If you then do switch banks independently the headhunter who has got your details can sometimes try and get some blood money by claiming involvement.

Later that evening, my mobile rang and I heard James Cassock's unctuous tones: 'Steve, what we're looking at here is a fantastic opportunity [they always use this word] at a large European investment bank' [they never name the bank at this early stage in proceedings].

I listened to his spiel, thinking Mr Cassock would have benefited from listening to David's wise words about not bullshitting a bullshitter. After a bit, I made it clear that I was interested and a meeting was arranged with the relevant analyst. What the hell – I had nothing to lose and, if nothing else, it would be interesting to discover my 'market value'. The results of the latest Institutional Investor survey had just been published and Banque Inutile's utilities team had just managed to achieve a 'runners-up' mention which was good though it still meant we weren't top five. Irritatingly, Mighty Yankbank's utilities team was number one again with Hugo gaining the most individual votes in the whole sector. Pleasingly, however, within my own lowly ranked team I had received significantly more votes than my diligent but uncharismatic colleagues. All those liver-destroying lunches, rugby games and pop concerts I'd taken clients to during the November voting period had clearly done the job. I knew that my ranking was the only reason I had been called up – without it I would have been way below the radar.

I had only endured one City interview prior to this meeting and it had not been a resounding success. In reality, I had only decided to pass through the venerable doors of Cazenove's headquarters on Ropemaker Street out of curiosity. Prior to its alliance with JP Morgan in 2005, Cazenove was truly the most English of institutions. It was one of the last-remaining major English investment banks, with nearly all the others having been acquired following Maggie Thatcher's Big Bang in 1986 which had helped open up the Square Mile to foreign banks. In 1998, Cazenove was still a force to be reckoned with, being corporate broker (i.e. the representative to the City) to over a third of the FTSE 100 companies.

I entered a stuffy old room in a building whose low ceilings and sloping floors betrayed the fact that it had been around for a few centuries. Within the fusty room, there was an even fustier old man wearing an old-school pinstripe suit and a demeanour that seemed largely untouched by modernity. I half expected him to whip on a bowler hat at any moment and start banging on about Smith New Court or Strauss Turnbull – independent

English stockbroking firms that had long ceased to exist. The interview could have gone better – truth be told, it started off poorly, got even trickier in the middle, and then trailed off really badly. On sitting down, I asked this extraordinary character if I could take my jacket off.

'Potatoes wear jackets. Gentlemen wear coats,' was his terse response.

That pretty much set the tone for the next half-hour. At a later stage in this dreadful ordeal this farcical individual explained his profound take on life: 'Never trust a man with a beard; he's trying to hide a weak chin. And for God's sake never ever trust a man without laces in his shoes.'

As he uttered this incisive piece of advice I self-consciously tucked my slip-ons under my chair and stroked my chin which had supported an appalling bum-fluff monstrosity barely two years before. Funnily enough, that particular interview process ended there and then and I was spared the experience of working at that most secretive and traditional of investment banks.

On first meeting Michael, the expression 'a face fit for radio' sprang to mind. He was small and, despite being weedy, seemed to somehow possess both a slight hunchback and a tiny pot belly. His sallow skin, his thinning hair that spiked up unintentionally, and his NHS glasses combined to make him resemble a bespectacled mole – albeit one not yet out of the nest. A surprisingly erudite salesman would later joke that he had 'a face that launched a thousand quips', while the oil team's rather cruel secretary would dub him 'potato head'. However, despite having a face that only his mother could love, he displayed an understated, but clearly solid, confidence that I would quickly realise was justified by his vast, pulsating brain. Michael was the UK energy analyst at Scheissebank – an ambitious German bank that was a bit higher up the pecking order than Banque Inutile but still by no means a premier league institution. Most of the so-called 'bulge bracket' banks (i.e. the largest and most profitable) were American, though there were a few European banks like Deutsche and UBS biting at their heels. Although Michael was not the head of his team (that joy was left to an ineffectual German chap called Hans), it seemed clear to me that he pretty much ran the show.

'So, what do you think of United Utilities' cost-cutting initiatives?' he asked after the initial pleasantries were over. United Utilities was a water and electricity company based in the north west of England that I covered as an analyst.

'I think they should do the trick. There are clear synergies to be attained from owning an electricity network contiguous with a water network.'

'Really? Funny that they are towards the bottom of both the water and electricity regulator's recent comparative efficiency assessments. Strange that United Utilities' unit costs and employee/customer ratios fare poorly against all of its peers of a comparable size.'

Oh shit! I had recently been on holiday and clearly missed some regulatory announcements. What essentially was happening here was that someone who covered a different sector knew more about my supposed specialist subject than I did. Nobody likes to see that; especially not at this level.

However, despite a dodgy start the rest of the interview went reasonably well. I impressed Michael with the list of clients I believed I had a solid relationship with (a group that was suspiciously composed of young men who liked a drink) and by the end of the forty-five-minute meeting we were actually having quite a laugh. The old Steve Jones charm was paying dividends and getting me out of a potential tight spot once again.

Within minutes of seeing how brilliantly Michael's brain worked I knew he was the man I needed on my team. He had a way of dissecting every statement I made, unearthing the underlying assumptions and then finding evidence that contradicted those assumptions. The lightning-quick workings of his razor-sharp mind were a veritable pleasure to behold, even when it was your own argument that was crashing down all about you. I also knew that there was no way his team should only be ranked ninth when they had the bastard son of Albert Einstein and Stephen Hawking as their key analyst. I quickly realised that not only should his ideas, with the right marketing, make him one of the highest-ranked UK electricity analysts but that he could also help me think up clever angles for my own sector. For his part, he probably felt that we could work as a very complementary team – with me sorting out the client relationships (i.e. boozing and blagging) and he providing the intellectual ballast. When I watched the film *Schindler's List* a few years later, something Oskar Schindler said chimed with my early prescient vision of what would become of Michael's and my working relationship. When questioned by his hard-working Jewish colleague about what exactly he brought to the party, Oskar Schindler responded that he'd see that the business had a certain panache. That was what he was good at. Not the work . . . the presentation.

I liked this concept and pictured a very acceptable scenario: Michael would do all the hard work that required maths and spreadsheets and tedious nonsense like that and I would just package it and sell it to the suckers out there. As Scotty on the Starship Enterprise may well have exclaimed, 'It's a long shot, Captain, but it might just work.'

Anyway, this first interview must have gone all right because I was called in to have eight more to be held between 12 p.m. and 4 p.m. on the following Wednesday. At first, I was gobsmacked and annoyed that these jokers were demanding three hours of my precious time. Then, after I got my calculator out and realised it was four effing hours (as I said before, maths has never been my strong point) I was even more pissed off. I knew that investment banks often demanded numerous interviews because the package (i.e. the basic salary plus guaranteed bonus) that they offer is generally pretty offensive to any right-minded person. But eight! Fabricating some long, boozy client lunch so as to get the time out of the office was not the problem. It was just the thought of sitting there answering the same tiresome questions from a bunch of charmless automatons that I didn't find overly appealing. Frankly, given the choice between that and scooping my eyes out with a blunt teaspoon would have been a close-run thing.

No matter how I tried to deceive myself there was no escaping the fact that my upcoming ordeal was going to be similar to a German joke – i.e. no laughing matter. However, I knew it was an ordeal worth enduring because the list of interviewees included senior people, like the head of research and the head of sales, and that showed that Scheissebank meant business. If they were willing to demand the time of some fairly hard-core MDs, then that boded well for how much they wanted me and, more importantly, that in turn boded well for what they were willing to pay me. I licked my metaphorical lips and prepared for battle.

My confidence about the upcoming trial stemmed from the fact that I knew that if there was one thing I could do well it was look people straight in the eye and convince them I was the man for the job. I had done this to get into Cambridge University and also with David Flynn two and a half years before. Hell, half the girls in West London would be willing to attest to my ruthless powers of persuasion . . . well, my tiresome persistence at least. Interview technique, like seduction, was all about assessing the needs of the audience and then giving them what they wanted. Furthermore, I would put exam technique in the same bracket and that truly was my forte. Not a single GSCE, 'A' Level or degree exam was ever mistimed or poorly prepared for. My school, Latymer in Hammersmith, had made sure that we were well indoctrinated in exam strategy and I, realising that a few cheap tricks would mean I didn't have to work so hard, had listened intently. Most public schools understood the power of exam technique and that, more than anything, helps explain why around fifty per cent of Oxbridge students came from them. Of course, Cambridge had been full of swots, but there were also chancers like me who understood what achieving the bare minimum was all about. Smart exam technique, convincing interview strategy and efficient seduction tricks – these were the unholy trinity that had got me where I was and those arse-wipes at Scheissebank were just about to find this out.

The first interview set the standard for all the ones that followed. Some huge lumbering cretin, who looked like he was on day-release and had accidentally scoffed his week's supply of Mogadon, wearily trudged into the room, sat down and slowly asked me some eminently predictable questions:

'Who are your principal client contacts?' 'What are your key bull and bear stocks and why?' 'Which valuation techniques do you favour in your sector and why?' 'How do you calculate the weighted average cost of capital?' etc., etc.

All the time I was responding to these obvious questions, which any right-thinking applicant would have prepared for, I was just thinking that I should probably hurry up so that this bloke could get back to auditioning for *The Addams Family* or whatever horror film it was that required some thick-as-pig-shit Frankenstein lookalike.

The rest of the interviews followed a similar pattern but just involved different members of the Addams Family. After Lurch came Morticia, who had a nervous disposition that suggested she hadn't seen any action since the eighties . . . the eighteen eighties. It was when Uncle Fester came in that I thought I'd have some fun and turn the interview around just as I had discussed with Tony a year before. I had already heeded his advice and told everyone I'd met that I wanted to join Scheissebank to make as much money as possible; now it was time to ask them why I should deign to work at their 'moody little outfit' when I had bulge-bracket Yank banks 'constantly knocking on my door'.

This was a high-risk strategy and Uncle Fester's clear shock at my audacity, which manifested itself with him dropping his jaw as if I'd just suggested selling his daughter into the white-slave trade, initially made me think that I'd overstepped the mark. However, once Fester had picked his jaw up from the floor and begun to stutter an impassioned defence of all things Scheissebank, I knew that the ruse had succeeded. He had assumed that my arrogance resulted from me being really sought-after and that I was more important than my paltry two and a half years in the City suggested. I liked this ruse and, when all the Addams family had buggered off and called in their mates, the Munsters, I tried the same gambit again. Despite a slight contretemps with Hermann Munster himself, who started mocking Banque Inutile in a transparent 'attack is the best form of defence' kind of way, the plan seemed to work reasonably well.

After four painful hours of this nonsense I felt bruised and battered as if I'd just completed the twelve labours of Hercules . . . rather than the slightly less onerous 'eight tests of Steve'. All that mattered was that I had completed the ordeal and although I didn't feel quite as joyous as Hercules probably did on capturing Cerberus, I was vaguely exhilarated. It was now just a question of wait and see. Though I'm loath to admit it, I was pretty nervous over the next few days, knowing that being in a team with Michael was the key to my future success and Hugo's demise.

Three days later, James Cassock called my mobile: 'Good news, Steve. They like the cut of your jib. They want you, my friend.'

I took umbrage with him using the expression 'my friend', not just because I wasn't his mate (I was merely the potential source of £50,000 or so), but because of my association with those particular two words. During my travels around the world I generally heard those words just before being horribly ripped off by some carpet seller in Marrakesh or being hideously conned by some jewellery trader in Rajasthan. If ever there were two words that have come to mean the exact opposite of their English dictionary definition they are surely 'my friend'.

Anyway, the point was that they wanted me and now it was time for one last chat with the head of research at Scheissebank to discuss remuneration. James had actually asked me what salary and guaranteed bonus I expected a couple of days before and I had refused to answer, merely saying that I wanted 'the market rate' – especially since I was happy where I was. This is a generally sensible approach in these situations, as trying to give them a steer is more likely to result in you underselling yourself (because you have not realised their desperation) or you saying something silly and pricing yourself out of the market. It's much better to get them to make the first move. All that I had told James was the salary that I earned and the size of the previous bonus; so that's a £60,000 basic and a £65,000 bonus. Perceptive readers may notice that I wasn't a hundred per cent honest on either issue, but what harm could a couple of white lies do? I knew that they would have to offer me a premium to my current salary and so had upped it just a teensy weensy bit. What's a few grand between 'friends' anyway? There was a very small chance that they'd ask to see my P60 or something, but if it got to that stage I'd just call the whole thing off.

With hindsight, this silly risk I took just to get an extra £20,000 or so more on my first year's package was not the smartest thing I've ever done. It wasn't that there was any real chance of getting into trouble or losing my job over it; but had Scheissebank asked for proof of my salary then it could have jeopardised me joining The Genius's team, which was so clearly where my destiny lay. I did it for the same paranoid reasons that resulted in me having impostor syndrome throughout my career. I felt I had to make as much cash as humanly possible as quickly as possible before the powers that be rumbled me and kicked my sorry arse out of the Square Mile. That conviction resulted in me always going for short-term cash rather than long-term career prospects throughout my City career. Still, it was a strategy that was working and my basic thought process was: if it ain't broke don't fix it.

The pay negotiation was simple. I was called up by Scheissebank's head of research who told me I was being offered £75,000 basic and a one-year guaranteed bonus of £85,000. I mumbled something about it not being quite what I expected and that I'd think about it and call him back. This, of course, is standard practice and I probably would have done it even if they'd offered me all the tea in China. I made sure I left it until the next day and then called them up saying I'd move for £80,000 basic salary and a £100,000 guaranteed bonus. This was an audacious request but I was feeling ballsy and thought 'what the hell'.

Much to my amazement, they agreed! They must have been really fucking desperate because I was simply not worth that money. I would later find out that the head of research had been given a remit from his ambitious masters in Frankfurt to somehow get Scheissebank a top-five ranking and that money was no object. This was why they'd accepted my counter-offer and this was why, after less than three years into my City career, I was going to 'earn' (a word I use very loosely in this context) almost four times my father's salary. That is despite the fact that my father had been a diligent, successful public servant for over thirty years. It is a sick and twisted world we live in, make no mistake.

What is even sicker and more twisted is that the offer I received on that wet winter's day in early 1999 was not actually very impressive compared to thousands that my peers would receive in the madness that encapsulated the City during those last gasps of the twentieth century. Never has there been a greater contrast than between the vast rewards Cityboys across the Square Mile were being offered in 1999 and 2000 for doing bugger all and those their grandfathers and great-grandfathers had received fighting to preserve freedom in that most violent of centuries. One set of spoiled, pampered, overindulged idiots sat there complaining about 'only' receiving two guaranteed 'half a bar' bonuses (i.e. half a million pounds) while decades before, their forefathers had been eating dog meat and dodging bullets in the muddy trenches of Flanders for tuppence ha'penny a week. I'm sure if the Tommies from the First and Second World Wars could see that their huge sacrifices had meant that twenty-five-year-old brats could drive German sports cars through the streets of London swigging champagne with Henrietta and Camilla they would have felt that it had all been worth it.

So, with hindsight, I had somewhat mistimed my first job move although, as they say, one sees everything twenty-twenty with hindsight (I, for one, know that I have never made a bad stock recommendation retrospectively). The latter stages of 1999 and the first half of 2000 must have witnessed some of the most preposterously huge pay deals this God-forsaken city has ever seen. A combination of flying stock markets, a plethora of companies being floated on the stock market, and a bunch of wannabe investment banking newcomers desperately trying to participate in this exciting feast, meant that as we started the new millennium we City types were about as sought-after as a cucumber at a nunnery. My package, although farcically large relative to those that 'civilians' earned, had probably been somewhat negatively impacted by the recent turmoil in late 1998 when Russia had defaulted on its loans, South American currencies had gone into free-fall, and the supposedly indestructible Long Term Capital Management fund had gone bust. Indeed, in early 1999, people still remembered the comments Alan Greenspan, the Chairman of the US Federal Reserve, had made about the 'irrational exuberance' of stock markets back in December 1996. Within months, banking executives had foolishly forgotten his wise words. That was because no one wants to listen to a Cassandra when the good times are rolling and in 1999–2000 they really were rolling.

There are numerous stories from this bubble about analysts in their mid-twenties who covered the technology, media or telecoms sectors (TMT) being offered two- and sometimes three-year packages of well over two million pounds. These lucky bastards would have guaranteed bonuses sometimes lasting up to 2003 no matter what they did. In theory, once they had survived their three-month probation period they could just sit around squeezing blackheads and scratching their nuts and still receive these huge pay packets that were multiples of what our very own prime minister receives. All they needed to do was make sure that they were not kicked out for gross misconduct because that was the only legally watertight way banks could renege on these obligations. Since being fired for gross misconduct required doing something like openly snorting a fat line of Charlie off your boss's desk or booting a colleague in the meat and two veg, even the most disreputable of stockbrokers could generally survive.

There were even some lucky tossers who received guaranteed bonuses for two or three years and then did not have to work a single day in order to receive the full whack. This apparently happened to a Dutch bank that was trying somewhat belatedly to join the investment banking bonanza in 2000. Unfortunately, or so the story goes, this bank never actually obtained the required licences to begin trading. What was even more unfortunate for the firm's shareholders was that it had only managed to persuade new employees to join the bank by using huge multiple guarantees. Once the markets turned and these new employers backtracked on their hastily composed plans to join the sexy world of investment banking, there were a bunch of stockbrokers who had never traded a single share who were owed vast sums of cash.

This fantastic scenario also happened when banks merged, as BT Alex Brown and Deutsche did in 1999, and a recently employed analyst or trader who had just received a guaranteed bonus or two from one of the merging banks was found to be surplus to requirements due to job duplication. Sometimes, the bank and the departing banker came to a mutually agreed compromise pay-off but, if the broker in question wanted to play hard-ball, he or she could generally stick it out for the full whack despite never working at the merged bank. If ever there was proof that investment banking is great for investment bankers, it was during those two absurd years of plenty.

Of course, all these guaranteed multiple bonuses that were flying around back then made a mockery of the belief that the City system of remuneration is based upon incentivisation and hence is a more risky form of salary than what the general public receive. This is significant because one of the many piss-poor justifications for our vast salaries is that our earnings are much more risky and temperamental than those of non-City workers. Well, anyone who's been in the City for any time knows that, on average, about half your bonuses tend to be guaranteed either as a result of moving bank or threatening to do so. Even if this isn't the case, I think I'd still risk taking a £100,000 basic salary and a bonus of between zero and perhaps seven times that rather than risk my life as a fireman or policeman and earn a 'predictable and safe' £40,000. You don't have to be a rocket scientist to work that out . . . which is probably why all the rocket scientists are now calculating algorithms on huge computers in the derivatives departments of your average investment bank and not actually building rockets.

Once I'd received the contract and signed it, all that was left for me to do was the rather unpleasant job of resigning from Banque Inutile. This meant confronting and betraying my guru, David. Despite my steadily becoming a more hard-nosed bastard, this was going to be no fun at all. Resigning from a bank is never what I would call a 'laugh a minute' at the best of times but when you have to say adieu, or whatever the correct French word is, to the man who has nurtured you in this crazy world of finance, it is particularly unpleasant. Just as my own father had shown me how to survive in the wider world, David had played this role when it came to the City. The day after signing the contract I gingerly approached his office with a resignation letter in my jacket pocket, experiencing a whole conundrum of emotions.

I had been warned by James Cassock that extricating myself from Banque Inutile was going to be no walk in the park and that my bosses would try every trick in the book to persuade me to stay. For some reason the manoeuvres I had been warned about reminded me of the famous 'five stages of grief' that patients are supposed to go through on being told that they have a terminal illness. However, instead of denial, anger, bargaining, depression and acceptance, I had been well briefed that my bosses would exhibit the following:

1. Emotional blackmail: 'But Steve, we trained you up . . .'
2. Financial bargaining: 'We'll match whatever they've offered.'
3. Angry threats: 'We'll make sure your name is mud.'
4. Demeaning the new job: 'Everyone knows your new bank is falling apart.'
5. Acceptance: 'All right, then, you've made up your mind . . . so fuck off.'

Of course, sometimes things don't turn out exactly as you've been led to believe . . .

'So, Steve, you're here to resign, aren't you?' David bellowed just as I was shutting the door to his office behind me, and before I had even opened my mouth. Had David heard something on the grapevine? Had my inability to look him straight in the eye over the last few days betrayed my nefarious scheming?

'Dear boy, don't look so shocked. It's been a long time coming. You have a way with clients and you've figured out how to work the system very quickly. You've also correctly worked out that your prospects at this bank are limited. We, of course, will go through all the motions to retain you, but you've got a look in your eye that tells me we'll be wasting our time. I don't blame you and, although I'm sad, this is the City and this is what happens.'

What a great man! He was making everything so easy for me. Of course, some of his colleagues, especially the head of investment banking and the head of sales, would prove to be not half as agreeable but I didn't give a tinker's cuss about those fuckwits. It had been the thought of David's disappointment that had been keeping me awake at night but he had generously chosen to smooth my passage, and in some ways, had even given his benevolent blessing to the next stage of my odyssey.

Once Banque Inutile had accepted that I meant business I was told to pack my stuff up and bugger off home to await a phone call. There was now only one issue that preoccupied me. Would these comedians make me work my one-month notice period, or would they insist that I didn't come back to the office while also not allowing me to join my new bank either – all the time on full pay? This so-called 'gardening leave' has to be about the best goddam invention I'd ever heard of. The theory is that there is no point asking stockbrokers like me to work my notice period if I and my clients know I'm going to be joining a new bank. If kept in the office, all I would be doing is using my bank's resources to promote myself and my new employer. I'd also probably be disruptive and bad for morale. Hence, nine times out of ten when you move bank you get a holiday on full salary during which you're legally not even allowed to work for your new bank (which, of course, I would have loved to have done had it been possible, or so I said to my new masters). This can be a damn good incentive to move bank every few years – especially since more senior bankers have notice periods of three and sometimes six months.

As soon as I put the phone down after David had informed me that I was free as a bird for the next five weeks on full pay, I literally screamed as loudly as I possibly could, 'Yesssssssssssss!' Such was my unbridled ecstasy that I think the neighbours probably concluded that I was just reaching vinegar strokes at the denouement of a *ménage à trois* with Helena Christensen and Claudia Schiffer. Either that or QPR had just scored the winning goal in the FA Cup Final. Funnily enough, I'm not sure which scenario is more unlikely.

Even before David had passed on the good news I knew exactly what I was going to spend my free time doing – chilling out on the beaches of Goa with my good pal Alex who was living as a yoga-practising artist out there. There was, however, one final duty that I was obliged to undertake before I could do that: I had to organise my leaving drinks. This is not only a polite thing to do when leaving a bank but it is also an extremely sensible thing to do. You never know if some of those characters you're leaving behind might one day be colleagues at a different bank or perhaps even clients. The rule of thumb in the Square Mile is 'if in doubt, be everybody's mate' . . . or at least pretend to be.

I chose a Thursday for my leaving drinks and, showing tremendous originality, selected 'The Moon Under Water' as the venue. As I've already mentioned, Thursday is the traditional day for boozing with colleagues in the City, and leaving drinks tend to occur on that day too. I wasn't particularly looking forward to the somewhat awkward ordeal of pretending to have a pleasant drink with a bunch of people with whom I generally wouldn't choose to hang out. I was also concerned that some of them probably thought I was a tosser, having used Banque Inutile to train myself up before buggering off at the first sign of a better prospect. Another reason for dreading these drinks was the City tradition that the departing broker was obliged to pay for all the drinks at his leaving do. I knew that there were some bitter arseholes at Banque Inutile who were going to do their damndest to make me rue the day that I had dared get ideas above my station and leave them behind. They would invariably try and hit me where it hurts – my wallet.

The actual leaving drinks were tolerable. As usual, there were at least ten liggers I didn't recognise who had just come along for the free booze. The reader will be tremendously surprised to hear that I very quickly got absolutely wankered as did most of my soon-to-be-ex colleagues. David held court in the corner of our roped-off section of the bar and told amusing anecdotes about times gone by. Listening to his hilarious stories made me conclude that nostalgia sure ain't what it used to be. Meanwhile, Tony was being his raucous, wonderful self. By the end of the night the intensity of my sadness actually shocked me. When David and Tony left I actually felt tears welling up in my eyes. I think the fact that I was moving on and leaving behind a few decent people had sent me a bit emotionally leftfield. It was either that or the £600 bill I had just been handed . . . or perhaps the nine pints of wife-beater I'd consumed.

It almost goes without saying that when I woke up the next day I knew almost immediately that I had been revisited by those same cruel little bastards who'd come to me in Edinburgh. Once again, they had clearly spent most of the night performing their sick, sadistic ritual for reasons that still remained a mystery. One day I'd get to the bottom of their agenda and then they'd suffer, but in the meantime it was me who'd be doing the suffering.

As soon as I arrived in Goa and felt the familiar wall of heat as I left the aeroplane despite the early hour, I felt a huge weight lifted from my shoulders and the knots in my stomach unravel. After passing through the customs at Dabolim airport I was met by Alex on his Enfield Bullet 350CC motorbike. I attached my rucksack to the bike's back and we drove north towards Anjuna beach. Gazing out at the palm trees, the paddy fields, the azure sea and the white sandy beaches, with my top off and the wind in my hair, that one-hour journey felt like heaven on earth. By the time we'd reached Alex's beachside house at Anjuna I felt reborn. I just wanted to see and do all the things that I had done a few years before when I had spent months here living a righteous hippy life. I felt alive for the first time in years. All my senses which had been so numbed by the monotony of work and the drudgery of a grey London existence burst into life. I was convinced that I could see everything more vividly and that I could smell and taste everything more acutely. I was blind but now I could see. As Wordsworth put it rather poetically a couple of hundred years ago: 'Bliss was it in that dawn to be alive, But to be young was very heaven'.

The next month was one of the happiest of my entire life. It doesn't get much better than lying in a hammock smoking Manali Cream (India's finest hash) and reading rubbish blockbuster books about gangsters and other such mindless crap. Occasionally, I'd order another beer, eat some beautiful seafood or have a swim in the warm, gentle sea. Life was simple and life was great. Why on earth was I and everyone else in Britain putting up with another hideous winter getting stressed out and worrying about unimportant shit?

At some point during week two of my break, while I was chilling at one of the beachside restaurants, the owners started playing a pirate video of a film that had just been released called *Fight Club*. Sitting there, high as a kite with my good pal Alex and a bunch of stoned hippies, I thought Brad Pitt's character Tyler Durden was talking directly to me when halfway through the film he declared that we spend all our lives working in jobs that we hate so we can buy shit we don't need.

The huge significance of his words were not lost on me and I sat there contemplating them for several minutes, listening to the sound of waves behind me and watching the smoke from a dozen joints curl upwards in front of me. I was not alone in appreciating Tyler's sentiments. On hearing him sum up modern life so perfectly there had been a general cheer all around me and shouts of 'right on' and 'you tell 'em, brother' from people who shared his view and had dropped out of society. They looked healthy, happy and calm. They knew life was short and had to be grabbed by the short and curlies. Since I'd been in India I'd been laughing more than I'd laughed for years and hadn't felt as healthy, happy or relaxed since my last travelling adventure. This was who I was. This was how I was supposed to feel. What the fuck was I doing even thinking about going back to Blighty?

Of course, I did come back. I suppose there wouldn't be much of a story if I hadn't . . . or at least there would be a very different one. Perhaps a better one. Who knows? I suppose it was my 'mature' side, the lack of obvious alternative career paths, the knowledge that I could secure my financial future after just a few years' hard work and my unwillingness to break the apron strings to my parents that ensured I didn't just 'turn on, tune in and drop out' there and then. However, I have to say that I almost didn't make it. On my penultimate night Alex and I went to a rave at a 'venue' in a jungle clearing called Bamboo Forest. These free parties are weird enough anyway but after a tab of the notoriously strong Hoffman acid and enough ecstasy to keep Ibiza rocking for a few days you needed the mental strength of Gary Kasparov to not lose your marbles completely. After a mind-blowing drive on the back of Alex's motorbike on unlit, pot-holed roads, dodging sacred cows and the occasional elephant we finally came to our destination. I'd been to quite a few of these three-day raves in Goa before at this venue, Hilltop and Disco Valley, but I'd forgotten just how truly freaky they were.

After alighting from our trusty stallion we walked towards the thumping base line that heralded some hardcore Israeli trance music. We passed about thirty chai ladies serving cakes and tea on mats outside the main 'dance floor', if you can call a clearing in the jungle such a thing. God only knows what those poor local women made of all the saucer-eyed Western layabouts jumping up and down to a noise that had little if anything to do with what they considered music. There were robed and painted sacred cows walking around with bells on their horns and the trees supported huge spider webs of bright fluorescent rope. As if everything wasn't odd enough, whoever had organised the party had generously ensured that there were massive hallucinogenic portraits of aliens and other psychedelic images surrounding the dance floor. Most of them were 3D . . . or, at least, they seemed that way to me. We arrived on day three of the party and the casualties that surrounded us were something to behold. It wasn't just the drugs in my system that made me see them as zombies. After three days of nonstop drug ingestion and dancing you, too, would look like one of the living dead.

I went on to have one of the best dances I'd had for years. To stoop to using an oft-heard cliché, 'I became the music, man'. My body, fit and healthy from regular swims, great food and all that sun, allowed me to jump around without a care for hours. It was almost too much. I was ready to explode, such was my overwhelming joy.

That's the thing about acid. It merely accentuates the mood you're in and I was feeling great already so I just felt even better. Admittedly, acid also opens doors in your mind that most people would like to remain firmly closed. But if you're not prepared to deal with certain uncomfortable truths then you haven't faced your darkest fears, and if you haven't done that then how do you learn about yourself? Just as Dylan Thomas never trusted a man who didn't get drunk, I have always found it difficult to trust people who haven't tripped on acid. I mean, what are they trying to hide?

Whoa . . . sorry about that! What a load of nonsense! You can see that by week four of my idyllic holiday I was really getting carried away by all that hippy shit. Anyway, by that stage I had had a sufficiently wonderful time that the prospect of getting up at 6 a.m. every morning to work twelve-hour days as a stressed-out stockbroker at Scheissebank in a wet and cold London just didn't quite cut the mustard. So I formulated a plan. I had heard from some low-life that I'd met at Arumbol beach that the doctors at Calangute would, for a few rupees, be happy to sign a letter stating that I had contracted something like malaria or dengue fever and hence was unfit to travel for a few weeks. I actually got on Alex's motorbike on the morning I was supposed to fly home and headed towards Calangute so that I could execute this ruse and so procure a couple more weeks in paradise. Halfway there I slowed down and stopped. After a few minutes of deep introspection by the side of the dusty road I gradually turned the bike around and headed home, but only after I had promised myself that I would only be a stockbroker for, at most, another five years. I guess the fact that I was having to resort to negotiating with myself about how long a 'sentence' I was prepared to endure shows that I wasn't massively enthralled by my life choice.

After a tearful goodbye hug with my old pal Alex, who seemed to me to be living the dream, I embarked upon my aeroplane and glumly sat there for nine hours wondering what fate had in store for me back in dreary old England.

The shock to the system that the first day at Scheissebank delivered was intense. The contrast between the idyllic, relaxed Goan life that I had touched upon and the intense, hectic, stressful drudgery that I had condemned myself to could not have been more extreme. About three hours into my first day's work, the knots in my stomach returned and this time they invited their best mates over: a dull throbbing ache in my temples and an acute pain in my eyes caused by staring at my computer screen for the first time for five weeks. All I could think was that if Marvin Gaye had been confronted by the same scenario he might well have sung, 'This ain't living . . .'

In that first week of work I was so depressed that I could barely get myself out of bed. The 1980s legendary CEO of Salomon Brothers, the so called 'King of Wall Street' John Gutfreund, famously required that stockbrokers and traders wake up every morning 'ready to bite the ass off a bear'. Well, for that first week back, the best I could manage was to perhaps throw a pebble at a squirrel or maybe use strong language at a chinchilla. Such was my low that even doing those things seemed like a big ask. There was nothing for it but to get my act together and remember the objective: the merciless destruction of Hugo Bentley. I had been out of the market for five weeks and I was slow – like a boxer who hadn't fought for years and had gone to seed. They say that a week is a long time in politics but in broking it can sometimes feel like a lifetime. Companies' strategies change, stories move on and clients and competitors change employer. I felt like Martin Sheen at the beginning of *Apocalypse Now* when he despairs of not being in the jungle fighting his Vietnamese enemy. If you exchange the name 'Charlie' for 'Hugo' and 'bush' for 'Le Gavroche', then just as Mr Sheen said, every day he spent in his room he got weaker while every minute Charlie squatted in the bush he got stronger: words that almost perfectly encapsulated my psyche.

I needed to get out there and start wining and dining my clients like billy-oh. I needed to start thinking and behaving like the stockbroker I was or my mission was doomed. There was no doubt that smoking dope killed your ambition . . . unless your ambition happened to be chilling out on the beach or watching daytime TV.

So that's what I did. I took every single client I had out to boozy lunches and gave my first month's expense account at

Scheissebank the kind of battering a tag team of George Best, Peter O'Toole and Oli Reed would have struggled to match. Far from being unhappy with my flagrant display of old-school broking tactics, Michael and my new boss Hans were very pleased . . . which is more than I can say for my poor, distended liver and my struggling lower intestine. Within a month I swear I went from looking like a tanned, healthy, slender young man to a spotty, pale, bloated shadow of my former self. Whereas once girls had occasionally admired my half-decent looks on the tube I now received quizzical glances of concern. Once, a lovely-looking redhead opposite me leaned across from her seat on the tube to say something. My ever-expanding ego assumed she was going to perhaps ask me on a date. In fact, she simply wanted to know if 'everything was all right'. A particularly rich and boozy lunch combined with a surprisingly hot April afternoon had resulted in me getting the sweats so badly that I had completely drenched my shirt and, as an off-duty nurse, she had felt somewhat concerned. The sound of my ego shattering as it fell to earth must have been audible at the other end of the carriage.

It was around May 1999 that Michael published what would prove to be a ground-breaking research note that would quickly establish his reputation as one of the finest UK electricity analysts in the market. With hindsight, the argument was quite simple but the conclusions were ballsy. Recently built power stations were going to result in oversupply which, combined with a more refined electricity market mechanism, would invariably cause the artificially high UK power prices to fall dramatically. This meant that investors should sell their shares in virtually all the UK electricity companies. His theory was coherent and backed up by compelling evidence. The stock recommendations weren't the usual ten to fifteen per cent upside bullshit. He was saying that some of the stocks he covered were worth about half their current share price! It is extremely brave as a relative newcomer to tell the market (i.e. all your competitors and your clients) that it has overvalued certain share prices by a factor of two. If this didn't make holders of shares in UK electricity companies think it was worth having a meeting with him then nothing would. All I needed to do now was think up something equally cunning to say on the UK waters so that we could be a double whammy – that way we'd really make a splash. I decided I'd write a really bearish (i.e. negative) note on the UK waters too (partly just to copy Michael). We might not paint the town red but we would be painting Reuters screens across the City red. There'd be blood on the streets once our message got across and that tit-wank Hugo would have no choice but to sit up and take notice.

Truth be told, I had been struggling about what to say in my UK water note and I needed to come up with something quickly if Michael and I were to execute a pincer movement on our clients. It took Michael coming over for a little chat to show me the way.

'Look, Steve, just have a view. Just give them a superficially plausible story. Your sector is so sensitive to unpredictable things like movements in interest rates, politicians' pronouncements and sector rotation that it's a bit of a bugger's muddle anyway. Why don't you just say something like upcoming regulatory announcements, a non-supportive Labour government and exaggerated bid hopes all mean that the sector's got around twenty per cent downside.' So that's what I did. I would have asked him to write the note, too, but it seemed a little rude. I had to at least pretend to my team that I was doing my job properly.

As soon as my note was published I organised a damn good marketing schedule for the both of us, even if I say so myself. We went to nearly every major client in London, Edinburgh, Glasgow, Dublin, Frankfurt, Paris, Madrid, Milan, Zurich, Geneva, Stockholm, Oslo, Copenhagen and Helsinki. We were a formidable double-act, like Batman and Robin or Butch Cassidy and the Sundance Kid. Having said that, I have to admit that it sometimes felt a bit more like Jeeves and Wooster or Wallace and Grommit . . . with me playing the thick one. That was the problem about presenting next to Michael: relative to his consistently magnificent performance anything I did seemed pedestrian at best. But it didn't matter and I went into all our meetings calmed by the knowledge that any complicated questions on my sector about accountancy or valuation would be answered perfectly by my faithful Sancho Panza. Before long we had a whole bunch of prearranged 'spontaneous ad-libs' with which to entertain our clients and our ideas were going down a storm. Even better, the stocks we advocated selling were beginning to drop in value and our bank was making loads of commission from the investors whom we had talked into selling down their portfolios. It didn't matter that a large reason for the sell-off in the utilities sector was because everyone was buying technology, media and telecom shares and selling off defensive 'old economy' shares. We were getting it right, even if it was for the wrong reasons.

After we had 'done' Europe there was one major place left to visit: the good old US of A. I had never been to America and was especially looking forward to checking out New York. The schedule was daunting – involving about six or so presentations every day for the best part of a week and sometimes requiring major distances to be travelled between meetings. We were also going to visit some properly weird places too like Des Moines and Wilmington. All this was necessary because we had to convince the Yanks of our brilliance, since their fund management institutions had a reasonable weighting in those all-important surveys.

I suppose one's first experience of New York is a bit like that first line of coke – and it can never be repeated. There can be no comparison to the buzz in the air that I felt as our yellow taxi, of a type that I had seen in so many movies, went over the

Williamsburg Bridge from JFK airport and entered what can only be described as an enormous movie set. My only complaint was that the actors on the street were a bit hammy; they were over-acting big time and giving such exaggereated performances of stereotypical 'Noi Yoikers' that they really needed to tone it down. Not only did I feel I was in a Hollywood blockbuster but I also felt like I was the hero in this particular film. This city better wise up, I thought, because there is a new sheriff in town. And, even better, he's got a deputy who's gonna kick your arse . . . sorry, I mean ass.

On our first night in New York Michael and I had no choice but to go on the razzle dazzle. It might not have been the smartest preparation for a four-day marketing schedule but I wasn't going to forego an opportunity to check out this great city.

Over the previous month's marketing Michael and I had begun to form a nascent friendship based on mutual respect – with my respect for him based on his huge intellect and his for me based on . . . I'm not quite sure what. Anyway, we genuinely got on well and enjoyed each other's company. Michael had slight autistic tendencies, which meant that his interaction with others was sometimes odd, but that was the price he paid for being so clever. Indeed, I would say that the majority of great City analysts whom I've met are borderline autistic or at least sufferers of Asperger's Syndrome. These guys who live in peculiar formulaic unemotional worlds have a distinct advantage over us 'normal' types when dealing with something as abstract as shares or derivatives.

Still, whatever his faults young Michael sure could piece together a convincing argument as two unfortunate drunken Yanks from some shit-hole like Iowa discovered when they started a conversation with us at some dodgy bar down in the Meatpacking district (or fudge packing district, as an amusing colleague dubbed it). On discovering that we were stockbrokers, these two mullet-sporting lumberjack-shirt-wearing rednecks took us to task claiming that all stockbrokers are 'heinous assholes, dude'.

While I was thinking about leaving this dive and attempting to find some better company Michael stepped up to the plate and showed them some good old-fashioned rhetoric: 'Tell me, Hank, do you love your grandparents?'

'Why, sure I do.'

'Then you should be thanking Steve and me because we've come all the way from England to help them out.'

'What the fuck is this Limey talking about?' asked an exasperated Hank to Rusty.

'Your grandparents almost certainly have a pension which is mostly invested in a mutual fund. It is Steve's and my job to advise that fund so that they invest your grandparents' money in shares that go up and not ones that go down. If we do our job properly then they'll have more cash and that means that their annual trip down to Florida to get some winter sun can keep happening.'

That shut them up, but not for long because Michael had another question: 'And tell me, Rusty, are you a Communist?'

'No fucking way, dude. I believe in the American dream and everything it stands for.'

'Really, then you should surely be patting me and Steve on the back because we help keep the American dream alive.'

'Oh yeah? How's that, then? Are these guys for fucking real?' Rusty asked his compadre.

'The American dream, as I understand it, rests principally on the tenets of free-market capitalism and the opportunities that such a system affords the individual. Steve and I are people who work tirelessly to ensure the continuation of this system. We tell people to buy shares in companies that are well run while telling people to sell shares in inefficient companies. Soon the well-run companies' share prices rise while those of their unproductive neighbours fall. Over time the efficient companies acquire the poorly run companies and impose their own superior working practices. You see, Rusty, we are at the very cutting edge of meritocratic capitalism which, in turn, is at the heart of the American dream and which only functions if hard work is rewarded with financial success. We make sure this process runs smoothly.'

Shit – even I was impressed by that! However, Rusty and Hank didn't look quite as impressed. In fact, they got off their bar stools and looked like they were about to kick the shit out of us. Having two suited English blokes use lots of long words while explaining that they were here to help their aged relatives and keep the American dream alive was probably a little too much for their tiny brains. I hurried Michael out of the bar. In his autistic bubble he probably failed to realise the danger he was putting us both in.

As I was leaving I heard Hank shout: 'We kicked you out in 1776 and we'll kick you out again, you fucking Limeys!'

I virtually had to cover Michael's mouth with my hand to prevent him being heard as he responded: 'Actually, we weren't kicked out until 1783 and besides, the term "Limey" generally refers to English people and I'm of Irish descent . . .'

Once we were a safe distance way, almost crying with drunken laughter, I asked Michael whether he really believed all that stuff.

'Don't be a fucking idiot!' he exclaimed, much to my surprise. 'Firstly, it's a zero-sum game so if we help one mutual fund by persuading them to buy shares in companies with good prospects they'll probably buy them off another mutual fund whose pensioners will thus not benefit from any ensuing share-price appreciation' – good point, well made.

'Secondly, as you know the quality of management comes way down the pecking order when I am assessing reasons to buy a company's shares. Valuation based on a fundamental analysis of industry trends and macro shifts dictates my recommendations.' Well, that showed me. Perhaps I had somewhat underestimated

Michael's sense of humour and overestimated his autism. After a few more drinks we got a taxi back to the Parker Meridian Hotel near Central Park. It was 3.30 a.m. and our first meeting was in four hours. As my head hit the pillow I wondered: why do I continually do this to myself?

Considering that my sadistic night-time visitors had actually got on an aeroplane and followed me all the way to the Big Apple (or had called up some distant mafia cousins and asked them to perform 'the usual'), our presentations went reasonably well on that first day and got better thereafter. Never once was Michael asked a question that he couldn't answer fantastically. No matter how many meetings we endured, I never once got bored of watching the way Michael's magnificent brain destroyed his adversaries' counter-arguments. It truly was a pleasure to behold, except for those stupid enough to try and take a contrary view. After our plane had arrived back in England we parted company at Heathrow airport. Before a rather formal shake of the hand we both concluded that the trip had been a resounding success. Things were beginning to shape up nicely.

The only other notable incident that happened during that first year at Scheissebank was on 1 May 2000. We had been warned that there were going to be possible riots and, as a historian of revolutions and the Paris troubles of May 1968 specifically, I was really looking forward to the day's events. Our security professionals had insisted that we were not to wear suits on that day. Amusingly, most of my preposterous colleagues thought that a uniform of chinos, loafers, polo shirts and sports jackets (i.e. their standard 'dress-down Friday' look) would constitute a perfect disguise. In actual fact, their appearance screamed stockbroker from about four hundred yards, especially since most of these buffoons carried copies of the *Financial Times* under their arms. As far as I could remember rioters didn't carry copies of the *FT* around . . . oh no, they much preferred the *Daily Telegraph*.

It was late morning before we heard any trouble; I guess these soap-dodgers liked a lie-in even if there's a revolution to be organised. At about 11 a.m. a colleague exclaimed 'the peasants are revolting' but since I'd heard most of my workmates express such sentiments many times before it took the sound of breaking glass for me to realise trouble was afoot. Now we're talking, I thought. My confused left-wing sentiments were somehow making me support the very people who had come to hassle us. The truth is that I was enjoying the excitement of it all and, despite protestations from my team-mates, went down on the street to investigate. Unlike my colleagues I had come in wearing jeans and a baggy T-shirt and just for today I'd leave the FT on my desk.

What I saw on the streets disappointed me enormously. There were a few of the dogs-on-string brigade but it all looked really tame. I later found out that there'd been some action on the trading floor of LIFFE (The London Financial Futures and Options Exchange) but that sounded like a resounding victory for capitalism. Apparently, those amusing future traders in their multicoloured jackets had made hundreds of photocopies of fifty-pound notes and thrown them down on their would-be aggressors. When a few of the braver rioters had tried to climb up the escalator into the building its direction was reversed, which apparently resulted in all of them falling down and collecting in a big heap at the bottom. Even in Trafalgar Square, where things had got a little more exciting, all that had really happened was that a statue of Winston Churchill had been defaced and the window of a McDonald's broken. This was all very disappointing. This was not by anyone's definition a proper attempt at a revolution.

The fact is that the May 2000 riots were pointless and achieved nothing. It was clear that the participants were just a disparate bunch of groups with diverse and ill-thought-out objectives. If the 'Wombles', who were one of the groups involved, had actually targeted cleaning up Wimbledon as their namesakes had done, rather than random vandalism, they would have achieved significantly more because they may have gained some public support. History shows that it is possible, even in modern times, to make changes through direct action but you need to have achievable, unifying aims that find sympathy with the general public. I clearly remembered witnessing the anti-Thatcher Poll Tax riots at Trafalgar Square in 1990, which essentially succeeded in bringing down Thatcher and having the Poll Tax removed. The beauty of those particular riots was that they were based on a single unifying issue and one that chimed with public opinion. Admittedly, Thatcher and her cronies were always going to have a problem introducing a concept that had not got any more popular since it was first mooted six hundred years before and kicked off the 1381 Peasants' Revolt.

I returned from my sociological expedition back to the office feeling somewhat dejected. An egotistical part of me thought that I should be out there using my analytical abilities like a management consultant to organise a proper revolution. I had the historical knowledge and knew the enemy well. It was only when I remembered that I was a stockbroker and hence was 'the enemy' that I realised what utter nonsense I was thinking.

A month after those pitiful riots something of much greater significance happened. The 2000 Extel survey was published and Scheissebank's utilities team was now in sixth place. We were moving up the rankings fast. Our marketing blitz, my incessant client entertainment, and the fact that our stock calls were going so well had made us leap up the league table. The game's afoot, I thought. Just you watch out, Hugo Bentley!

It was only a few days after this great news that I had the misfortune of bumping into Hugo at a water company's full-year results presentation. Of course, he was still head of the number-one team and, much to my chagrin, Mighty Yankbank's percentage of the total vote had actually gone up. Hugo only exchanged a few words with me but he had selected them perfectly so as to cause maximum irritation: 'Well done, Steve. Keep trying. God loves a tryer, you know.'

He didn't realise that he was just signing his own death warrant. I had almost forgotten just how much I hated that man but that one short encounter reminded me of all the humiliation that he had meted out to me when we were at Edinburgh. He was going down . . . down to Chinatown (whatever that means). It would take meeting just one more man to make his downfall a racing certainty but before I did that it was time to have some fun . . .

5

THE CLIENT

When the revolution comes, let's make sure it's those hedge
fund boys who are first up against the wall. Never in the field of
human capitalism has so much been earned by so few for doing
so little. Quite a few of these clowns earn more in a week than a
teacher or nurse does in a year and their salaries often dwarf
those of the 1980s New York bond traders – the so-called
'masters of the universe'. Although I'd like to pretend that my
outrage at this situation is solely based on some altruistic wish
for a more egalitarian society I'd be fooling no one – least of all
myself. My competitive nature ensures that even after my
'breakthrough' I can't deny a smidgen of jealousy about their
gargantuan pay packets. Now when I think about hedge funds
my brain is filled with images of just one man – Richard
Montague.

Richard was, and as far as I know still is, a partner at one of
the most aggressive and successful hedge funds in London.
When I first met him in January 2000 he was in an ebullient
mood. I didn't know it then but he had just been told the size of
his bonus and he was as happy as a pig in shit. Normally, hedge
fund managers are a notoriously secretive bunch who would

never disclose what they earn, but later that year at some appalling Soho club, when buzzing like a maniac on Bolivia's finest toot, Richard confided in me that his bonus in lieu of 1999 had been $4.5 million. Richard was twenty-six.

The rise of hedge funds began in earnest around 2001. By then stock markets had been in decline for around a year after the bursting of the tech bubble. With no end to the bear market in sight investors wanted to make returns that were not geared to the performance of the stock market. They wished to make an absolute return even if stock markets fell. They demanded what Cityboys, in their never-ending mission to confuse the general public and appear intelligent, like to call 'Alpha' not 'Beta'. Hence, hedge funds became increasingly popular since, unlike conventional 'long-only' funds, they can 'short' shares. That is to say, they can sell shares they don't own by borrowing them off a conventional fund so that when the share price falls they make a profit by buying them back at a cheaper price. As the bear market continued cash began pouring into these funds and certain small but successful funds like Richard's (that initially only had around £200 million under management) grew to four or five times their size.

The significance of the dramatic increase in the size of the funds under management relates to the way hedge fund managers are paid. Generally they receive a two per cent management fee and a twenty per cent performance fee. This means that those running a fund with £1 billion worth of assets, like Richard's was by 2004, receive £20 million a year for doing absolutely nothing as well as twenty per cent of any increase in the fund's value. So a twelve-month rise of twenty per cent in Richard's fund would result in about five or six characters sharing around £50 million (after £10 million of costs) for one year's 'work' – though it ain't exactly smelting iron for a living. The lion's share would go to perhaps two or three senior partners but no one was exactly going to go hungry – not for about three centuries anyway. The amount of people required to run a fund of £1 billion and one of £10 billion is not necessarily that different. Hence, the ever-increasing size of some of these funds has led to some guys in America 'earning' almost unbelievable amounts of cash – with 2006's top twenty US hedge fund managers and private equity boys on average receiving $675.5 million each that year personally. So, in 2006, these guys, and it is nearly always guys, earned in ten minutes what the average Joe in America took one year to earn. Nice work if you can get it.

Admittedly, some of these people are extremely shrewd investors who can make money no matter what markets do. However, I have noticed that many hedge funds' performances exhibit a far greater correlation to the stock market than they would care to admit. Since the FTSE 100 rose around eighty per cent in the three years after its low in March 2003 Richard's fund would have gone up by around £800 million even if all the money had just been invested in the market via a passive tracker fund and Richard and his friends had spent the whole time scuba diving in the Maldives. In this scenario Richard and his fellow partners would have earned £160 million. Acceptable remuneration for checking out Angel fish in the Indian Ocean.

As these hedge funds multiplied and grew, investment banks had no choice but to prioritise them relative to their old, traditional long-only clients because some of these crazy guys *really* like trading shares. Whilst your typical pension fund might, on average, hold on to a share for a year or more I've seen certain hedge funds buy in the morning and sell in the afternoon. Hell, I've even seen buy and sell orders in the same stock within an hour! On certain days, one of the biggest hedge funds, GLG, has been said to be behind five per cent of all the trades in the FTSE 100. Understandably, investment banks liked the vast amounts of ensuing commission so much that they started helping set up hedge funds but only on the proviso that they were the hedge fund's 'primary broker' through which it did the majority of its trades. This helped to fertilise the hedge fund boom, or bubble as it is likely to be, even further. Such was the investment banks' love affair with all things hedge fund that they even started setting up their own internal ones, making their own quarterly profits even more vulnerable to the vagaries of the stock market. If those internal hedge funds don't occasionally benefit from inside information as a result of being part of a huge bank that is involved in hundreds of corporate deals I'm a monkey's uncle – but we'll come on to that later.

This whole process resulted in numerous consequences, some of which may have affected you – especially if you live in London. Firstly, stock markets became much more volatile as short-term hedge funds traded like whirling dervishes as they desperately tried to make a profit on even the flimsiest pieces of newsflow. This made the stock market a more risky place to put your money into, be it directly or via your ISA or pension fund. It meant that even certain blue-chip stocks went 'up and down like a whore's drawers', to use one of the less pleasant City expressions.

Secondly, certain hedge fund managers started gambling rather than investing. If your remuneration is directly correlated to the performance of your fund and you're living in the short-term hire-and-fire world of finance, then the temptation is to take big bets on volatile stocks. This is because you know that if these bets come good then you will personally walk away with vast sums of wonga. This recklessness results from a combination of get-rich-quick greed and the pleasing fact that it's not your money that you're gambling with. Admittedly, if your bets go really badly wrong you might lose your job but my experience suggests that most failed fund managers can generally obscure the reason for their departure and often find a position elsewhere, such is the size and inefficiency of the global financial services job market.

Short-term gambling is also not just restricted to the buy-side. The whole bonus culture that dominates the sell-side ensures that many traders at investment banks take punts that are much riskier than they would care to admit to their bosses. If bets work out you can be sure that the compliance department will turn a blind eye to the risk controls that were momentarily breached and that you will receive a huge bonus. If the punts fail, although you may lose your job if the loss is major, you don't actually have any money removed from your bank account. This is why the bonus system encourages short-term gambling – there is an asymmetrical financial risk to taking punts and most traders are smart enough to have sussed that out after about two days on the job. It may be uncovered that the huge bets that Jerome Kerviel, the alleged rogue trader from Société Générale, took in early 2008 were motivated by his belief that if they worked out he would receive a massive bonus and his boss would forget all about the risk procedures that weren't adhered to. Hence, the £3.7 billion loss made by Société Générale may be explained by a logical analysis of the bonus system that is currently used by all investment banks! There may be trouble ahead . . .

The most famous recent example of the buy-side's gambling tendency relates to a fund called Amaranth (crazy name, crazy guys). In September 2006 this large, well-respected fund apparently lost about two thirds of its value ($6 billion!) in a week or so mainly as a result of its bet that the US gas price would go up proving to be erroneous. Several other funds had followed suit. Now, this huge punt was itself based on the assumption that hurricanes usually caused gas supply disruptions in the States around that time of year. So investors lost over half their cash because some comedian took a bet on US weather conditions! You wonder whether these people had ever heard about the effect a butterfly flapping its wings in China can have. Frankly, investors in Amaranth (unbeknownst to them) might as well have had a flutter on 'Little Joe' at the

12.15 at Doncaster or waltzed into a casino and blithely put all their chips on black.

Another consequence of the rise of hedge funds was more specific to me and my fellow brokers. Before the rise of hedge funds I could generally be sure that I earned more than the clients I broked to. This basic truth meant that the dynamic of any client presentation – an underlying acknowledgement of my superior status – was as it should be. Once those hedge fund boys started multiplying and earning salaries that made a mockery of my own I had to begin facing the humiliation of trying to persuade them in meetings that they should listen to me knowing full well that their salary dwarfed my own. This was all wrong! I began to go into meetings feeling about as confident as a baby chihuahua facing a coked-up pit bull.

It was in these circumstances that I had my first encounter with Richard. I had spoken to him on the phone a few times and had got in his good books with a few decent stock calls that had made him some cash. Michael and I went over in early 2000 to deliver a PowerPoint presentation with the enthralling title: 'Prospects for the UK utilities sector in 2000'. Richard had agreed to see us because our bearish notes of the previous year had proven to be so prescient and hence he was interested in what we predicted for 2000. In the black cab over to Mayfair (the home of many hedge funds) I explained to Michael that this was a potentially very lucrative account and that Richard was one hell of a smart cookie. Arriving at his beautiful Mayfair office piqued my envy as I thought about how infinitely more pleasant that vibrant area of London was relative to the sterile Square Mile which is so dominated by its tedious City workers. And at least people around here did things other than push around bits of paper and talk about how rich they were. They were so rich they didn't bother with such pointless flim-flam.

The first thing that struck us on entering Richard's office was how small it was. There were about ten employees (including secretaries) running the whole show and these guys were in charge of a few hundred million squid! My immediate thought was: what a great life these guys had. They didn't have to wear suits or ties. They rocked up to a beautiful office near Hyde Park at a relatively civilised 7.45 a.m. They didn't have to run their investment ideas by committees as happened at Fidelity and other big buy-side institutions. They didn't have to engage in the mind-numbing administrative horseshit that any large company necessarily requires. These guys just sat there and thought all day about what stocks they should 'long' and what stocks they should 'short'. What's even better than all that is that they had both a pool table and a darts board. They made more money than us, had a more interesting job than us and could hone up their pub game skills while they were at it. Lucky bastards!

Michael and I were ushered into a small meeting room, offered tea and coffee and asked to wait while Richard 'finished some rather important business'. We waited, and then we waited some more and finally after about twenty minutes we were graced by the presence of a completely unflustered Richard. He had an air of such relaxation that my first thought was that his 'important business' probably involved smoking weed while knocking one out in the toilets.

Richard was good looking, around six foot tall and had the broad, muscular shoulders of a man who was no stranger to the gym. He wore the classic hedge fund uniform of loafers, chinos and polo shirt but showed a slightly outré side by wearing a big, thick woolly 1970s cardigan, the like of which hasn't been seen since *Starsky and Hutch*. He casually offered his hand to us, uttered a barely audible 'sorry about that, chaps', and sat down with a big cheesy grin on his face that said 'life just couldn't get much better'. I should have hated him immediately but something about him interested me.

'So, Steve, how are you going to make me some money this year? You know I love money, don't you!'

Michael and I immediately took out our carefully constructed PowerPoint presentations and passed one to him. He ignored it and said, 'Fuck that bullshit! Just tell me your two best ideas and if there isn't over twenty-five per cent upside in six months' time then you're wasting my time.'

Christ almighty! We've got a live one here, I thought. I could see Michael was getting a bit tetchy but he was an important client so we had to remain calm. Without further ado I went on to explain why he had to own shares in Thames Water and then Michael gave him an infinitely superior appraisal of why he needed to own shares in Powergen too. All the time we were giving him the spiel Richard looked a little bored, though his questions betrayed the fact that he was listening and that he was one sharp motherfucker.

The thing is that Richard knew he was smart. He was also good looking, physically fit and rich with the potential to become much richer. A combination of these features might turn even the most humble Buddhist monk into a bit of an egotistical swine and Richard could be excused for believing himself to be slightly superior to the 'pond life out there' – which is how he referred to ninety-nine per cent of the population. I could see that even at this relatively early stage in his career he was somewhat arrogant but I would find out later that this was nothing compared to what he became when he started earning 'serious' money in a few years' time. His personality in early 2000 would probably be described as unassuming relative to the monster that he would turn into. One of my vaguely humorous colleagues would later claim that God had a Montague-complex.

Arrogance and the City go together like port and cheese or cocaine and talking total gibberish. The perennial question that has been posed at dinner parties across London for decades is: does the City attract arrogant tossers or do they become so as a result of their job? Richard was a case in point but the evidence was inconclusive. I never knew him before he was at the City but

I imagine he wasn't short of confidence. What I do know is that after a few years his City experience transformed what was formerly an almost acceptable human being into the bastard son of Paris Hilton and Russell Crowe.

I think there are three main reasons why the City can instil such extraordinary arrogance in those who choose to waste their life there. Firstly, most people enter the City so young (i.e. at about twenty-one) that their personalities are not fully formed and so, when they begin to earn serious cash, it goes straight to their heads. Fortunately for me, I entered the City at the relatively senior age of twenty-four and hence managed to retain my undeniably perfect personality without any hint of arrogance.

Secondly, and this applies mainly to buy-side analysts and fund managers (i.e. 'the clients'), self-importance can rear its ugly head as a result of the constant arse-kissing that they are subjected to. With too many brokers chasing too little commission even some lowly client from some God-awful little institution finds himself the recipient of offers for the kind of client entertainment that the average Joe would give their eye teeth for. Many of them become so blasé that they feel able to cancel their attendance at expensive events like Wimbledon with virtually no notice and no excuse. Even more amazingly, some don't feel the need to even give an excuse and simply don't bother turning up – sometimes to events that cost three or four hundred pounds! I suppose if enough people kept offering you tickets to see Champions League football games or the latest Madonna concert you too might become a pampered prima donna, but I always found this behaviour extraordinary. They say that one definition of madness is doing the same thing again and again and expecting different outcomes, but this capacity that clients had to be so goddam rude never ever ceased to amaze me throughout my career.

Finally, Cityboys (and occasionally Citygirls) become arrogant because their job often requires them to do so. Every day a trader or fund manager buys or sells a share they're implicitly saying that the market (i.e. everyone else) has GOT IT WRONG and mispriced the asset. Hence, an egotistical decisiveness is key to their job. That's why Hamlet would have been a dreadful broker while I'd have Lady Macbeth on my team any day of the week. Unfortunately, this professional arrogance tends to seep into other aspects of Cityboys' world view such as their view of their attractiveness to the opposite sex. I remember clearly Richard telling me early on in our relationship that only girls 'who were blind, rug-munchers or one stop past Dagenham' (i.e. Barking) would fail to fall for his charms. Much to my chagrin, my experiences out partying with him suggested he wasn't talking total twaddle.

So, next time you're at a dinner party and you find yourself sitting next to some dreadful tosser from the City braying on about how fantastic he is, remember two things: firstly, it's probably not the poor chap's fault but rather it's his job that's destroyed his personality; secondly, be aware that he needs to be an arrogant buffoon in order to carry out his job properly. 'To understand is to excuse,' say the French philosophers ... although having said all that it's still probably worth asking the host if you can swap places before you move on to the next course.

The meeting was a relative success and we must have convinced him because on our return to the office our trader Gary informed us that Richard had placed some big orders in both the stocks we had recommended. That was the beauty of these hedge funds – you gave them an idea and, if they liked it, you got an almost instant reward. He bought around £20 million worth of each stock which gave Scheissebank about £80,000 in commission. Not bad, for an hour's work. These hedge funds were so much more satisfying to broke to than their slow, ponderous long-only cousins. With those jokers you might, if you're lucky, get a vote in their next internal survey which theoretically would then result in commission being sent your bank's way – but not necessarily in your own sector. The way hedge funds traded was so much more fun and definitely appealed to my MTV generation's need for instant gratification.

The next part of my cunning plan to make sure Richard was 'on side' was to invite him to the Cheltenham races a couple of months after our first meeting. If I could get him to think he was my 'mate', as Tony had advised me, then the sky would be the limit for commission.

There's nothing a Cityboy likes more than a day at the races with clients gambling his 'hard-earned' cash. These trips tick all the boxes: copious amounts of free booze, massive consumption of overpriced food and, the cherry on the cake, the ability to competitively flash the cash with colleagues. Our love of trips to the races may also be because they involve a bunch of young men gambling lots of cash (sometimes on insider tips) and talking confidently about things they don't really know about, which is pretty much home from home for your average stockbroker.

So me, Richard, Michael and a client of his called Bertrand boarded the 8.15 a.m. train from Paddington to Cheltenham and set up camp at our table in the first-class carriage. The champagne drinking began at approximately 8.22 a.m. and the inane banter had begun sometime before that. All Michael and I had to do was ensure that the clients' glasses were never empty. As the drink kicked in we marvelled at the Fedora-wearing tweed-clad idiots that surrounded us and relished their ruddy faces that must have taken a few generations of inbreeding to produce. This sure was better than a day at the office.

By the time we arrived at Cheltenham we were already half-cut which, seeing as it was only about 10 a.m., meant that we had more in common with the Tennents Super-drinking pissheads on the street than the average human being. What was slightly daunting was that the first race began at 2 p.m. and even a poor mathematician like myself knew that that meant we had almost four more hours of champagne-quaffing nonsense to endure before the racing began. It's a dreadful job but somebody has to do it, I suppose. We spent much of the intervening time betting on anything we could think of. At one point we bet on the bra size of some poor salad-dodger standing at the bar. Needless to say, I was nominated to find out the correct answer and the lady in question's terse 'fuck off' response meant that no one won that particular bet.

The other main topic of conversation as we drank ourselves into oblivion in the enclosure was gambling strategy. There was lots of analysis of the horses' form, the jockeys and the 'running'. Apparently, the ground was 'good to soft', which pretty much described the state of my brain come midday. I personally had a slightly less complicated approach to selecting winners which was taught to me by my aunt Beryl when I was six. It's quite simple really – you bet on the horse with the name which has some vague significance to you. I didn't tell the others my strategy because I didn't want to lose my competitive advantage. They also may have drawn some unfair (but completely correct) conclusions about why I chose 'Exotic Dancer' and 'Roll-a-joint' in the 3.15 p.m. race.

Once the betting began in earnest our egos predictably ensured that we bet more and more on each race trying to make sure everyone knew who the big swinger was. What began as a forty-pound flutter soon grew into £250 by the time of the last race. Any winnings were boasted about as if they were confirmation of the gambler's analytical brilliance but all losses were laughed off to ensure people knew we were rich enough not to care.

Predictably, by the end of the day my companions, with all their clever analytical strategies, were all down between about £200 and £400 while yours truly with my 'Auntie Beryl strategy' was up over £200. It just confirmed what I've always believed: that gambling, like stock picking, is basically all about luck unless you have some good inside information – though I wouldn't know anything about that, of course.

On the way back Richard drunkenly suggested continuing the fun in the West End – ideally at some posh bar first, and then at a nightclub. We had all been getting on fine and although Richard was essentially a dickwad he was tolerable and had a good sense of humour. I was up for it, knowing that the more mischief we got up to the more Richard and I would be bonded. I was also pretty arseholed and up for some fun. Michael and Bertrand, however, tried to beat a hasty retreat making piss-poor excuses about their wives or something. After a few comments about them being under the thumb and their wives wearing the trousers we allowed them to leave.

Richard and I certainly got up to mischief that night and I, for once, was slightly taken aback by the level of naughtiness we attained. While we were sitting down at some appalling bar on Kingly Street in Soho, Richard disappeared for a minute and returned with a glint in his eye. 'Get your laughing gear around that,' he said, passing a small wrap of something surreptitiously into my left hand. Oh, I see . . . that's what he'd been organising when he was having those muffled telephone conversations as we pulled into Paddington. Without a second thought I stood up and marched to the toilets.

Believe it or not, I had never tried cocaine before that night. I had sampled pretty much every other mind-bending substance but, for one reason or another, had never experimented with marching powder. When I was a student it was too expensive and it was not the kind of drug that you generally find when travelling around Asia. As for my first years in the City, it was always the devil's urine and not his dandruff that I indulged in (oh, and the odd joint of skunk . . . but only on days with a 'Y' in them). So this was going to be real interesting.

It wasn't just 'interesting'; it was ABSOLUTELY FUCKING AMAZING. About three minutes after having completed the soon-to-be-familiar ritual of racking up two fat lines on the toilet seat and snorting them both using a rolled note, I started feeling so powerful and euphoric that I just wanted to rip all my clothes off and explode. I wanted to stand on my bar stool and, with arms raised and an insane look in my eyes, scream like Dennis Hopper in *Blue Velvet* that 'I WILL FUCK ANYTHING THAT MOVES!' As soon as Richard had returned from his own visit to the cubicle we began an extremely intense chat that was more passionate than any conversation I'd ever had.

Except it wasn't really a conversation. It was two coked-up dickheads shouting self-obsessed monologues at each other. Generally, the connection between what I said and what Richard said was tenuous at best and that's because I was talking about some really important stuff like how great I was and he was refusing to participate in this extremely interesting discussion. In fact, he was banging on about some fairly pointless subject – something about how fabulous he was or some such nonsense. I'd wait as patiently as I could for him to finish his babble because he was my client but I was constantly chomping at the bit to get my important message across which was simple: I am a fucking amazing individual, who is hung like a mountain lion, gets loads of fit birds and is devilishly good looking. It was a simple message – why didn't he just nod in agreement and let me continue to discuss in greater detail my unbelievable intelligence, my tremendous wealth and . . . I don't know, anything else you wanted to compete over.

We spent the rest of that night making regular trips to the toilet and continuing our enthralling debate about who, out of the two of us, truly was the greatest human being ever to step foot on this planet. Despite him being my client I mounted a pretty strong defence of my own argument and would have been willing to continue into Sunday. Until the gak ran out, that is, and then I straightened out a bit and I saw sense. Richard was an important client and I should, as the saying goes, be willing to bend over backwards for him. Eventually Richard allowed me to go home but only once I had unequivocally accepted that he was virtually the Son of God, if not slightly better.

Charlie (or nose candy, toot, chang, blow, quiver, wallop, gak, beak, bugle, yeyo, Gianluca Vialli, Boutros Boutros, etc.) has been around in the City since the mid-1980s. However, in the good old days I hear that it used to be the preserve of the select few, usually brokers. I have heard tell of a memo that went around a certain investment bank in the late 1980s asking traders to use the toilets, rather than their desks, if they did insist on snorting coke. Whether that's true or not is debatable but what is undoubtedly true is that London was becoming infested with cocaine by the late 1990s. That's why Robin Williams's famous quote that 'Cocaine is God's way of telling you that you are making too much money' was no longer valid by the time I got to the City. By the early twenty-first century, because of the steep decline in its price, it's just as likely to be the tea boy as it is the head of trading who invites you to powder your nose.

I've seen many press reports suggesting that every broker in town has permanently got a rolled-up fifty stuck up his hooter. However, I think outsiders may be surprised at just how straight City types are becoming. This is mainly because stricter rules and random drug tests (even if they are apocryphal this side of the Pond as my experience suggests) can prove quite a deterrent when you're earning half a million a year. That said, there is still a diehard bunch of bugle monsters, who seem to manage to make millions and avoid getting their P45 while buzzing like Peter Doherty at a Bogota house party. Word on the street is that there's quite a trade out there in untainted urine just in case those compliance boys come calling.

Still, risking your job aside, hoofing a load of gak is not going to do anyone working in the City too many favours. I can think of few jobs in the world that are less healthy than being a Cityboy (apart, perhaps, from being Ron Jeremy's fluffer). A stockbroker's life generally consists of stress, alcohol, sleep deprivation and rich food and on that basis many of us burn out before we're forty. Add cocaine into the mix and your ego's writing cheques your body really ain't going to be able to cash. Unfortunately, I didn't know that then and that's why I started taking coke pretty damn regularly and would soon end up developing the kind of habit that Keith Richards would have considered excessive. But I'm getting ahead of myself – that night with Richard was just the start of a not-so-beautiful friendship with this most pernicious of drugs. Over the next months that friendship blossomed into a relationship but even in late 2001 the white lady was still only a regular bootie call. It wasn't until perhaps 2002 that we started getting serious and I guess we formalised our relationship and went 'exclusive' around 2003. It was on a cold winter's day in early 2004 that I gathered my courage, got on one knee, took a huge nasal ingestion and asked Madame Cocaine for her hand in marriage. Of course, she said yes . . . because she loved me too.

So things were going absolutely swimmingly with Richard. The main thing was that I was making him money and that has always been the way to a Cityboy's heart. Forget about getting there through his stomach (though a few Michelin-starred restaurant meals can help), it's got to be the direct route via his wallet every time. That's why I became even more firmly entrenched in his good books when Thames Water was acquired in September 2000 at a forty per cent premium to what he had paid for his shares. On hearing the news he had rung me up to congratulate me from a yacht in the Mediterranean with such an obvious smile on his face that I could almost see it down the phone. And rightly bloody so! I later estimated that the premium that the German giant RWE paid for Thames meant at least an extra £100,000 for Richard's bonus. I reckon my superb advice probably only resulted in me gaining perhaps a tenth of the benefit Richard had gained from it. Still, an extra £10,000 to my

2000 bonus wasn't too bad – especially since it had been Michael's idea anyway.

Richard soon became my first client call every morning and within months he was giving Scheissebank more utility commission every week than the next three clients put together. I continued to pretend he was one of my best mates and we'd regularly go out for coked-up evenings at dodgy City bars picking up gold-diggers like they were going out of fashion (which of course they never will). He and I became partners in crime; our bond strengthened by a mutual understanding that our knowledge of each other's drug habit would be sufficient to destroy each other's career if we so decided.

The only downer for our burgeoning relationship was that Richard had been one of the many clients I had pushed into buying shares in a little company called Scottishpower. It was in late 2000 that a power station blew up in Utah and . . . well, I think you know what happened then. Fortunately, he and most of my other clients forgave me. After all, it wasn't as if Mormons were well known for their mechanical incompetence, so no one could have predicted that particular event. Indeed, even my boss and Gary the trader eventually let me off for losing my bank £1.2 million since most of my other calls came good. My meeting with the head honcho on the day it happened had gone acceptably, all things considered, though he made it clear that another fuck-up could be 'detrimental to my career prospects'. I also managed to persuade most of my colleagues that I'd suffered from regular nosebleeds since childhood and that they were brought on by stress. Most people seemed to buy that bullshit though a few hilarious wags on the trading floor insisted on referring to me as 'Charlie Chang' for the rest of my time at Scheissebank.

Richard and my other clients forgave me even more quickly when, in April 2001, Powergen announced that it was to be acquired by another greedy German behemoth, E.ON, at another huge premium to its share price. About three minutes after the announcement popped up on my Reuters screens, Richard rang me up screaming so loudly about what a total genius he was that I had to hold my telephone's earpiece away from my head. It was a sign of his increasing arrogance that he had conveniently forgotten that it was Michael's idea to buy shares in Powergen. This is something I've noticed with many clients. When they act on your ideas and they work out well, they convince themselves that it had been their idea all along. However, when your stock recommendations prove about as successful as the Sinclair C5, you won't be allowed to forget that they were definitely always your ideas. As JFK once said: 'Victory has a thousand fathers, but defeat is an orphan.'

Richard decided that we should celebrate *his* fantastic success by going out for a big knees-up courtesy of uncle Scheissebank. Since he was throwing money at my bank like a lottery winner at a Stringfellows' stripper I had no problem applying for an £800 expense allowance. Interestingly, the fact that he probably earned £800 in about two hours never, for all the time I knew him, detracted from his unwillingness to spend his own money if he could get my bank to part with the readies. I suppose that's how the rich stay rich – justifying their tightness with some tired cliché about 'looking after the pennies and allowing the pounds to look after themselves'.

It's a sick and twisted world we live in, of that there can be no doubt. And it's also a very expensive one, if you happen to live in London. The amount of cash that I spent on that day in May 2001 with Richard revealed to me just how pricey things were becoming in old London town and made me wonder how the hell ordinary 'civilians' have the cash to go out of an evening without taking up a sideline in dealing bugle or mugging grannies.

The evening started with cocktails at a renowned private members club in Mayfair (where Richard was a member via some family connection). Surrounded by rich Arabs, dreadful

City types, a smattering of Eurotrash, the odd member of the landed gentry and a few classy Eastern European hookers we immediately got stuck into cocktails and inane banter – by then, a tried and tested formula. It was a crying shame that we hadn't invited Carol Vorderman along because the bill quickly became very scary and difficult to calculate. We consumed around five champagne cocktails of various types and bought two Romeo Y Julieta cigars (which at seventy pounds a pop had better have been rolled on the thighs of young virgins or I wanted my money back). So that was about £320 with tip and the evening had barely begun . . .

We then went off to eat at Petrus. Somehow, while we talked at each other about how great/well hung/rich/sexually attractive we each were, we managed to stack up a bill of just over £500 for a meal that was pretty damned good but not so tasty that Mummy was going to be receiving a letter extolling its virtues. Admittedly, most of the spend was on the wine and that was because I had made the schoolboy error of allowing Richard to choose the booze. Still, it could have been worse; I noticed that the most expensive bottle on the menu cost £30,000 – probably sufficient dough to keep a village in Africa alive for about five years. The fact is that the food was a bit wasted anyway because both of us were desperate to wolf it down as quickly as possible so that we could get on to dessert – which I had carefully concealed in two wraps in my wallet.

After paying the bill I declared that the bank was shut since we'd already breached my £800 limit. Of course, empowered by a few cheeky lines in Petrus's toilet Richard was having none of it. For once in his life, he showed a modicum of generosity saying, 'Fuck that, tonight we party hard and I pay.' We left Petrus marching off as if to war.

The long queue outside Chinawhite seemed foreboding for two unaccompanied men but Richard simply marched to the front and asked the bouncer how much a table cost. The £500 response almost made me projectile vomit my recently consumed foie gras but clearly presented no challenge to my pal. He took his wallet out and handed the bouncer ten crisp fifty quid notes and an extra one for good luck. Once we had been seated with two bottles of vodka in front of us we found ourselves immediately surrounded by a swarm of young, mainly Eastern European ladies. Call me cynical but I don't think it was our intelligent conversation that they were interested in. It's probably best if I refrain from saying how the night progressed in order to protect the innocent . . . as well as Richard and I.

I would estimate that our night, including cocaine and taxis, cost in total at least £1600 and that kind of evening became steadily more expensive as we worked our way through the first decade of the new millennium. The influx of cash from Russian oligarchs, oil-rich Arabs and ever-wealthier Cityboys combined with the City's boom times meant that even a 'gentle evening' out with clients would often cost at least a few hundred quid. By 2004 it really was a mystery to me how Joe Public survived in this City when I seemed to piss money away as soon as I stepped out of my front door.

Hence, it came as no surprise to me when a survey by *The Economist* published in 2006 revealed that London had become the fourth most expensive city in the world. After some of the costly frolics I've had there it amazes me that any city is above us (and to find out Oslo was 2006's most expensive city definitely confuses me – mackerel fishing must be damn lucrative). It's pretty clear that ever-increasing City bonuses have played a major role in pushing up the cost of living in London and making even me baulk at some of the prices that are being charged. When a successful stockbroker, as I was at that time, starts finding things a bit pricey you know that the world really has gone mad. Indeed, such was my self-loathing and disgust after my and Richard's bountiful night that I seriously considered going to live in the cheapest city in the world . . . although Tehran may have its drawbacks it can't be as appalling as a £1600 night in Piccadilly.

Richard and I were, unbeknown to us, riding the crest of a wave that was set to bring so much wealth into London that it felt like King Midas was in town and had a compulsion to touch pretty much every goddam thing in sight. Clearly 2001 was by no means a particularly great year, with stock markets continuing to fall until 2003, but the writing was already on the wall that if we managed to keep our jobs during these difficult years then the time of plenty was there for the taking. The only problem for most Londoners was that we Cityboys were beginning to make such stupendous amounts of cash that everyone around us, unless they happened to be a Russian oligarch or own a Saudi oil-field, felt comparatively poorer and poorer.

Of course, people argue that all this cash eventually flows down to all the poorer parts of society. I, however, have always felt that 'the trickle-down' theory is about as convincing as a former girlfriend's hypothesis that getting a joint bank account would 'spice up our love life'. OK, it does work to a small extent but when it comes to absurdly large City bonuses a lot of that cash is trickling down to Ferrari dealers, posh restaurants and hideous clubs like Chinawhite or Boujis. It also pours into Cityboys' favourite boroughs like Fulham and Battersea and makes property prices so preposterous that the chances of nurses or teachers buying a pad are akin to Dawn French's prospects of winning rear of the year.

One definite consequence of the recent boom times in the City is an increasingly divided, dissatisfied society. Cityboys' relentless ostentatious displays of wealth help make sure most other Londoners feel that they are working in Mcjobs and so act like the underclass that they are rapidly becoming. Between 1990 and 2005 the top one per cent of the UK's richest people's share of the national wealth moved up from seventeen per cent to twenty-five per cent and has undoubtedly risen further over the last three years. The rich are getting richer and the poor relatively poorer. Ironically, this has been especially true under Tony Blair and Gordon Brown's management of UK plc. Eighteen years out of power had made these jokers so paranoid about being viewed as 'old Labour' that every time Cityboys and entrepreneurs asked for 'business-friendly' reforms they rolled over and allowed tax and regulatory changes that facilitated the rich accumulating ever more capital. This very visible ever-widening disparity in wealth helps cause such resentment that an increasingly violent, crime-ridden society becomes a racing certainty. We are all Thatcher's children now living in a country where there is 'no such thing as society' – just a bunch of individuals competing with each other for the scraps on the table. In this unhappy dog-eat-dog world the only answer for many of the repressed is, as 50 Cent so sweetly put it, to 'get rich or die trying'. Call me old fashioned, but that attitude doesn't seem conducive to a healthy, joyous society.

Admittedly, this process has been helped by the decline in religion and the discrediting of its successor, left-wing idealism, by failed experiments in Russia and China during the twentieth century. Into the void stepped money as the one true God and the Gospel according to Adam Smith became the only one that anyone now listens to. I won't pretend that selfish greed was invented by us Cityboys but we have become its finest and most visible exponents. We are missionaries for the new faith and our conspicuous consumption foments the jealousy and discontent necessary to convert the masses. Capitalist economies can only survive if they grow and that requires people to be dissatisfied because only people desperate for material betterment will buy that flashier car or that smarter jacket. To ensure success we have enlisted advertisers as our propagandists to spread the word. These scumbags will sell us the ice cream that makes us fat and then make sure we buy the diet pill to make us slim. The trick is to make people as unhappy about themselves as possible so that they strive to spend the cash in the false hope that it will make them happy and sexy. The last thing we want is for you to be content because then you'll just stick with your beaten-up Ford Cortina and the whole system collapses.

The problem is that money is so clearly a false god and that striving for it single-mindedly generally brings nothing but unhappiness. Desperate attempts to keep up with the Joneses just breed discontent mainly because there is always some other joker who's got more than you. That's why we rich Cityboys are generally such an unhappy bunch. A study by Alden Cass ('the Frasier Crane of Wall Street') has shown that US stockbrokers are not achieving their 'unalienable right' to be happy as set out in their country's most hedonistic of constitutions. Apparently, they are 'four times more likely to be clinically depressed than the average male' and those 'who were the most depressed made the most money'. A study of Florida-based brokers found that they tried to alleviate their weltschmertz through 'sex, masturbation, alcohol and drugs' – which, while arguably all fine pursuits, should perhaps not be the be all and end all of one's existence. This unhappiness derives from the average Cityboy's competitive mentality and subsequent 'status anxiety' since there's always some wanker further up the food chain who makes you feel small in comparison. I suppose if you're called Bill Gates or Warren Buffet you may beg to differ, but who wants to be ugly losers like them anyway?

The question, of course, is why haven't the dispossessed got their shit together, realised 'all property is theft' and changed an unfair system that condemns them to living as second-class citizens? 'Bread and circuses' were used by the Roman elite to keep the plebeians in line and now we have Sky and KFC, football and McDonald's. As the radical William Cobbett said two centuries ago: 'I defy you to agitate a man on a full stomach.' Radicalising people to try to change a corrupt system is made even harder when the alternatives have been discredited by the likes of Stalin and Mao. The unity required for the masses to act is also not present as race and religion make dividing and ruling so easy for the elite. Anyway, our masters have successfully employed clever propaganda to feed our pathetic obsession with celebrities and so distract us from unjustifiable wars and the hideous unfairness of our socio-economic system. What's even worse is that the media have so successfully extolled the virtues of the market economy that most people blindly 'believe the hype' despite Public Enemy's best attempts to dissuade us from doing so. Hence, we live in a superficial, bling bling society that is neither happy nor peaceful. The seething anger that is necessary for revolution exists but is not used to change the system – rather it just results in the ever-present violence and aggression that are inevitable when there is such a blatant and ever-expanding gulf between the haves and have-nots.

I think I can safely say that these radical thoughts may not have been at the forefront of my mind when I decided to buy a top-of-the-range Porsche. My previous car, a fifteen-year-old Vauxhall Cavalier that my mum had given me, had been dubbed by cruel colleagues and friends alike 'the fanny repellent' and, anyway, the £75,000 price tag was only about a third of the £200,000 bonus I received in January 2001. The one-month waiting that was required before I could get my grubby mitts on the car suggested that I wasn't the only Cityboy who was having money chucked at him despite tricky markets. Richard, who was almost becoming a genuine pal, had been instrumental in persuading me of the virtues of treating myself to some toys. My pathetic new-found urge to show my own mates what a big swinging dick I was becoming also made me buy a £3700 Submariner Rolex watch and a £1900 Ozwald Boateng bespoke suit. Up until 2001 I had been wearing a combination of the classic six-pound number and a half-decent one from Gieves and Hawkes. The days of looking like a junior Burtons salesman were officially over.

The Extel survey of June 2001 showed that Scheissebank's utility team were fourth with Michael and I receiving by far the most individual votes for our team. We were rising up the league table at a rate of knots and our competitors were beginning to take notice. I could now hold my head up high among my peers at corporate jollies and results presentations. Of course, those tosspots at Mighty Yankbank over in Canary Wharf were still number one, but we were catching them up. For the first time in three years their share of the overall votes actually declined but they still had a whopping thirty-one per cent of the vote compared to our eleven per cent. Still, Hugo wouldn't be quite so cocky next time I saw him.

Or so I thought. After a riveting corporate presentation by Severn Trent on the prospects for its waste division I was approached by Hugo: 'Well done on the old Extel survey, dear boy. Keep up the good work. At this rate we might even consider you competition in a few years' time.'

'Fuck off, Hugo. We're coming to get you and you're scared shitless.' All pretence of social nicety had long since left our relationship.

'Sorry, old bean . . . "scared"? I'm afraid I don't know what that word means; you'll have to explain it to me.'

'Yeah, I heard you were retarded and needed things explaining to you. I'll tell you what – if you're so fucking confident, why don't we have a little wager?'

'Look, boy, if you even dream you beat me you'd better wake up and apologise . . . though, if you want to give what little money you have to me, then that's your choice.'

'Coolio Iglesias, cocksucker. I bet you a grand that I'm in a team that beats you in the Extel survey within . . . three years.' I had to be realistic with the time frame because they were still a hell of a long way ahead of us and moving up the top three was invariably going to be an arduous process.

'Ohhh! Aren't we brave? The game's simply not worth the candle, dear boy. You need to put your money where your mouth is. You need to up the ante. One measly grand? That, you little pipsqueak, is why you will always be small time – because you think small time.'

'Yeah, so you think you're big time? Well, you're gonna fuckin' die big time,' I said, misquoting a classic Pacino line from *Carlito's Way*.

'Why don't we make it interesting? How about we play for ten grand?'

Oh shit . . . things were getting a bit silly now. The ego had well and truly landed. At that time, £10,000 sounded like quite a lot of money to me and I wasn't that confident in beating a team that had dominated the survey for years. There was only one possible response to this total dong.

'Nah – fuck ten G's. If we're gonna do this, we're gonna do it right. Let's make it . . . twenty.' I had actually wanted to say fifty but just managed to restrain myself in time.

'So be it, and remember – a gentleman's word is his bond,' he said, offering me his hand to seal the deal. I walked off as casually as I possibly could . . . cursing my pathetic ego for having forced me into a preposterous bet that was going to be really tough to win. What the fuck had I just done?

It was only the next day that Richard called me: 'Listen' (he started pretty much every sentence commanding you to listen), 'me and some of the boys are going over to Ibiza next weekend for the opening parties. Someone's dropped out last minute and I'd like you to come. We're flying over there in my mate's private jet and we've already booked one of the flashest villas around. Shouldn't be too pricey – nothing for a man of your means, anyway!'

This sounded like an interesting proposition. Going on holiday with a client must surely be the ultimate bonding session. It would be good for commission and would absolutely cement Richard's vote in the all-important surveys. More importantly, I hadn't gone raving hard since Goa and needed to let loose the juice. Just like Glastonbury and Goa it would be a colonic for my mind making me return all the stronger to beat

Hugo. Anyway, those were my pathetic attempts at justifying what would simply be a debauched weekend aimed at consuming as many pharmaceuticals as humanly possible.

The Gulfstream 200 touched down in Ibiza at 11 a.m. on Saturday morning. The nine-seater plane had been modified and we sat in perfect luxury on spacious, comfy cream-leather seats surrounding a central table. The flight over involved the three C's: champagne, cocaine and cards and had been a real eye-opener. I hadn't realised that people like Richard's friends actually existed other than in satirical parodies on Channel Four. I spent the best part of three hours in an aeroplane with some of the biggest (but richest) tossers this side of Kathmandu and by touchdown was seriously regretting my decision to come along. François, Brad and Dimitri made Richard look like Mother Teresa, such was their unbelievable arrogance and contempt for all human beings not part of their rarefied world. The pilot was barely acknowledged because he was just a flunky paid to do his duty and his occasional attempts at humour over the tannoy received outraged quizzical looks from my fellow passengers as if they could not believe that someone had dared interrupt their vitally important conversation. The banter itself was the usual self-aggrandising horseshit and only ever stopped long enough for a fat line of Charlie to be aggressively snorted. My weekend pals truly were oxygen thieves of the worst possible kind.

By the time we reached Ibiza I was totally wired and jittery as fuck – not helped by the fact that I'd lost £700 at poker. I had struggled to get my voice heard at the beginning of the journey but by the end I simply sat there, pretending to look out the window and wondering if I would survive were I to open the emergency exit and jump into the welcoming sea. After about the fifth time I heard Brad bang on about his fucking Ferrari or François complain about his 'four-million-euro apartment' in Monaco being a 'trop bijou', I didn't really care if I would or not.

The fact is that my fellow would-be ravers had got my number within approximately two seconds of meeting me at City airport. My relatively average wardrobe, my pedestrian Rolex and even the way I held myself made them realise that I was just an also-ran, a wannabe. These guys were high-rollers and everything from their Louis Vuitton luggage to their expensively coiffured hair styles screamed MONEY in big, fuck-off neon letters. I suspect that the fact that they were sharing an aeroplane with someone whose net worth was clearly under £10 million irritated the piss out of them.

You couldn't make up the backgrounds of my fellow passengers. Dimitri was a good looking, tanned, short version of Adonis and was the only team member younger than me. I never really did find out what he actually did for a living. All that mattered was that papa was a Greek shipping magnate who was worth almost a billion. His favourite things seemed to be smoking, fornicating, smoking . . . and fornicating. That man's poor lungs creaked whenever he breathed and he was only twenty-five. I had some insight into his interesting perspective on life from the charming toast he blessed us with before we downed our first glass of champagne on the plane: 'To fast cars, cheap whores and no taxes.'

François was tall, tanned and almost as handsome as he thought he was. His family, as far as I could see, owned half of Belgium, but this hadn't stopped him becoming an extremely successful hedge fund manager in his own right. His fund was purely dedicated to shorting stock (not all hedge funds take a 'market neutral' approach) and so the market turmoil of that time suited him down to the ground. When I found out a little more about his repellent personality it made a lot of sense to me that his salary was directly correlated to the financial suffering of pensioners whose investments were being decimated by collapsing markets. François was one of those nutters I'd meet throughout my City career who had been born into outrageously rich families but felt some strange urge to make even more money. Greed clearly knows no bounds and these privileged City types seem unlikely ever to be satisfied. I used to always wonder why they couldn't just gallivant around their country estates and follow a traditional country pursuit like developing a smack habit so that other people can have a piece of the action. François was probably the wealthiest of the three and had an advantage over his peers when it came to the never-ending competition over who was more arrogant – he was half-French. Two millennia before, Roman emperors used to have a slave walk beside them in ceremonial processions whispering in their ear 'Remember, you are mortal' so as to keep their feet on the ground. If there's some Italian descendant of one of those slaves around now who's willing to carry on the family tradition, I met an outstanding potential employer on that plane. Though I somehow suspect it will take more than a few cursory remarks to get that wanker's feet to touch the ground.

It was our American partner in crime, Brad, who was the real larger-than-life star of the show. Loud, brash, obnoxious – he ticked all the boxes for a stereotyped Yank financier. Brad was, at thirty-one, the oldest amongst us and was a partner at an extremely successful private equity fund. He was a tall, blond gym monster and possessed an extraordinary and almost enviable lack of self-awareness. Confusingly, the others often referred to Brad as Patrick. I soon found out that this was in celebration of their mutual hero Patrick Bateman, the eponymous protagonist of Bret Easton Ellis's disturbing book *American Psycho*. It didn't seem to strike them as ironic that their hero was a serial killer who liked to do rather unpleasant things involving rats that were never featured in any pet healthcare manual that I have ever read. When on drugs (which was frankly all the times I ever saw him in Ibiza) Brad revelled in his alter ego almost as if it gave him licence to act like a complete animal. On this hellish holiday, whenever someone we met asked him what he did he would gleefully say 'murders and executions' (rather than mergers and acquisitions) which would be followed by an inevitable high-five with one of our team – and even once with me, I regret to say.

The one thing that these boys all had in common, apart from their uncontrollable egos, was their unfathomable wealth. They had spondulicks in buckets and clearly weren't afraid to use them. Within ten minutes of walking on that plane I realised that this was going to be the most expensive weekend I would ever enjoy . . . or rather endure. Among my old school friends I was considered close to the top of the financial premier league but compared to these boys I wasn't even in the second division. Shit, I wasn't even Vauxhall Conference.

My inferior status was further confirmed when, halfway through the flight, I vainly tried to curry favour with my disturbing new mates by complaining about the tax man taking forty per cent of my earnings. All three of my fellow passengers looked at me aghast as if I was an alien species. 'You pay taxes?' asked François incredulously. 'They're just for the little people,' added a clearly bemused Dimitri (unintentionally quoting the hideous billionaire New York hotelier Leona Helmsley who was, I'm pleased to say, eventually caught by the IRS). It turned out that all three had clever accountants who ensured that the poor old Inland Revenue received, at most, ten to fifteen per cent of their domestic salary. Every trick in the book, from schemes involving the financing of UK films to investments in renewable electricity projects in Italy were combined with off-shore bank accounts in places like the Cayman Islands to minimise their tax bill. Brad found it even simpler since his private equity fund exploited a tax loophole aimed at encouraging new start-up companies. This particular abuse of a well-intentioned incentive was especially repellent and made many outraged headlines in 2007 when it was pointed out by trade unions that the cleaners in certain firms owned by private equity financiers paid a higher percentage of their income in taxes than their multi-millionaire owners. Brad, François and Dimitri clearly felt that spending their cash on cocaine and fast cars was a far more socially valuable form of expenditure than wasting it on silly things like hospitals, schools and the unemployed. I thanked them effusively as they gave me the phone number of a specific accountant that they all used and thought it best not to mention the moral obligation that the rich should have to look after the more unfortunate members of society. The very rich, as F. Scott Fitzgerald observed in his book *The Great Gatsby*, really are 'different'. That's right . . . they're usually total wankers who have become rich and stayed rich by shafting all those around them and thinking only of themselves.

Apart from my alarming new friends' immeasurable wealth, what shocked me most on that plane journey was the delightful attitude they exhibited towards women. They had left their wives and girlfriends at home and were using this boys' long weekend to get a few things off their chest. I'd like to think that I don't have a sexist bone in my body (well, perhaps just the one), and I found the sheer contempt and objectification that women received genuinely extraordinary. Weakly, I did not open my mouth to protest at some of the more outrageous comments, but in my defence, m'lud, to have done so would have made me lose friends and alienate people so quickly that it would have made Toby Young's efforts in New York look amateur. That is what is so insidious about these appalling sexist discussions that men often indulge in – to protest is to be labelled a humourless do-gooder who probably can't fuck for toffee, and so you have little choice but to acquiesce. So I sat there listening to how Brad's wife 'could suck the chrome off a hubcap' while his mistress 'could suck a golf ball through a garden hose'. Dimitri had my peers in stitches with a tale about meeting a girl with a pussy like a 'wizard's sleeve' and how 'even with my enormous schlong it was like waving a sausage in the Albert Hall'. Like some kind of coked-up quisling desperately trying to ingratiate himself with the enemy

I tried to tell my own humorous anecdote. Unfortunately, my tedious story about an encounter with a red-headed chick that confirmed the old adage 'rusty roof, smelly garage' went down like a shit sandwich. These arse-wipes weren't even sufficiently polite to pretend to laugh and I vowed to keep my mouth shut until we grounded.

We were picked up at Ibiza airport by a stretch limo driven by a suntanned tattooed Scouser called Danny. It soon became apparent that Danny worked as a 'fixer' for loaded ravers. Like some kind of modern-day take on the tourist guide he would show us the sites and make sure our holiday went 'smoothly'. However, instead of holding aloft an umbrella while boring the pants off us about some ancient ruin Danny would hold aloft a bowl of coke and provide us with VIP tickets to all the big club nights. Clearly, François had used his services before as they greeted each other like long-lost friends. The fact that this character was afforded any respect by my otherwise dismissive peers immediately suggested to me that he was associated with some heavy guys who ran things – probably illegal, nasty things. It was either that or my paranoid, snow-blasted brain was putting two and two together and making five.

Admittedly, when I had been in the plane's cramped toilet I could have sworn that I had overheard my new pals conspiring to spike my drink, so I wasn't necessarily interpreting everything entirely accurately at this stage. Still, I've always believed that just because you're paranoid it doesn't mean they're not out to get you. The suspicious look I gave my glass of champagne on my return was a source of much amusement for my lovely new mates.

After brief introductions we were walked towards the stretch limo complete with tinted windows and boomerang thingy at the back. After a theatrical pause Danny opened the door and with a cheeky grin said simply, 'Gentlemen, enjoy.'

Inside the shadowy car I could just about discern two naked female forms sitting demurely on the back seat. Like hungry lions who've spied a herd of gazelle my pals lost no time in getting into the car while I stood around like a lemon. The sight of these naked temptresses and the sound of some really deep, dark house music emanating from the car made it look like I was being tempted to enter Hell itself. Things were turning weird real early and I needed to get a grip and quick.

But thousands of questions plagued my drug-addled brain. Were these prostitutes? Were these jokers going to have sex with them in the back of the motor in front of each other? Would I have to get involved? Would I be considered a bad sport if I didn't? Taking into account all the bugle I'd hoofed, was there even the remotest chance that I would be able to get a boner? I suddenly realised that my pause was going to be a dead giveaway for my anxiety and, prompted by a beckoning finger from the clearly coked-up Asian chick nearest the open door, I nervously walked towards the car. I clumsily shuffled into my seat and saw in the gloom my three 'colleagues' all sitting with their respective new lady-friend. They were all snorting yet more lines of cocaine that our ever-so-thoughtful hosts had prepared for us on little mirrors. Like a total twat I offered my hand to Suki with a formality that a 1950s accountant would deem excessive and stutteringly said, 'Er, hello . . . my name's Steve. Er . . . pleased to meet you.' The hysterical laughter that greeted my totally uncool first impression will plague me to my deathbed. Despite there being very little light in the car I think saw Richard put his sunglasses on, such was the heat emanating from my ever-reddening cheeks.

My embarrassing gaff had the pleasing effect of breaking the ice and my equally coked-up pals were probably pleased that what was quite an unusual situation was made easier to deal with now that the resident prat had been identified. They took the opportunity to introduce themselves to their ladies in an equally formal way, laughing while I tried to disappear into the crack in the leather seat.

By the time we were approaching St Raphael I began to calm down a bit and realise that this was not all bad. I was surrounded by dickheads but it was thirty degrees and I was in Ibiza. Thankfully, things hadn't got too silly in the car. Some clearly fake tits got felt up and some nonsense got talked, but that was about it. At one point I think I saw Dimitri 'feed the pony' but no one's pecker left their underpants – which was a Brucie bonus if ever there was one, since I don't think I could have found mine had it reached that stage.

Soon we drove through an impressive gateway and up a remarkably well-kept drive surrounded by a beautifully manicured lawn. After about fifty metres we turned a corner and I saw a gaff that was so unbelievably flash I literally gulped. It was not just the sheer opulence of the villa that forced me to swallow. Truth be told I was scared shitless just thinking about how much cash I was going to have to spend for five days' bed and board. I had made the huge error of asking Richard on the plane how much the villa was going to cost each of us but had been soundly berated by François who condescendingly said, 'Stiv, if you 'ave to ask the cost then you can't afford it.' He was speaking more truth than he knew.

The villa was located at the top of a hill and was three storeys high. The views over the surrounding countryside were truly breathtaking. The south-facing front was all balconies and windows which glittered in the midday sun. In front of the villa was a beautiful heart-shaped swimming pool surrounded by sun loungers. Standing stiffly in the doorway was a butler in traditional formal attire holding a hooded silver platter by the side of his head. If you wanted to design the perfect place for unadulterated hedonism this was it. It was definitely the perfect Bond villain's pad although whether Blofeld could actually afford it was a moot point.

We and our brazen hussies stumbled out of the car and walked towards Jeeves – as we immediately dubbed him, despite his name being Juan. If Jeeves was surprised at four naked chicks running around giggling, he didn't show it. Some of the girls immediately jumped into the pool while Danny rabited on about the various amenities: 'forty-two-inch plasma TVs in every room, sauna, steam room,' etc., etc. Every single mod con that he mentioned just made another 'kerching' noise in my head as I tried to estimate the vast expense that five days with a bunch of fuckwits was going to cost me.

When Danny came to Jeeves he revealed that he had forgotten none of the theatrical exuberance that he had demonstrated at the airport. As our butler lifted up the hood of the silver platter Danny uttered a soliloquy worthy of Shakespeare, if not perhaps as profound: 'And here, gentlemen, are your nutrients for the week. I have assembled for you the best gear this island has to offer and, believe me, I've got a fucking Ph.D. in buzzing so I know exactly what I'm talking about. This cocaine is the genuine pellet straight from the gash of some lovely Colombian bird. It is known as "mother of pearl" due to the way it reflects the light and if you can feel any part of your face within two hours of snorting it you can you have your money back, guaranteed. I've got twenty grams of that – so four each. The MDMA I have procured for you would pass any Pepsi challenge. Fuck, this stuff truly is rocket fuel. It's so poky you could put it on *Top Gear* and Jeremy Clarkson would be dancing like a pilled-up sixteen year old. There're twelve grammes of that. I've put fifty Jack and Jills in there, too, just for good measure, but I'd stick to the "Mum and Dad", if I were you. As for the damage – all this is going to set you back is a mere two thousand euros.'

Fuck me! I considered myself a seasoned caner but these boys definitely meant business. I imagined that most of this stuff would be used to persuade horny coke-sluts and fit pill-heads back to the ranch, but still, it was a hideous amount of pharmaceuticals. I was definitely not happy about having to fork out four hundred euros before we had even eaten anything or been anywhere but, of course, could not protest and risk losing face in front of my minted pals. I reached into my jacket pocket for my wallet but stopped as Dimtri handed Danny a roll of forty fifty-euro notes and told me not to worry about it. All I could think was that, just like in *Withnail and I*, it was free to those who could afford it and very expensive to those who couldn't. Still, the drugs haul seemed like total overkill to me, especially since Richard had mentioned he might be doing a little bit of work on Monday and Tuesday! Frankly, I'd never seen such vast quantities of mind-bending substances in my entire life and came to the rapid conclusion that surviving this trip was now my principal objective. As far as I could see, there was simply no possible way on earth we'd ever get through all those drugs.

We ran out on day three. The sheer gut-wrenching mindless debauchery of a weekend spent doing nothing other than dancing, consuming drugs and shagging cannot be overstated. Ibiza was made for hedonists by hedonists and, frankly, what they don't know about partying ain't worth knowing. Europe's spiritual capital may be Rome and its artistic capital may be Paris but Ibiza is Europe's partying capital, of that there can be no doubt. As a wise man probably once said – if Ibiza didn't exist then someone would have to invent it. But it does exist and every few years another generation of Europe's teenagers discover the joys and woes of nonstop pleasure seeking. Call me hypocritical, but if I ever have daughters and they try and go there I would simply laugh them off the stage. There's no fucking way I'd ever let any daughter of mine meet people like me as I was then or my appalling weekend pals unless they were old enough to have the wisdom to see through our incessant bullshit.

Whatever faults my companions had, and frankly, between the lot of them they covered the whole gamut, they certainly knew how to party. Richard had said early on that 'sleeping and eating is cheating' and he was a man of his word. We were driven to every club by our ever-faithful Scouser Danny and managed to get in without ever having to queue which, according to Dimitri, 'was only for the plebs'. It was champagne and girls on tap combined with some good 'old-skool' raving. However, after having been partying for thirty-six hours solid at Pasha, Space and DC10 with the occasional break at the villa, I was not in a great physical or mental state come Sunday afternoon. At approximately 4 p.m. I tried and failed to have one last dance in the sun on the terrace of Space. Sweating like a paedophile at Disneyland it was only when my calves seized up that I knew my time was finished. I virtually had to be carried to Danny's ever-present limo but at least my handicap meant that I was finally allowed home by my hard-partying colleagues. As soon as my head hit the pillow of my luxurious emperor-sized bed I fell into a blissful sleep that lasted nineteen hours.

I awoke late on Monday morning to the sound of Richard talking business on his mobile on the terrace. If he was feeling even a quarter as bad as I was then this was truly an extraordinarily impressive feat. I simply lay there, not daring to move, knowing that my merciless night-time visitors would have almost certainly paid me a visit and that any movement would reveal to me what particular torture they had dreamed up. Despite my bleary-eyed befuddled state I soon realised Richard was up to no good: '. . . he's a junior in the corporate finance department at the bank handling the acquisition, you say? Have we used him before? OK, then this sounds like a runner. How much does he want? Woah – does he think we're made of money? Oh yes, we are, aren't we! OK, give him the fifty grand – cash; you know which accounts to use. So, if it's being bought on Friday then we need to get our skates on. Let's go in big but subtle – little bits and bobs using lots of different brokers. I want us to get at least sixty million's worth – nah, that's too greedy, that could raise suspicion. Let's get forty million squid's worth. If the take-out price is at a thirty-two-per-cent premium to where it's currently trading, then that'll make us around twelve and a half big ones. Not bad for three days' work!'

So that was his game: insider trading. If there's one thing that really gets people's goat about us Cityboys, it's insider trading. It upsets 'civilians' that a bunch of jokers choose to supplement their already hideously large pay packets by trading illegally in shares on information that only they are privy to. It also confirms the general public's absolutely valid suspicion that the City is a close-knit club dedicated to making its members as much cash as humanly possible as quickly as possible. I estimated that Richard's 'fortunate' investment would probably net him personally around £500,000. Cityboys give each other profitable tips about what shares to invest in all the time. However, this was my first direct encounter with this crime although I had known for some time that it was endemic in the City.

I wasn't the only one who realised this. In July 2007 John Tiner, the outgoing head of the City Regulator, the Financial Services Authority, exclaimed in a major interview in the *Financial Times* that insider trading was 'rife' in the Square Mile. Apparently, in the same interview he made the equally controversial claims that bears sometimes defecate in forests and that Dolly Parton generally sleeps on her back. The fact is that the City regulates itself and is thriving partly because of its relatively loose regulation (unlike, for example, Wall Street). Hence, the interesting thing about Tiner's statement was who was saying it rather than the conclusion.

But I didn't need this character's confession to make me realise that something was rotten in the City. Even by that stage in my career, I had seen many companies being forced to issue a statement because of an extremely rapid rise in their share price stating that they were indeed in talks 'that may or may not lead to an offer'. In 2004–7, five companies in the UK utilities sector alone (Viridian Group, Anglian Water Group, East Surrey Holdings, South Staffordshire and Kelda) did this. In each case the company was obliged (usually by the Takeover Panel) to reveal publicly that they had received a 'preliminary approach' by another company wanting to buy them. The dramatic share-price appreciation that had obliged them to issue the statement results from an unusually large amount of stock being bought in a short space of time. So every time a company makes this kind of announcement (and they're pretty damn frequent) it suggests very strongly that there has been some serious insider trading going on. If there were any justice in the world, every single person or firm whose buying had pushed up the share price in the day or two before these announcements should be investigated by the Financial Services Authority.

However, there is a major problem getting evidence to convict insiders and hence the number of successful prosecutions can be counted on one hand. Even if the FSA had definite proof that a notoriously loose-tongued corporate financier involved in a specific takeover had a candle-lit dinner with some greedy toe-rag the night before the latter purchased shares in the target company, it would be hard to get a conviction. If there were no witnesses or tape recordings, how can it be proved that they talked about nothing more innocuous than which one of the Spice Girls floats their boat? That's why Ivan Boesky, Michael Milken and Martha Stewart's insider trading convictions were the exceptions that prove the rule and why most insider traders can sit at home counting their ill-gotten gains as happy and innocent as O.J. Simpson.

Everyone in the City knows insider trading goes on and everyone realises that there's virtually bugger all you can do about it. That's because there are too many people involved in preparing for the dissemination of non-public price-sensitive information. For example, the average takeover of a company requires weeks of work by corporate financiers, accountants, lawyers, PR advisers, printers, etc. before the actual announcement. Since human nature hasn't moved on since Alexander Pope first declared 'to err is human' three hundred years ago it is natural that several greedy bad apples will choose to profit from their inside information and, using an anonymous mobile phone or email address, get their long-lost Auntie Marge or some loosely connected chap abroad to buy shares in the company being acquired. Since the problems in securing a conviction are well known, there is little genuine disincentive to naughtiness and that's why this scourge is prevalent. I also have little doubt that self-serving cabals operate amongst the more aggressive hedge funds feeding each other inside information for their mutual benefit. Fuck, I thought, that's probably what these four got up to.

Some claim that insider trading is a 'victimless crime' but it's not; every time some scallywag uses his inside knowledge to make a fast buck by, for example, investing in a company that is about to be acquired, the sucker he bought his shares off suffers as a result of no longer owning shares that would have benefited from the premium that a predator is willing to pay. Since these schmucks are often the people running your pension or ISA, these insider traders are stealing directly off you. Furthermore, these bad apples damage the City's already battered reputation. It's no wonder that when I go to certain dinner parties I find myself about as welcome as a turd in a swimming pool – though come to think of it, that was the case long before I joined the City.

So Richard was a naughty boy, but his nefarious business didn't end there. Almost as an afterthought he asked the trader at his fund, who was clearly his accomplice on the other end of the phone, about a company in the UK water sector that he had invested in, despite my protestations that it was expensive.

'John, by the way, where's United Utilities trading? Really, down again, eh? OK, we're gonna need to pull a number here. I'll do a little bit of reverse broking with some salesmen and you do the same with some of your trader pals. The usual thing, you know . . . hearing rumours about a takeover, around a thirty-percent premium to the share price, big US private equity fund. That should do it. We'll see if we can get Reuters and Bloomberg to bite and, once it's up four or five per cent, let's get out. Shouldn't be too hard, eh? We've done it a hundred times.'

I then heard Richard ring up several salesmen and analysts at various investment banks and say pretty much precisely the same spiel: 'Hi, Tarquin, it's Richard. Yeah, yeah living the dream in Ibiza. Anyway, what's this I'm hearing about UU? You haven't heard anything? I'm hearing that a large US private equity fund's been nosing around. There's talk of a seven-hundred-and-fifty-pence take-out price. Can you ask around? Great – I want to know if this is bollocks or not. Call me back in a few hours.'

OK. Richard was definitely not mucking around. This could help explain why his fund's performance was so damn good. Not just trading on inside information but spreading false rumours which contravenes City regulations – what a stand-up guy!

Why do certain hedge fund managers spread false rumours? The same reason why dogs lick their balls – because they can. You don't have to be a rocket scientist to work out that although spreading bogus rumours is illegal, it's a pretty rational thing to do for naughty hedge fund managers because the risks are minimal yet the rewards can be disgustingly huge. Provided the rumour you choose to propagate is vaguely credible it will spread and even some of the less plausible rumours work. I mean, if the Queen can get away with the obvious nonsense she spread decades ago that swans can break your legs by beating their wings, which she clearly did to protect her favourite source of food, then you can get away with a lot!

So, if a cunning hedge fund manager like Richard had bought shares in United Utilities and then told a few gullible sell-side contacts that it could be taken over, before long mobile phones and Internet sites across the world would be buzzing with the story. If the ruse works then the original rumour-monger would eventually be rung himself by a Johnny-come-lately to the story. In this situation I can imagine a sly smile spreading across his greedy face as he utters the immortal words: 'This confirms exactly what I thought.'

Since hedge funds can short-stock too, the rumours they spread can also relate to profit warnings or other events that would have a negative impact on a share price. This means they can 'trash and cash' as well as 'pump and dump'. I remember when it was falsely rumoured that the chief executive of Centrica (the company that owns British Gas) stormed out of a meeting with two key investors shouting, 'You don't understand my fucking company.' Two telephone calls to the relevant buy-side analysts quickly revealed to me that this rumour was utter horseshit but not before the stock fell four per cent. It was also once rumoured that the publication of Scottishpower's US accounts had been delayed due to the discovery of an accounting error. Again, this proved to be total nonsense, but since this rumour was spread at the time of general accountancy-related fears sparked off by the Enron debacle, the shares fell around seven per cent before recovering. You can bet your bottom dollar that a few cunning hedge fund managers had been shorting both stocks and sat around giving each other high-fives after the successful implementation of their ruse.

Profiting by spreading false rumours is the oldest trick in the book. However, it really started spreading like a malignant cancer this decade and the fact that this happened during the rise of the hedge funds is, I believe, no coincidence. Unlike conventional funds that invest for the long-term, many hedge funds are extremely short-term. Although some hedge fund boys may be reluctant to 'manipulate markets' for ethical reasons (well, perhaps one or two), very few would not do so for fear of being caught. That's because being prosecuted for being the very first person to spread a rumour is about as likely as John Prescott being named Britain's Poet Laureate and Mr Universe in the same year. The beauty of this gambit is the sheer impossibility of proving that a specific individual was the first ever to mention the rumour. The rise of the Internet has further aided this particular trick and nowadays informal investment websites and chat rooms are often the first port of call for a rumour-monger. Again, the swindle works best if you can execute it in tandem with a few pals and, again, this is what happens – with Richard and the boys almost certainly working as a team dedicated to filling their already-bloated wallets.

I lay there trying to process this new information about my most lucrative client. So, he was a criminal. He was almost certainly working in tandem with his alarming chums. He trusted me enough not to feel the need to cover up his flagrant wrongdoing. What should I do? Any action would lose me my best client and really screw up my reputation in the City. This kind of greedy, selfish behaviour pissed me off (at least at that stage in my career), but it wasn't exactly mugging grannies. I would also struggle to prove any wrongdoing had occurred since it would be my word against Richard's. He and his trader were clearly speaking on mobile phones so the conversations would not be recorded. Any court case would be a major ball-ache and probably not result in a conviction. My association with any such court case would also probably make me a pariah in the City – and certainly an analyst that few hedge fund managers would seek to chat to. After a fair amount of soul-searching, I concluded that the only thing to do, was to do nothing. I didn't approve of what he was up to but, as Michael had always told me, 'If in doubt, leave it out.' I was aware that inaction can be just as much a crime as action and had always baulked at the excuses made by people who had stood by while the Nazis rounded up Jews for death camps but this was just a few guys making a bit of dodgy cash on the side. That's it, I decided, I'd do nothing.

What I actually did do, was slowly try and get out of bed.

Unfortunately, as soon as I stood up it was revealed to me what imaginative brutality my nocturnal foes had meted out. I screamed in pain and fell back on the bed – the little buggers had clearly been injecting polyfilla into my calves all night. Either that or it was the effect of almost nonstop dancing combining with the lack of food and fluids that I had stupidly forgotten to consume. As usual, I came to the more rational and less self-critical conclusion that I had been revisited by my malicious tormentors.

The rest of the break was somewhat more muted than the first two crazy days. I could barely walk but still managed to go out and have a little party time at the Jockey Club and the Blue Marlin where I mostly sat around chatting inanely to the beautiful people whose superficiality was only rivalled by their vacuousness. My new 'pals' were also taking it a little more gently and before long we were heading back home in our private jet all suffering from the kind of come-down that makes you question everything you've ever held dear. We hardly spoke in the plane back and the only noise was the occasional snore from Dimitri and Brad.

My melancholy back at Blighty was only heightened by an email from Richard which arrived two days after we got back stating nonchalantly that the total bill for my five days of depravity was, including villa and jet, £25,000 – roughly the annual salary of a primary school teacher! I both hated and celebrated the preposterous size of this bill which probably meant nothing to any other member of my group but was still pretty breathtaking for me. The sheer exuberance of my holiday told me that I'd arrived and I ceaselessly mentioned it to as many of my old friends as I could despite sensing that they were finding me increasingly less tolerable. While at a dinner at my parents' house, my brother complained that I was becoming a 'money-obsessed Cityboy cliché' and that he had 'unleashed a monster'. He had recently given up his job in the City and was training to be a vicar, so I couldn't really accuse him of hypocrisy. One of my oldest school friends, Angus, told me that my ego was growing out of control while an ex-girlfriend asked what had happened to the lefty hippy she had known and loved. I just didn't really care what they thought. I had a mission to fulfil and if they couldn't handle my success then they could fuck right off. It was while I was in this unwavering state of mind that I received a phone call from someone who, I immediately knew, would make my mission's success completely inevitable.

6

THE LEADER

There are some really fanatical, hard-working motherfuckers in the City. I've seen men, and it is mainly men, sacrifice their marriages, their kids and their own lives just to thrive in that soul-destroying industry. Working all hours God sends, some of these characters have a drive and energy that would even embarrass James Brown – by all accounts the hardest working man in show business. But compared to Neil Jameson these people were part-timers and also-rans. They were uncommitted time wasters whose hearts weren't really in it. Hell, if Neil had lived in Stalinist Russia, Aleksei Stakhanov would have stepped aside and let my former boss show him what dedication to coal mining really meant.

Just one day after my return from Ibiza I received a call from Neil. I knew of him from his previous role as utilities team leader at a second-tier French house. I also knew that he had recently been taken on by Megashite bank with a mandate to form a strong utilities team following the wholesale departure of their own team to another bulge bracket US bank. As soon as I recognised his voice on the telephone I knew that this was a great opportunity to move to a hard-core bank that was willing to commit serious resources to creating a number-one-ranked team. They had their reasons for such a pointless task but I had my own and the fact that our interests were aligned meant that I should do everything in my power to get myself and Michael to go and work for Neil.

'Steve, it's Neil Jameson. We met a few months ago at the Edison electricity conference. I'm hearing good things about you. You may have heard I'm building a team over at Megashite and I was wondering if you'd be interested in coming in for a chat.'

ABSOFUCKINGLUTELY! This was exactly the bank I needed to work at. It had a great brand name, a massive sales force and was involved in loads of corporate deals. Some major clients felt they didn't need to hear the views of analysts from a mid-tier bank like Scheissebank but that would never be the case at Megashite. Michael and I could really thrive there. With Michael's Mekon-like brain, my world-class bullshit and the backing of Megashite, the sky was literally the limit. Despite the fact that I was virtually becoming tumescent, such was my excitement, I said as unenthusiastically as possible: 'Well, truth be told, I'm pretty happy where I am. I'm willing to come in for a little chinwag but I have to say right now that I can see little real reason to leave. I'm achieving great success with my colleague Michael at Scheissebank and any disruption to our momentum could cost us dear.'

If Neil had even three brain cells to rub together he would have seen through that horseshit immediately. But, if he did, he was polite enough not to show it.

'I understand. Still, why don't you come in on Friday?'

By Friday, I had just about recovered from the kind of drugs come-down that was so intense it was a miracle that my wrists were still fully intact. I had spent the previous days and nights questioning everything about my personality and my circumstances. I had dwelled on my inevitable death and the loneliness inherent in the human condition. I had gazed into the middle-distance with a Vietnam Vet-like thousand-yard stare contemplating the sheer cruelty and meaningless of life. In short, my serotonin and dopamine levels were severely depleted. Still, on that fateful Friday, I pretended to my colleagues that I had a lunch with a client from Morgan Stanley Asset Management and took the tube from Bank to Canary Wharf. From there I walked to the huge phallic tower that housed the esteemed house of Megashite, trying my best to anticipate the questions that my potential new boss would pose.

'Hello, Steve, good to see you again,' Neil said extending a hand. His face had the grey pallid look of a man who rarely saw the light of day and his skin had the premature wrinkles of someone who worked all the hours God sends, and then some. He was only forty years old but I reckon it had been decades since a New York barman had felt obliged to ask him for ID – and those fuckwits 'card' pensioners for fun. Still, he had a youthful glint in his piercing blue eyes that hinted at an intensely sharp mind.

The interview was quick and efficient. Neil didn't bother with many of the usual questions. I remember privately thanking God that he hadn't asked me some tedious valuation question such as how to calculate the weighted average cost of capital. By that stage I had forgotten that kind of nonsense, having delegated those kinds of silly technical things to The Genius. Frankly, the fact that my team was ranked fourth in the surveys and that I was personally ranked ninth did all my talking for me. Hence, Neil could dispense with the usual formalities. The conversation lasted forty-five minutes and was mainly aimed at ensuring that we could vaguely get on with each other as well as making sure that my clients were the same as those that Megashite targeted. This latter exercise was fairly pointless because as far as I could see, every bank was chasing the same dickheads across the globe – those conventional houses that had the biggest funds under management and those hedge funds that ran less cash but traded shares like whirling dervishes.

I could tell the interview was a resounding success, but I suspect it was for reasons other than my innate brilliance. Megashite were desperate to replace their lost team as quickly as humanly possible and were clearly after a top-five team who could hit the ground running. I, or if I'm being honest, The Genius, had analysed the potential list of people Neil could choose from and the list was smaller than I had imagined once you discounted those who had recently moved shop or were happy where they were. This boded extremely well for our bargaining position. I had informed Michael that I was going for this interview and had told him that he should join me at the new bank, pretending that I was doing him a favour when, of course, I knew that I would be shown up as an intellectual flyweight without him covering my back. Before the interview was up I had to make a pitch for The Genius, who was less of a showman than I was, and hence less well known by the market. I just had to make sure I didn't reveal Michael's brilliance too enthusiastically or he might get the larger portion of whatever cash Neil had to allocate on behalf of Megashite.

'Listen, Neil, you don't just wanna hire me. You wanna think very seriously about getting my colleague Michael to join as well. He's quite a smart cookie and he's beginning to shape up. With my guidance I think we can mould him into a pretty decent analyst. Truth be told, we're a bit of a double act anyway, and I'd be somewhat reluctant to leave without him.'

'Really? I have heard good things about him but he's not as well known by the clients as you are. I'll tell you what, get him to come in early next week and then we'll see. We want this whole thing to be wrapped up asap, so make it Monday.'

Michael's interview predictably went like a dream and, after a series of meetings with the usual suspects at Megashite, Neil called me with an offer merely a week after we last met. These boys really meant business and that was the best goddam news possible. Neil rang me on my mobile at around 2 p.m. on Friday and said that he was calling to discuss money. I looked around suspiciously at my unsuspecting colleagues and as calmly as possible asked him to ring me back in ten minutes. I grabbed my jacket and then I grabbed Michael, saying loudly in an appallingly self-conscious fashion purely for the benefit of my unwary colleagues, 'Michael, we're late for that meeting I arranged this morning with . . . John. Come, come quickly.'

Anyone in the team who had been paying attention would have realised immediately that something dodgy was going on. My dreadful acting ability made Liz Hurley look like an Oscar winner, but fortunately my team-mates were all preoccupied working out their companies' free-cash-flow yield or some such pointless nonsense. We nervously left Scheissebank's offices, desperate to find somewhere appropriate for 'the conversation'. Both of us were in a state of anxious anticipation though we were trying our damndest to mask our trepidation so as not to appear uncool to each other. As we randomly walked around Cannon Street, hearts pumping with excitement, we suddenly spied St Paul's Cathedral and, in an unspoken agreement, set off towards that most majestic monument to Christianity. It would be in its garden that our most unholy of discussions would take place. With hindsight, Sigmund Freud would have had a field day analysing my subconscious urge to cleanse myself of religious guilt by gravitating towards the house of God – but fortunately for me that pipe-smoking cokehead was not present to pass comment. Before we reached the gates I felt obliged to condescendingly inform Michael how to conduct this all-important conversation.

'OK, Michael, it's squeaky bum time. This is when you find out about yourself. Time to fucking step up to the plate. The difference between playing this right and lunching it could easily be a hundred grand or so. These jokers want us badly and they want us quick. If Neil asks you what you expect cash-wise, don't bite – ask what he's willing to give. We are not going for less than two guaranteed bonuses and we are not going for a basic under six figures. Whatever they offer, appear unsatisfied and demand more. I have a figure in my head for what the two guarantees are gonna be for me and I suggest you think of one too. Now add about fifteen per cent to that. Now add about twenty grand to that and that's what you go for. We are talking telephone numbers, my son! Let's show these fuckers that we're not going to have the piss taken out of us. Not only does smart negotiation now bode well for our near-term remuneration but it also immediately ties our flag to the mask and shows them that we ain't doing this shit for the love of the job. If they know we're mercenary mother-fuckers that should keep 'em on their toes for however long we stay at this shit-hole. OK? Let's not fuck this up!'

In reality, I was talking as much to myself as I was to Michael.

I had the mobile in my hand and I was going to be first. I virtually jumped out of my skin when it rang and my trembling hand almost dropped it as I put it to my ear. Michael was probably looking at me and thinking what a total muppet I was but I had entered 'the zone' and was ignoring all around me. I walked away from Michael and listened.

'Hi, Steve, it's Neil. So, let's cut to the chase. We are willing to offer you a basic of a hundred thousand and two guaranteed bonuses of two hundred and fifty grand.'

What a total buffoon! What is wrong with these fucking idiots? These total losers think that I'm worth almost seven hundred thousand pounds over the next year and a half! The sick fucks! There are kids starving on the streets! My dad earns a fraction of what they're offering and is a diligent, clever man who has worked really hard all his life. Don't they realise I'm just a stoner hippy who got lucky? Those were the main thoughts that were bouncing around my short-circuiting brain but I needed to buck my ideas up and present a slightly different attitude if I was going to adhere to my own advice.

'Ehem, that sounds in the right kind of ball-park. But I've got to be honest with you – the basic's a little light . . . I mean, I'm virtually earning that already,' I lied.

'OK, we can make it one twenty.'

'Cool . . . and I was kind of thinking of something closer to three hundred for the two bonuses.'

'I'll tell you what, we'll make it two eighty and, if you deliver, you'll find you get more than three hundred.'

I didn't buy that shit for a second. Lucifer will be throwing snowballs long before a guaranteed bonus is exceeded by an investment bank. But frankly, I could hardly believe my future employer's absurdity and finished the conversation feeling like the cock of the north. After Michael's suspiciously brief chat we went to a local wine bar and celebrated in style with a £300 bottle of vintage champagne. I didn't know what this Yank bank thought we were gonna do for the cash they were offering us but, frankly, provided what they required wasn't going to wear my knees out or result in life-threatening diseases, I didn't give a rat's fart.

The contract arrived in the post two days later and I signed it with unhealthy speed. My brother had told me to have a lawyer check it out but I wanted this deal wrapped up as quickly as possible before Megashite realised what a horrific mistake they'd made. I was also thinking about the three months of gardening leave that awaited me over the summertime which, in itself, would have been sufficient incentive to move bank.

Leaving Scheissebank was a lot easier than my rather emotional departure from Banque Inutile. I'd been there far less time and I'd forged no decent friendships. There was no Tony and no David that I was betraying and having Michael in the same boat certainly helped reduce the solitude you felt during these difficult times. Hans and the Head of Equities tried the usual tricks to make us stay but Michael and I were resolute and they soon realised the pointlessness of their efforts. Within two weeks of Neil's first overture we were leaving Scheissebank with a cardboard box each of our personal items. Theoretically, we were supposed to leave all our spreadsheet models at the bank since they were officially our employers' property. Of course, we had saved them on to disk and carried them out the day before we gave HR our resignation letters – as all analysts do. There was no way in hell that we were gonna waste another few months composing these all-important models.

On the day we were marched out of our office, we called Neil to inform him that, much to our great chagrin, Scheissebank were insisting that we do not work for Megashite for the next three months and that effectively those inconsiderate bastards were demanding that we take the whole period as holiday on full pay. He had anticipated this gardening leave and optimistically (or foolishly) gave us some tasks to achieve at home while we 'waited' for the pleasure of starting work again. As soon as I walked into my house I filed the documents he had handed me in the big, round filing cabinet under the sink in my kitchen. Our start date at Megashite had been set as Monday, 10 September 2001 and I fully intended to utilise my time up to then having as much fun as humanly possible. If I remember correctly, Michael went off and did something pointless like marry his childhood sweetheart. I still remember wondering whether she realised that any potential future divorce settlement had just been made significantly more lucrative.

It was 21 June and I had three months of unbridled debauchery to look forward to. The sheer joy I felt at my new-found freedom was intense and I couldn't help grinning from ear to ear as I walked down the road to my house. Within five minutes of entering my abode, I immediately called up my old pal Sam to pass on the good news. Within ten seconds, I was informed by my extremely jealous pal that he and two friends were driving up to the Glastonbury festival in Somerset in two hours' time and that they had space in the car for one more reveller. PERFECT! ABSOLUTELY FUCKING PERFECT! IT SIMPLY GETS NO BETTER!

I hastily assembled my 'Glastonbury survival kit' – which mainly consisted of Rizlas, cigarettes and Absolut vodka bought from the local off-licence. I think I may have brought a spare set of clothes but past experience suggested that such organised preparation was generally a waste of time. The car journey up was spent in a haze of dope smoke and, as usual, we were caught in a horrific traffic jam around Shepton Mallet. We finally parked the motor at around 11 p.m. and then had the fun of breaking into the grounds, which was almost always the best part of any Glastonbury experience. None of us had any tickets but this was before the organisers got their shit together to make the festival near-impossible to break into. We began circling the fence at around midnight, trying to look as nonchalant as possible but buzzing with excitement. After about half an hour, we came across a friendly Scouser carrying a fifteen-foot ladder. For the paltry price of ten quid a pop he let each of us climb over the fence, hang down and drop on to the ground. For the mere price of forty quid, we were all in and the fun was about to begin.

Apparently, there are some quite serious bands that play at Glastonbury but I've never seen any. The time there, as always, was simply spent getting wankered, throwing shapes in the dance tent and wondering around the Lost Vagueness area feeling very lost and very vague.

It was at about 9 a.m. on the Sunday, having been up all night talking codshit to any poor sucker dumb enough to hang around me, that something truly bizarre happened. As I was walking towards the hideous long-drop toilets by the Glade ready to 'drop the kids off at the pool', I suddenly saw Neil Jameson walking towards me with a young girl by his side. I, of course, assumed it was merely a hallucination – albeit a rather more convincing one than those that had been entertaining me over the previous twenty-four hours. However, as this human form neared me it soon became very clear that I was either having the most realistic hallucination of all time or that, for some sick and twisted reason, my future boss was hanging out at Glastonbury with some young chick! It was almost inconceivable but it was true. As I was trying to process this information I could see Neil's eyes light up in recognition and he walked straight towards me. Since it was too late to run away, I did what any sensible caner would do in that situation. I put my sunglasses on.

'Hello, Steve,' he said with unabashed surprise in his voice. 'You didn't tell me you were a fan of Glastonbury.'

Christ almighty! You couldn't make this up! Here I was still tripping on some extremely potent Mexican magic mushrooms, having been up for the best part of two days, about to have to engage in a serious chat with my future boss – a managing director at a major investment bank. Steady yourself, son! Think before you speak. Keep it simple and try to extricate yourself as quickly as possible. Most importantly, for God's sake never take your shades off.

'Oh . . . hi, hi, Neil. What on earth are you doing here? Ehm . . . I've just woken up actually and . . . I'm going to get some breakfast. I haven't been up all night, definitely not. Silly thing to do, dreadful business . . . must be stopped . . . at all costs . . . Ehm . . . the bands are great, aren't they?' Christ, I was fluffing this badly and ranting like a man possessed. My attempt to project a calm disposition wasn't helped by the fact that Neil's face was melting in front of my very eyes.

'Yeah, who have you seen so far?'

FUCK! I didn't have a clue what bands were at this festival. I was in big fucking trouble now!

'Oh . . . you know? Er, loads of bands – rock and pop and all that . . . er, the Manic Street Fighters, for example' – phew, I remember hearing someone talk about this band last night. That's got me out of trouble.

'You mean, the Manic Street Preachers?'

'Er, that's exactly who I mean . . . I've just woken up, bit tired, had a few drinks last night – d'you know what I mean?'

'Funny you've seen them already . . . they're playing tonight.'

'Oh are they? Er . . .' goddam it, think man! 'It must have been a little surprise show they put on just for those in the know. That must be it' – I was really, really struggling here. This was career-threateningly appalling.

'Yes, of course . . . that must be it,' he said, clearly not buying any of my horseshit. 'Anyway, this is my daughter Rachel. We're after breakfast too. So why don't we go to that café over there together and . . . have a chat.'

This was going from bad to worse. I couldn't refuse him but just thinking about food made me want to projectile vomit. Also, the way he said 'chat' sounded incredibly ominous – or was that just my paranoia kicking in . . . again?

I nodded acceptance and wearily trudged through the glutinous mud towards the huge yellow and red striped tent from which emanated the sickening smell of fried food. I ordered bacon and eggs but had no intention whatsoever of eating it, knowing full well that if I did so I would a produce a Technicolor yawn that no amount of bullshit could explain. I sat there pushing my food around my plate with the peculiar wooden cutlery I'd been given and tried my best not to destroy my career whilst feigning joviality. As I listened to Neil drone on about each band that he and his daughter had seen and how he had come on his daughter's behest because his wife had not allowed Rachel to go on her own, I hatched a plan about how to escape this hellish ordeal. I excused myself and went to the bog from whence I called Sam telling him to ring my mobile in five minutes. I returned to our table, keeping my shades on despite the grey skies and near-torrential rain.

When my phone rang I apologised to Neil and answered it. I

immediately acted out a scene that I had been rehearsing in my head for the previous few minutes.

'What? She's hurt herself? Really? She's cut her leg on a nail? Look, I've got the plasters and antiseptic in my bag here. I'll come over right now.'

I don't know if Neil or his daughter bought this utter nonsense but by that stage I was way past caring and I left in a hurry babbling on about 'tetanus' and 'lock jaw'. As soon as I was out of range, I breathed a huge sigh of relief. Unfortunately, the rest of my Glastonbury experience was somewhat marred by my constant paranoid visions of this gruesome twosome. By the end of Sunday I must have seen Neil and Rachel about three hundred times (or not, as almost certainly was the case) which put a bit of a downer on an otherwise perfect festival.

On arriving home I felt as if I had just undergone an SAS assault course. I weighed myself on the bathroom scales and what was revealed simply confirmed that what I had endured had been no holiday. I had lost three quarters of a stone over four days. To this day I think that Glastonbury should be advertised as a health spa where people can lose their love handles and tone up their 'summer bodies' ready to impress our Continental brothers and sisters on the Mediterranean beaches in July and August. I think the 'Glastonbury diet' could catch on; I'd call it the 'G Plan' if that hasn't already been taken.

After a three-hour soak in the bath, which rapidly turned a rather disconcerting brown colour, I went through the routine of reading the mail that had come to my home in my absence. I immediately noticed one from Megashite. I gingerly opened it and was horrified to see the words 'Medical Required' at the top of the page in big, fuck-off letters.

The problem was that I fully intended to fly off to South America with Alex for two months in about a week's time and these jokers wanted me to undergo a medical within a month. There was only one thing for it; I'd have to call my brother.

'Hi, John, it's your brother Steve. How are things? Yeah, well listen – I need you to take a slash in a jam jar and Fedex it to me asap.'

'You're taking the piss, aren't you?'

'That's right, your piss to be precise. Look, after Glastonbury I've got so many drugs in my system that anyone engaging in a golden shower with me would be taking a very serious risk with their health. Shit, my piss is probably corrosive. You're training to be a vicar and, unless I'm very much mistaken, are living a clean and pure life. I need your piss for a medical that Megashite are insisting I take and I need it by Thursday. Please don't let me down!'

Blood is thicker than water and so, it turns out, is piss. My brother delivered the goods and within two days I was signing off for a bubble-wrapped jam jar of the finest unadulterated urine this side of the Vatican. Even better, it was piss from a genetically similar male who was only a little older than me so the chances of me being found out as a fraud seemed remote. The fact that I had to promise to give a Christian charity five hundred pounds to persuade my brother to participate in my evil scheming showed that he had not lost all his financial nous since his move to the Christian brotherhood. He still knew how to negotiate a good deal, though his intentions were admittedly somewhat more worthy than when he was merely a self-serving capitalist.

On the Thursday before I flew off to Lima, I waddled into the medical centre off Bishopsgate with an uneasy gait. Walking normally with half a pint of your brother's piss in a bladder sellotaped to your inner thigh ain't as easy as it sounds. I had read on the Internet that piss poured straight from a jar would be suspiciously cold to the touch, which could be a dead giveaway if the doctor were to handle his receptacle soon after I had supposedly urinated. By strapping it to my inner thigh, the piss would be close to body temperature.

After filling in a long questionnaire and undergoing the usual tests (blood pressure, heart rate, etc.) I was left alone in the toilets for a few minutes to provide a urine sample. Congratulating myself on my cunning plan I took out the bladder of piss and, in a scene reminiscent of *Withnail and I*, proceeded to decant it into the little plastic vessel that had been left for me on the shelf. However, unlike Withnail, I got away with it. When those boys from Megashite read my urine analysis and saw its divine purity they must have thought a puritanical Boy Scout was coming to the firm instead of a coke-snorting, semi-alcoholic degenerate.

Alex arrived from India on the Saturday and we left for a two-month jaunt around South America on the Monday. I had persuaded him to come over by telling him that 'this trip was gonna make Goa look like a Christian Union meeting'. Oh, and also by promising to pay for his flights and giving him £2,000 spending money. He was broke when I had called him up to invite him on my mission and so I did the decent thing. None of this mattered, though, as we left to check out a continent that neither of us had ever visited.

The trip to South America was both breathtaking and frustrating. Unlike Asia, where you felt able to get off the tourist trail and discover the real deal, this proved extremely difficult to do in Peru, Chile and Bolivia. Alex and I faithfully followed the 'gringo trail' and kept meeting the same people whether it was at the Nazca lines, Cuzco, Machu Picchu or the Salar de Uyuni. It felt as if we were being ferried around a vast fairground and were going on tried and tested rides with all the other punters. I suppose the fact that our Spanish extended to '*Dos Cervezas, por favor*' didn't help. Still, two particular adventures stand out in my mind.

The first seriously weird experience occurred when we visited the main prison in La Paz. Our *Lonely Planet* guide mentioned that, for some surreal reason, if you stood around the prison gate on a Thursday you would, for the equivalent of five English pounds, be allowed to enter and check out what a genuine South American prison looks like from the inside! This seemed like too good an opportunity to have a weird time to miss. Sure enough, as we self-consciously waited around, we suddenly heard a voice shouting, 'Hey, touristo, over here.' We paid the prisoner/tourist guide, Miguel, our money (some of which was immediately handed to a prison guard) and with a German couple and some moody-looking Dutch hippy began our tour of the prison.

San Pedro prison is divided into seven main courtyards. Prisoners have to buy their cells and then sell them on their release. The 'poshest' ones in the Los Pinos quarter cost around $3000 and have luxurious interiors, cable TV and Playstations, while the poorest ones are virtually uninhabitable, rat-infested shit-holes and cost around a hundred dollars. There appeared to be no prison guards within the confines of the prison walls and there were many wives and children who live with their criminal husbands. Eighty per cent of prisoners were in for cocaine-related crimes. Miguel told us that there wasn't much violence during the day but at night things could get 'un poco loco'. That's partly because everyone was getting arseholed on the local hooch called 'chicha' and partly because the purest cocaine in Bolivia was manufactured by the prisoners of San Pedro. We had a stocky prisoner covered in stab wounds and sporting a Beatles mop-top haircut circa 1965, who had just spent five days in solitary confinement for a knife fight, acting as our bodyguard, so we felt relatively safe. Miguel told us that prostitutes were often brought in by prisoners and for a hundred dollars a prisoner was allowed out for the night accompanied by a prison guard. Since money was all-important, most inmates worked within the walls selling food, giving haircuts, showing tourists around and so forth. Essentially, life here didn't seem so different from that in the Bolivian shanty towns we'd seen around La Paz and all I could think of as we were given 'the tour' was the anarchic town depicted at the beginning of the film *Mad Max 3*.

It was when we were being shown around a $3000 cell that I once again made a schoolboy error. I'd obviously been taking my brave pills because when Miguel's rich prisoner friend, whose cell we were briefly invading, asked if any of us would like to buy any 'coca' I immediately put my hand up. He sold me two grams for about seven pounds and then offered me a CD cover to have a line on. I racked out two fatties, did one and, on finding that no one else wanted a 'cheeky', did the other. Within about three minutes I lost all sensation in the entire lower half of my face and within about six minutes I was buzzing like Kate Moss at a fashion party. It was when Miguel suddenly asked us to stop on a gantry overlooking a particularly ramshackle courtyard and left us, that my old friend paranoia decided to come a-knocking.

Why has he stopped us? Where's he gone? Shit, I've got two grams of gak down my sock and I'm already in a South American prison! These fuckers don't even have to nick me! They can miss out the middleman! Do not pass Go, go directly to jail! You're already in fucking jail. This is all a scam designed to fleece idiot tourists like me. He's gone to get some prison guards and they're gonna strip-search me. I'm going to spend the next five years getting buggered by sweaty coked-up, chicha-swilling AIDS-ridden Bolivian arse-bandits. Christ alive, you fucking cocksucker . . . you've really done it now. When will you learn? Why don't you chuck the two G's away? But it's really good shit and this could just all be in your head . . .

Needless to say, it was all in my head. Miguel had simply gone out briefly to pick up two other tourists who had come to the gate and soon we resumed our tour. By the time Miguel rejoined our group I was sweating like a rapist in a line-up and a knowing look from our guide suggested he knew exactly what was going on in my poor, drug-addled, paranoid little brain.

The interesting thing about San Pedro prison, apart from its extremely high-quality nose candy, was the way that even within this theoretically enclosed microculture a tremendously pure form of capitalism entirely ran the show. Miguel had said that if you had cash here 'you could live like a king' but that without money 'your life was nothing'. In San Pedro money could literally buy you anything, but a lack of it meant you had nowhere to sleep and that you could lose your life at the drop of a hat. It was an existence entirely dictated by unmitigated market forces. There was no welfare state or NHS diluting true 'dog eat dog' capitalism here. It was the ultimate untainted capitalist state where the law of the jungle ruled . . . and it was horrific. There were four murders a month and anyone without cash lived in a state of constant fear. The only thing preventing mass riots were the prison walls and the armed guards. It seemed to me that the elites of Western societies had cleverly ensured that the states we live in had the bare minimum of support mechanisms in place. They had done this so that capitalism would thrive, ensuring that their privileged lives continued, but it was also not so unremittingly harsh that an underclass existed with so little hope that they would attempt mass insurrection. The clever bastards!

The other interesting experience that made me reflect on the effects of capitalism on the individual came to me somewhat surprisingly when we went on a nine-day trip into the Amazonian jungle. Our guide Pedro spent a lot of time discussing the sheer harshness involved in the everyday struggle to survive that the jungle vegetation experienced. The desperate need for light meant trees grow incredibly quickly and often attacked other trees around them. If any trees fell creating a hole in the canopy, then other trees would enter a live or die race to reach the sunlight – sometimes attacking each other as they did so. The trees often fell down because they had short roots as a result of the thinness of the top soil. Pedro also explained that many of the trees had nasty spikes, acidic leaves or were poisonous. All these defence mechanisms had evolved to give them an edge in the never-ending battle to survive and the acidity and poisons were apparently a direct product of the poor-quality soil that nurtured them. Maybe I was reading too much into it, but it struck me as a great analogy for the poor's struggle to survive in modern capitalist societies. The sheer never-ending competition to be one of the few to make it when there is such a lack of light/hope and the necessity of building defences and weapons to achieve that goal seemed a true reflection of 'ghetto existence'. The fact that this life or death struggle often resulted in the competing individual becoming poisoned in the process also seemed to ring true.

Anyway, I'd obviously been smoking a little bit too much of the local produce when I was thinking those thoughts. The reality was that by that stage of the trip I felt a strong need to get back to Blighty and start my career at Megashite. I needed to make sure I survived the three-month probationary period and I needed to stop wasting my time with all this hippy shit. I needed to get back on the gravy train and make sure that prick Hugo rued the day he ever set foot on this God-forsaken planet. For the first time in my 'travelling career' I was preoccupied with thoughts about going home and making lots of cash. Alex noticed this strange development but was polite enough not to take me to task over it. All I could think was that I needed to get back and we cut short the holiday by a few days and flew home so that I could prepare for the next phase in my career/mission. Most of all, I knew that our team needed a nice, quiet period which we could use to get to know each other, re-establish relationships with our main clients, and make a name for ourselves at Megashite. We started back at work on 10 September 2001.

The first day at Megashite was a real eye-opener. Neil had assembled a damn fine team with a lady called Nathalie covering the French and German utilities, a chap called Diego researching the Spanish stocks, and some character by the name of Luigi analysing the Italians. Neil would cover what was left (i.e. one company in Finland) as well as providing a leadership role and writing the 'guru' pieces on general industry themes.

It was clear from the word go that Megashite was a different kettle of fish from anywhere I'd worked before. This was your classic hire-and-fire, backstab-at-every-opportunity, work-your-arse-off hard-core Yank bank. The traders were in at 6 a.m. and never missed an opportunity to show you what aggressive twats they were. The salesmen took no nonsense and demanded that you see their clients whenever they required it. My fellow analysts were in at 6.45 a.m. and left no earlier than 7.30 p.m. and even then often did the old trick of leaving their jacket on the back of their chair to pretend that they were still in the office. The corporate financiers would call you up at home late at night and on the weekends without so much as a 'by your leave'. There was no pretence of friendship and it was clear that everyone was simply in it for themselves. I think on that very first day I actually heard a trader shout at some poor junior analyst the classic quote from Wall Street, 'If you want a friend, buy a dog.' It was immediately obvious that the senior executives at Megashite had successfully created a culture that was designed to excel at the unremitting, joyless maximisation of profits. Within about thirty-seven minutes of arriving I knew my life here was going to be no fun at all. However, if this was what I needed to put up with to be the best and to finally humiliate Hugo then so be it. Oh, and the $400,000 a year would make the whole experience a little more palatable too.

If the first day at Megashite was an eye-opener, then the second day was a genuine copper-bottomed ocean-going world-class shocker. It was around 3.30 p.m. when the first reports of a small aeroplane hitting the World Trade Center began to appear on Reuters. Soon the volume was turned up on the flat-screen TVs that were suspended from the ceiling every forty feet or so and we all crowded around them to hear what the fuck was going on.

As I watched the images of the aeroplanes striking the seemingly indestructible towers again and again and then of the towers falling I knew that I was witnessing history and that the world was going to be a very different place tomorrow. I remembered that as a seventeen-year-old boy I had watched the Berlin Wall being pulled down and that my long-suffering father had urged me to realise that I was watching history in the making. I remember thinking 'yeah, whatever', and wondering which pub I should meet my mates in and whether Jane fancied me or not. I was not going to make that same mistake this time. I was consciously trying to make myself acknowledge the enormity of what I was witnessing as I looked around and tried to take in the shocked faces of my new colleagues who surrounded the TV screens.

Many of the Americans in the office were desperately trying to call their loved ones in New York but the phones were all down there. One team had a member who was due to have a 9.30 a.m. meeting with Fiduciary Trust on the ninety-fifth floor of the South Tower and the secretary was really losing it trying to ring his mobile again and again without success. His near-hysterical wife was calling up every five minutes and no one could calm her down. It later turned out that the meeting had been cancelled and that he was in a taxi around 64th Street when the shit hit the fan. I remember wondering whether this chap's life would ever be the same again after he realised he owed his life to a cancellation. I remember wondering if he'd give up this whole caboodle and go and live a spiritual existence in the countryside having been given such a clear message from God. Of course, he did no such thing. He just shrugged it off as 'one of those things' and went on to work his arse off and become a top-rated research analyst. There's nowt as queer as folk – apart, that is, from investment banking folk.

Witnessing the distraught secretary reminded me that I had some clients whose offices were based in the World Trade Center.

So, in a fit of what can only be described as preposterous stupidity, I tried to leave messages on their phones asking, and I struggle to actually write this, whether they were still alive. Failing to get through to them, I actually wrote two emails to clients saying, 'I hope you're alive and well. Please write back to confirm you are alive.' I like to pretend that I was vaguely compos mentis when this whole event was unfurling, but the simple fact that I was leaving such crass, offensive messages makes me doubt that I still had my wits about me come 6 p.m. on 11 September 2001. By the end of the day, we all felt emotionally drained and our team and several others all went to the pub to try to process what we had witnessed. The bars and pubs were all full of people – partly because everyone had been evacuated from all the tall buildings, including Canary Wharf itself. There was nothing we could do and little that could be said. At some point a Yank raised a glass to 'fallen comrades' and even the self-conscious repressed English amongst us managed to raise a glass without feeling too awkward. If anything showed me that this was a world-changing event it was the fact that middle-class English people were able to overcome their innate fear of expressing their deeply repressed emotions.

We were still all in shock the next day but that didn't stop Neil from convening a team meeting aimed at deciding what our strategy should be, taking into account the 'brave new world' that faced financial markets. After we had sat ourselves down in a meeting room that our research assistant Suzanne had booked, Neil began his spiel:

'The way I look at it is this. The utility sector is inherently defensive and this clearly bodes well for its relative outperformance if the markets undergo some turmoil over the next few months as seems inevitable. I think the subsector that we should promote contains those regulated utilities whose earnings have little correlation to GDP growth since this may drop as consumer confidence falters. I think we should particularly recommend that investors buy those shares that have a high yield since this means that they offer some kind of total return in the absence of capital growth. Also, if interest rates start falling as central banks attempt to buoy up the economy, as is likely, then these bond-proxies should be the principal beneficiaries. So let's compose a two-page email now showing the proportion of enterprise value related to regulated profits and cross-referencing that against those with the highest yields. Steve, it looks to me like we're talking UK waters, National Grid and the regulated ones on the Continent, so I'm gonna leave this in your capable hands.'

We all agreed and shuffled out of the room. I, or if I'm being honest, The Genius, compiled the spreadsheet and within two hours we had created a pretty damn good email telling investors what shares in the utilities sector they should buy in a post 9/11 world. I showed it to Neil who liked it and we were on the point of sending it out to clients when a clearly nervous Suzanne piped up: 'Ehem . . . are you sure we should be doing this? I mean, isn't it a little insensitive? The rubble is still smoking yet you're telling people how to profit from this disaster. Don't you think the families of those who've just died might be unhappy about this? Don't you think that if the press get hold of this we are going to look like heartless bastards? . . . excuse my French. I would seriously urge you to reconsider.'

It took about 2.5 seconds for the whole team to realise that she was speaking total sense. It took another 3.2 seconds for me to realise that I had become so embroiled in this sick financial world that I had forgotten my humanity. We quickly agreed to put nothing out in writing that would show the world what tactless motherfuckers we were. Oh no, we would only tell clients by phone what they should buy and sell since we really didn't want the press to get hold of our musings and have a field day exposing us for the heartless cocksuckers we clearly were.

Strangely enough, lots of our peers and competitors showed

even less restraint than we did. Many salesmen on 12 September were sending out hastily composed emails and Bloomberg messages telling their clients to sell airline and insurance stocks and buy shares in companies involved in armaments and construction. You didn't have to be a rocket scientist to work out that those stocks would be particularly affected by this recent 'development'. There were even rumours that Osama Bin Laden had himself shorted airlines and insurance stocks just before the planes struck, knowing that their share prices would be decimated were his plan to succeed. If this story's true then it really is the purest example of working on inside information. Indeed, perhaps the CIA should stop seeking out Mr Bin Laden and let those ever-so-resourceful boys at the Financial Services Authority do their thang . . . they may have caught about three insider traders over the last decade but there's always a first for everything.

The thing is that the market is not a sentimental beast. In fact, the market has no place for emotions other than greed and fear (which in the context of financial markets is just the mirror-image of greed). I remember hearing certain clients claim in the days after 9/11 that the Dow Jones and the S&P 500 would actually go up once the New York Stock Exchange reopened as a result of 'patriotic buying'. I knew that this was utter horseshit the first time I heard some Yank voice the theory because, unfortunately, as Maggie Thatcher said with such unerring clarity, 'you cannot buck the market'. If some fool is willing to buy or sell a share for ethical, patriotic or socially conscious reasons, then there are a lot of other nasty bastards out there who will see an asset being mispriced and rush in to make a profit. The simple fact is that emotions like patriotism never paid off anyone's mortgage or bought them that fanny magnet of a car they've always wanted.

Interestingly, there is a long and inglorious tradition in the City of people profiting from disaster, and true capitalists accept that there is no time to sympathise with the victims of tragedy when there are big bucks to be made. One of the earliest examples of serious wedge being made on the back of thousands of deaths allegedly relates to the Rothschild family. The Rothschilds apparently had their own super-fast homing pigeons that flew back to London early with the news that Napoleon had been defeated at the battle of Waterloo in 1815. It is suggested by some scallywags that the Rothschilds, on hearing the news that Britain and her allies had won, gave the impression that Napoleon had in fact been victorious and bought every share that they could get their grubby mitts on during the ensuing stock market weakness. Once the truth was established British shares rose rapidly in relief making them a massive profit. Some claim that the wealth created by this ruse formed the basis of the Rothschilds' financial empire that grew so impressively over the nineteenth century.

More recently, there have been numerous examples of smart cookies not letting emotions get in the way of the never-ending task of 'maximising returns'. There is the story (possibly apocryphal) about the broker who came into work the day after the catastrophic storm that heralded the October 1987 stock market crash. Apparently this character had seen hundreds of boats washed up ashore on the news that morning. So he invested loads of cash in the only stock market listed UK boat repair company – thus making himself many thousands.

I have to admit to not always being totally on the ball when it comes to reacting appropriately to disasters. For example, when I heard a rumour in 2006 that two divisions of Israeli paratroopers had entered Jordan my immediate thought was simply, 'I'm sure it was fun at the time, but she's gonna be sore as fuck in the morning'. However, smarter people with less smutty minds quickly realised the potential geopolitical ramifications of a Middle Eastern war and immediately made a few quid by buying shares in companies that would benefit from the resultant higher oil price. The fact is that our clients want to make money, and excuses about patriotism and such non-financial nonsense will just result in our clients ceasing to be clients as they begin listening to more hard-nosed analysts. Until human nature becomes more refined the phrase 'money talks and bullshit walks' will prevail and that, I'm sorry to report, means that those in the City can look forward to a long and fruitful future.

The 9/11 tragedy could not have been better timed if Osama Bin Laden's evil plan was to disrupt financial markets. The technology, media and telecoms (TMT) bubble had burst in 2000 and by the third quarter of 2001 things were already looking a bit tricky prior to his violent actions. However, there was one man who seemed even more determined to fuck everything up for stock markets and investment banking than Osama Bin Laden and that was a US district attorney by the name of Eliot Spitzer.

The fact of the matter is that Mr Spitzer had every right to take radical action aimed at ending the egregious excesses of the late 1990s, and whether he was motivated by political ambition or not something was most definitely sick in corporate America. In 2001 and 2002 hardly a week went by without something reminding us analysts that our business was a corrupt and hideous one. Day in, day out, companies that had once been highly valued were going bust, or an accounting fraud was uncovered, or an investment bank was investigated for wrongdoing. In the period following March 2000 it sometimes felt as if we were waking up from an extraordinary dream. It was as if someone had finally had the courage to point out that the emperor really was wearing no clothes and we sat around in bars asking ourselves how we could have been such fools to believe that companies that made virtually no profits could be worth billions. The absurdity of the situation was that massively overvalued shares were used as a reference for the value of other shares being analysed, and so a bubble was created similar to the Dutch Tulip mania of 1636–7 or the South Sea Bubble of 1720.

Many stockbrokers, including myself, had bought shares in dubious Internet companies in 1999 and had briefly seen our holdings massively increase in value. Most of us were buying on the 'greater fool theory' that stipulated that the shares were preposterously expensive but that there was some idiot out there who would be willing to pay even more for them. It was like a sick game of musical chairs but only geniuses who sold in Q1 2000 when the music stopped came out smelling of roses. The initial public offer (IPO) of lastminute.com heralded the end of the good times and we all saw our paper profits diminish and then become major losses. Between early 1999 and March 2000 my PA (personal account) portfolio of mainly dodgy Internet shares went up in value from £50,000 to close to £250,000. Things began to go badly Pete Tong in March 2000. At one point I was losing between five and ten thousand pounds every day but stupidly only sold bits and bobs here and there due to a pathetic reluctance to sell a stock after it had fallen twenty per cent, not realising there was another eighty per cent to go. Predictably, The Genius had not only told me to sell all my equities in early 2000, but he had also never got involved in any of this inane madness.

I remember reading about the aftermath of the May 1968 riots in Paris and how the participants emerged dazed and confused from the extraordinary events, having dared to dream that the world could be changed. While the TMT bubble was the antithesis of the humanitarian optimism that May 1968 represented, being an ugly affair based on greed and deception, we were aware that we were living in extraordinary times. There was much talk of 'a new paradigm' – a new low-inflation world of high growth and plenty for all made possible by a revolution carried out on the Internet. In 2000 books were being published claiming that the Dow Jones Industrial Average could reach 20,000 soon. At the time, the Dow was trading close to 12,000 and was on the verge of falling around forty per cent over the next three years! Now, when I hear the words 'new paradigm', to paraphrase Hermann Goering, I reach for my gun. The only words that shit me up even more are: 'It's different this time.'

Between 2000 and 2002 a series of events occurred that exposed to the world the dark underbelly of unfettered capitalism and investment banking in particular. It got to the stage when even the most ardent believer in free-market economics was forced to question everything they held dear. It's worth discussing the major scandals that rocked corporate America during this period because they reveal just how ugly human behaviour can be when the potential rewards are so disgustingly massive.

In December 2000, Enron was an absolute darling of the stock market. It was the seventh-biggest US company by market capitalisation, its shares were trading just below their all-time high of ninety-five dollars, and it was just about to win the award for being 'America's most innovative company' for the sixth year running. Within a year its shares were worthless and it was about to file for bankruptcy under Chapter Eleven (which allows a company to continue operations despite being unable to service its debt). The problem was that the most innovative thing about the company was that its financial reports had absolutely nothing to do with reality. When it came to presenting their accounts to market, no one could accuse Enron's senior executives of not 'thinking outside the box'!

Around 1990, Enron had been just a normal, boring company which owned pipelines and earned the vast majority of its revenue transporting gas around the good old US of A. Over a ten-year period it had transformed itself into an asset-light entity that traded every conceivable commodity and a few new ones that they essentially invented like 'bandwidth'. The company lobbied US politicians into deregulating every conceivable market so that they could thrive and it comes as no surprise that its chief executive Kenneth Lay was one of the biggest financial supporters of George W. Bush. Lay was also the only energy executive to have a one-on-one with Dick Cheney when the Bush administration was framing its energy policy – showing the self-serving influence big business can have on even the most senior of politicians.

Apart from lobbying politicians into making changes beneficial to its strategy, Enron also went around the world buying up assets and getting steadily more indebted. I was actually a big fan of theirs because in 1998 Enron had for some God-forsaken reason bought Wessex Water for an absurdly high price. It is rumoured that the deal took four days to arrange and was engineered mainly to allow a bunch of Enron executives to have a nice shopping trip to London with their wives. They had no idea what they were acquiring but I didn't give a monkey's because I had fortunately written a big Buy note on Wessex three weeks before they made the acquisition which made me look real clever. Of course, in actual fact, I was just a jammy bastard. They say you make your own luck but sometimes *you* ain't got nothing to do with it.

All the Enron executives wanted to do was make their share price go up as quickly as humanly possible so that their stock options would make them multi-multi-millionaires, and they weren't going to let tedious things like accounting conventions get in the way of their God-given mission. Enron's trick to make the share price go up mainly revolved around fabricating earnings numbers while also hiding the company's indebtedness. Jeffrey Skilling, the chief operating officer, and Andrew Fastow, the chief financial officer, achieved this by creating a series of off-balance-sheet private partnerships that were not disclosed in the company's financial reports and hence removed from analysts' eyes.

I remember The Genius having a cursory glance at Enron's accounts in 1999 and concluding that he wouldn't touch it with a shitty stick because he couldn't see how the company made money. I seem to remember him concluding with the age-old City adage that 'If it looks like a duck and quacks like a duck, it probably is a fucking duck.' If any US analysts, many of whom had theoretically covered the company in depth for years, had even a tenth of Michael's ability, they should have seen that it was a paper tiger, a straw man, a total illusion. However, the vast majority of research analysts in 2000 were positive on the stock and any doubts were erased by its constantly rising share price. Enron was also notoriously aggressive to any analysts who dared question the company and who, like a bunch of spineless idiots, found themselves being bullied into being positive.

However, it wasn't just stupidity and cowardice that guided the analysts' recommendations. The simple fact was that an acquisitive, innovative company like Enron was handing out fees to investment banks like they were going out of fashion. Corporate financiers at Wall Street banks would lick their greasy lips every time they knew that the Enron boys were riding into town as they contemplated that pad in the Hamptons that these jokers were going to pay for. In the 1990s, banks were making billions from organising acquisitions, restructuring finances, and issuing debt for this wonderful company. A negative comment by a bank's analyst could jeopardise the bank's relationship to Enron and so corporate financiers made sure that nothing but sweetness and light was uttered by their banks' theoretically independent analysts. This, of course, contravened the supposed 'Chinese walls' that existed between corporate finance and research analysts but who cares about giving genuine objective advice to pension funds when there are big bucks to be made from keeping Enron on side? As City wags would later say: 'There were a lot of chinks in those Chinese walls.'

It is also clear that characters like Fastow and Skilling made sure that the corporate financiers were aware that anything less than gushing recommendations from their analysts would result in them taking their business elsewhere. Anyway, the 0.2 per cent commission that banks could make from the trades that a cleverly argued critical research note might generate was dwarfed by the gargantuan fees that Enron was splashing around to all and sundry. In the late 1990s the only negative analyst on Wall Street was John Olson, who was fired in 1998 by Merrill Lynch apparently after pressure was applied by Fastow. Unsurprisingly, Merrills were then awarded two major corporate deals worth $50 million. After this scandal some commentators asked for the Glass-Steagall Act of 1933, which forcibly separated investment banking from the business of lending, to be reinstated. The act had been repealed in 1999 but it was felt by some that investment banks could not be objective in their handling of a company if that same bank had lent it lots of dosh. No shit, Sherlock.

This same logic ensured that Enron's auditor, Arthur Anderson, which had the responsibility to check the company's finances, found itself accused of not being quite as diligent as it might otherwise have been. Andersons had a management consultancy arm that was making many millions from advising Enron (and actually occupied an entire floor of Enron's headquarters in Huston). Hence, many at the time argued that it had a huge incentive not to blow the whistle on the company's dodgy finances so as to keep the cash rolling in. It seemed a simple case of *Quis custodiet ipsos custodes?* or 'Who watches the watchmen?' Uncertainty about whether you can trust the people whose job it is to audit companies' accounts threw everything into question. If you can't trust the earnings figures that drive share prices then on what basis can you value a company? The market hates uncertainty but what certainty can there be when the numbers that are used to calculate ratios and growth prospects could be total horseshit? This is why the alleged accounting fabrication of this period was a massive issue and had to be dealt with quickly and harshly. Although several charges against Andersons would be overturned, the Enron debacle would eventually result in its collapse.

J.K. Galbraith's classic text on the 1929 Wall Street Crash *The Great Crash* observed that fraud rises when people are prosperous. Enron managed to create a mutually beneficial system based on a series of massive financial carrots and sticks designed to ensure corporate financiers, analysts and auditors all kept an illusion going.

Unfortunately, when the good times stopped it suddenly became clear that Enron was a house built on sand. It had few assets and massive debts in 'special purpose vehicles' that weren't disclosed in its accounts. The impact of Enron's collapse was phenomenal – especially for its 21,000 employees, many of whom lost their jobs.

What was even worse was that many of them had Enron stock as the main component of their pension plan, as had been encouraged by senior executives. Enron pensioners subsequently lost over $1.2 billion, which meant that their dotage was going to be considerably less rosy. Of course, Skilling and Lay sold off a large part of their massive holdings in Enron stock in early 2000 for good prices, when they realised that the writing was on the wall for their company (raising over a billion dollars for themselves!). Analysts had, with their characteristic incisiveness, failed to remark on this suspicious development.

No one came out of the Enron debacle looking especially good – particularly Lay, who died of a heart attack just before he was sentenced and Skilling and Fastow, who were sentenced to twenty-four and six years respectively. John Dingall, a member of the House Energy Committee, summed up the sheer horror of what happened best: 'Where was the SEC? Where was the financial accounting standards board? Where was Enron's audit committee? Where were the accountants? Where were the lawyers? Where were the investment bankers? Where were the analysts? Where was common sense?'

The answer for most of them was, of course, that they were counting their money, hoping not to get nicked by any investigation.

It was around this time that we analysts felt increasingly persecuted by the press and our peers. Whereas I used to just be dismissed by my more artistic (i.e. poor) friends as a greedy, money-obsessed tosspot, I was now also an evil deceiver whose main mission was to con pensioners, corrupt politicians and lose hard-working people their jobs. I, like most of my other thick-skinned compadres, cried all the way to the bank. The banks we worked for weren't so lucky, as Enron defaulted on the huge loans that they had made to the company.

The Enron scandal was just one of many that showed the average Joe that by the end of the second millennium after the birth of our dear Lord Jesus Christ it was greed and corruption that were well and truly in control of global capitalism. Arguments that these two bed-fellows were not so influential any more were shown to be fatuous by other scandals. Below is a brief list of a few of the other events that shook corporate America in the early part of the twenty-first century:

1. Worldcom: Bernie Ebbers was a bearded six-foot-four ex-bouncer and born again Christian who had built a vast telecoms company worth $180 billion (more than the entire economy of Greece) from very humble beginnings. To do this he had raised a huge amount of debt to acquire lots of other telecom companies, which was fine when the good times were rolling but wasn't so cool when the economic downturn began in 2000. Ebbers was a real hero in his close-knit local town of Brookhaven, Mississippi, having made many millionaires of the local populace. When he wasn't winning bidding wars against giants like British Telecom he was teaching Sunday school in the local church. If he was asked tricky questions about his company Ebbers would simply point to the vertiginous rise of his

company's shares saying, 'investors . . . only care if the share price goes up'.

Unfortunately, Bernie was the kind of good ol' boy who didn't take kindly to bad news. So when profits started looking none too clever his chief financial officer Scott Sullivan started cooking the books and got him and his boss into a right stew.

Essentially, around £4 billion of normal operating costs that should have reduced stated profits were redefined as capital expenditure, i.e. investment. A routine internal audit revealed this 'creative accounting' in June 2002 and corporate America's confidence was shattered to such an extent that even the earnings of blue-chip companies like General Electric began to be questioned. The highly indebted Worldcom filed for bankruptcy and poor old Bernie was sentenced to twenty-five years in prison (with Sullivan getting away with five years).

Again, we analysts came out of the whole debacle looking about as useful as a chocolate dildo in the desert. The most notorious bull of the stock was a clown called Jack Grubman who worked at Solomon Smith Barney. He was well known for getting very close to the management of the companies he covered and became a pal of Bernie's in the 1980s. Apparently, dear old Jack thought Chinese walls between companies, corporate finance and analysts were for losers and famously told the magazine *Business Week* in 2000 that 'what used to be a conflict has now become a synergy'. He went on to say that 'the notion that keeping your distance makes you more objective is absurd . . . Objective? The other word for it is uninformed.' Jack recommended investors buy shares in Worldcom even while it collapsed. Of course, the massive corporate fees that Worldcom were giving his bank had nothing to do with it.

Jack also famously turned bullish on the American telecoms giant AT&T in November 1999, apparently after Solomon's chairman Sandy Weill allegedly asked him to 'take a fresh look' at it. Shortly after Jack's sudden change of heart Solomon Smith

Barney was chosen by AT&T to handle the massive IPO of its wireless division which generated fantastic fees. Once the IPO had been completed Jack reverted back to his traditional negative stance on the stock. Amusingly, when Spitzer was investigating Wall Street abuses he apparently came across an email in which Jack suggests that he turned positive on AT&T to get Sandy Weill to use his influence to ensure that his kids could get into the 92nd Street Y preschool which apparently 'is harder than Harvard' to get into. Unfuckingbelievable! Jack the lad ended up paying a fine of $15 million, which was probably small beer relative to the cash he'd earned over his career.

2. Tyco: Dennis Kozlowski was the fat, bald chief executive of the US conglomerate Tyco International. In 2002 it transpired that he had avoided tax and had misappropriated around $400 million of company funds. He was also accused of artificially inflating his stock price while selling some of his shares. During the trial the press had a field day detailing the excesses of his lifestyle that seemed to be paid for by Tyco's poor (and soon to be poorer) shareholders. The company paid for Dennis's $18 million Manhattan apartment (which housed a notorious set of shower curtains that cost $6000!) without disclosing it in its accounts and paid for half of his wife's $2 million birthday party in Sardinia because he claimed it was corporate entertainment. Dennis proclaimed his innocence, stating that he was being persecuted because his 'pay packet . . . was almost embarrassingly big'. The judge told him to get real and gave the wanker eight years. His breathtaking extravagance made even the Wall Street boys stand up and take notice and that really is saying something.

3. Henry Blodget: Blodget (crazy name, crazy guy) worked at Merrill Lynch and was the number-one-rated Internet analyst during the dot-com bubble. It is alleged that he was writing notes

advocating buying shares in various Internet companies during this period in order to get corporate work for his bank. Unfortunately, when discussing certain piss-poor Internet companies that he officially recommended buying to the market, he would sometimes dismiss them as 'crap' or 'junk' in emails to his closer clients, and famously dismissed some as being 'p.o.s.' or piece of shit. In other words, Henry was allegedly happy to promote companies with shite prospects to gullible fund managers who were running pension funds in order to line his grubby pockets and those of his fellow bankers with corporate fees. Blodget was eventually fined and banned from the securities industry for life.

Of course, not every Cityboy accused of malpractice during this period was in fact guilty. Another famous scandal at this time involved a chap by the name of Frank Quattrone and, although he was sentenced to prison in 2004, he has since been proven innocent. Big Bad Frank was the head of a division of Credit Suisse First Boston that was bringing technology companies to the market day in, day out during the 1990s tech boom. He was the envy of his peers and it wasn't just that he had a 'tache to die for – the circa $80 million he apparently earned during that period also had something to do with it. Frankie boy was accused of 'spinning', that is to say, allocating shares in 'hot IPOs' to 'friends' of the bank to keep their relationship sweet. Put simply, if a share was likely to appreciate in value big time as soon as it was listed on the stock market (so that the lucky owners could 'flip' it, i.e. sell it immediately for a big profit), CSFB was allegedly making sure that senior executives at companies would be allocated these shares in return for them giving CSFB corporate fees at a later date. When CSFB was being investigated Frankie was accused of asking his co-workers to destroy incriminating emails. Good old Frank was in and out of court and eventually got sentenced to eighteen months in May 2004. However, the verdict was overturned in 2006 and Frank Quattrone can hold his head up high knowing he has been completely exonerated. Whereas poor old Frank may have been the innocent victim of Eliot Spitzer's purge of Wall Street firms, I have little doubt that 'spinning' was a fairly common practice at certain American banks.

There are other examples of wrongdoing by companies and investment banks alike from that period. Everyone who worked at an investment bank during the 1990s and even after knows that corporate financiers ran the show and that honest, objective advice to fund managers took a back seat. The pressure was sometimes subtle and sometimes very obvious, but if you didn't play ball your bonus was going to suffer and sometimes you might even get shown the door. Generally, a corporate financier would 'persuade' you to write a note on a specific company and then make sure that you fully understood that it had 'really good prospects'. You didn't have to be Brain of Britain to understand what was being asked of you – a positive note that could facilitate advisory fees, which is where banks made the real bucks.

So something really serious needed to be done to restore Brad and Marylou's faith in corporate America and investment banks. A much higher proportion of Americans own stock than us Europeans, and the post-dot-com bubble crash left many mighty pissed off and significantly poorer. When it transpired that the investment advice they had received was tainted by greedy scumbags only interested in inflating their next bonus, action had to be taken. There were two main outcomes from this malaise.

Firstly, in 2002, dear old Eliot Spitzer reached what became known as the 'global settlement' with ten investment banks which were forced to pay $1.4 billion in compensation and fines. Although his recent alleged involvement with a prostitute ring may have somewhat tarnished Mr Spitzer's carefully cultivated 'Mr Clean' image, he should still be congratulated for helping to make banks think twice before shafting investors with gay abandon, as was their wont in the late 1990s. Secondly, on

20 July 2002, a federal bill known as the Sarbanes-Oxley Act, became law. Sox or Sarbox, as it is commonly referred to, tried to address the specific misconduct that companies, auditors and banks had indulged in so expertly in the late 1990s. So companies were forced to enhance their financial disclosure, individual executives became personally liable for company wrongdoing, 'Chinese walls' at banks and auditors' independence were strengthened, and anti-fraud measures imposed. All these changes were backed up by more onerous penalties.

The jury is still out about whether banks have mended their ways though things are certainly better. Still, my experience of investment banking suggests that the system remains fucked simply because we analysts know which side our bread is buttered. Hence, we would rather please corporate financiers knowing it will increase our bonus (though it's now not supposed to) than offer untainted, objective advice – the rewards of which are less obvious. That's why I've noticed that whenever there is the prospect of a government listing a tranche of shares in a listed utility a whole series of Buy notes with inflated price targets suddenly materialises – sometimes from formerly negative analysts who work at investment banks hoping to gain fees from organising the sale. I have seen this phenomenon occur with many companies in the utilities sector such as Enel, Électricité de France, British Energy and Endesa, and am sure it happens across the market. Although things have improved since the bad old days, the whole system is still run by sick, greedy motherfuckers out to make a fast buck. Sometimes it felt like Harold Shipman had been put in charge of an old people's home.

Sox had one amusing unforeseen repercussion – London began to take over from New York as the financial capital of the world. The vast majority of scandals occurred in America and hence we in Europe felt under little pressure to tighten up our regulatory standards. By 2007, numerous articles were written claiming that London was bigger and badder than New York and Sox was often blamed or congratulated for this development. It was argued, for example, that the increasingly onerous regulatory demands on companies and the tougher penalties imposed made much more lax London a more attractive place to float your business. So when some dodgy Russian oil company wondered where to list its equity it would generally plump for the more 'flexible' London Stock Exchange. This helps explain why only one of the twenty-four biggest international IPOs during 2005 occurred in New York. Essentially this suggests that we in the UK are less concerned about whether a company is kosher or not, which certainly bodes well for our prospects of facing the next corporate scandal.

London now beats New York in terms of currency trading, the trading of foreign equities and over-the-counter derivatives, and is catching up on bond trading, private equity finance and securitisation. This helps explain why there are so many Cityboys who are becoming so unbelievably wealthy in London. The fact that our tax laws mean that foreigners who live in Britain but are 'non-domiciled' are only taxed on their British income, and not their world-wide earnings (unlike many other countries), adds further to London's attractiveness. It certainly ain't just the wonderful weather that's drawn the likes of Roman Abramovich to our fair shores. Such is the concern in New York that some are asking for Sox to be repealed and Mayor Bloomberg commissioned McKinsey to write a report on the subject. The USA's perceived post-9/11 jingoism doesn't help much either and nor do the tortuous queues that anyone who looks remotely brown has to endure in order to enter 'the land of the free'.

So, as a result of the TMT bubble bursting, 9/11 and corporate wrongdoing, Spitzer and Sox markets were in a bit of trouble in 2002. Truth be told, all I could think when all this malarkey was going on was 'thank fuck I've got two guarantees'. By all accounts my fellow stockbrokers' bonuses during the 2001–3 period were not impressive (e.g. perhaps generally only around ten times the average national salary) and jobs were being lost left, right and centre. Michael and I simply continued doing what we do best. He came up with innovative, thought-provoking investment ideas . . . and I took clients to Rolling Stones concerts and strip joints. That was the beauty of my particular client strategy – it was timeless, because pretty much everyone in the UK likes a drink, whether to celebrate the good times or drown their sorrows. We did notice that our target clients were an increasingly cynical bunch who took our words of wisdom with several cupfuls of salt. Fortunately, we managed to convince most of them that we weren't like those nasty analysts at Wall Street banks who fabricated stories dreamed up by their corporate finance department. Suckers!

Neil's approach to the difficult times was to work even harder. I have no doubt that he also had at least one guaranteed bonus and, if I were a betting man (which, of course, I am), I'd guess it was over a million. Still, the fact that his remuneration was fixed did not in any way de-incentivise the man. Neil was always in the office earlier than I was, despite living in some God-awful village in the stockbroker belt, and often remained there past 10 p.m. I would see emails in my inbox that arrived around midnight. I used to assume that he had just set his Microsoft Outlook to delay sending them to impress me and make me buck up my ideas. Unfortunately, a few late post-pub visits back to the office to pick up something I'd forgotten soon revealed that this was wishful thinking. The man was a machine.

The question was: what drove him and others like him to spend every fucking waking hour undertaking some pointless work bullshit when life is short, it's not a dress rehearsal and, most crucially, you could get run over by a bus tomorrow. As far as I was aware, no one on their deathbed ever said that they wished they'd worked harder. In fact, they generally said they wished they'd made love to more women or something equally life affirming. I distinctly remember poet laureate Sir John Betjeman saying 'not enough sex' was his major regret to a bemused interviewer in some TV advert. Neil had made enough money to retire and live the life of Riley if he so desired but instead chose to compose tedious spreadsheets, talk to irritating arrogant clients, and engage in tiresome office politics – things he had done for almost twenty years! WHAT IS WRONG WITH THESE FUCKING IDIOTS? Although Cityboys work harder than most, very few of them seemed to really love their work and many seemed stressed and unhappy as a direct result of it, so the question remained: why did they spend up to seventy per cent of their waking hours engaged in it? I was so perturbed by this tendency that I studied the hard workers around me in the City and compiled a list of the seven main reasons that could possibly explain their bizarre behaviour – which I dubbed 'The Seven Habits of Highly Defective People':

1. Insecurity: I once had a serious drinking session with a senior, and very rich, analyst from Megashite and asked this reasonably self-aware man why he bothered working his arse off taking into account our fast-approaching and inevitable doom. He took a sip of his thirty-pound-a-shot single malt whisky, looked me straight in the eye, and morosely said, barely holding back the tears, 'My mum loved my brother more than me.' His longstanding wish to seek his parents' approval had made him throw his life away and he knew it.

2. Competitiveness: This drive, of course, goes hand in hand with insecurity. I know a partner at a major London-based hedge fund who has been earning perhaps ten to twenty million a year for nearly a decade. He is not particularly extravagant and has long since ceased caring about the money (most of which he reinvests in his own brilliantly

performing fund). He simply wants the market (i.e. his competitors) to acknowledge his brilliance and works his arse off producing outstanding results year in, year out. I'm not complaining; I invested £50,000 in his fund in 2003 and he has almost tripled it since.

There can be no doubt that Neil was also intensely competitive and that his will to win was one of his major motivating forces. I remember playing squash against him in mid-2002 and not being sure if I should give it my all or not since pissing off the boss is never a good idea. However, I have been known to be a little competitive myself and overcoming my natural urge was never going to be easy. It was a genuine 'no-win situation'. Anyway, eventually I let him win a narrow victory and, with a pretend tail between my legs, went over to shake his hand. Amazingly, once he'd regained his breath he had the audacity to shout, 'Who's the daddy?' and then patted me on the back saying, 'Not bad for an old man, eh?' Now it was clear that he had major issues and when he finally asked the rhetorical question, 'Still lead in my pencil, eh?' I realised that this squash game was actually a simple opportunity for my boss to prove he was still a sexual tyrannosaurus. I don't think a single departmental booze-up occurred after that without my boss describing the game in detail and offering me some condescending remarks about my supposed 'defeat'.

3. Upbringing: The protestant work ethic that the sociologist Max Weber identified over a hundred years ago is alive and well in the Square Mile. There are also different variants of it with some extremely diligent second-generation Chinese and Indian kids beginning to make their mark in financial services. People who are still in the thrall of their parents' pressure to succeed may not know exactly why their lives are spent in the office but, as far as I can see, it's a cleverly

designed guilt-trip based on a 'you don't know how lucky you are' kind of vibe. Freud, I believe, said that the best thing a father can do is die when his son is in his teens. This is apparently the case with many world leaders and happened to my own father. The process ensured that he grew up extremely quickly into a responsible, hard-working adult . . . something I'm seriously considering doing at some point.

4. Denying life: Most people should have realised by their twenties that life, as Thomas Hobbs so eloquently put it back in the seventeenth century, is 'solitary, poor, nasty, brutish, and short'. While things may have become a little bit more pleasant since the days of the Great Plague and the Fire of London life is, arguably, still a pretty complicated and messy affair. One way to escape its chaotic absurdity and have some control, especially for us men who always have something of the autistic about us, is to throw oneself headlong into an obsession of some kind. Being a workaholic is just like being a junkie or a pisshead except work, rather than booze or drugs, is used to numb the pain generated by the ever-present knowledge that we will soon be food for the worms. As the unsurprisingly short-lived French romantic poet Baudelaire wrote:

One should always be drunk. That's all that matters;
that's our one imperative need. So as not to feel Time's
horrible burden – one which breaks your shoulders and
bows you down, you must get drunk without cease.
But with what?
With wine, poetry, or virtue as you choose.
But get drunk.

5. Fear: Investment banks are expert in never letting you

forget that if you underperform you will lose your job. Job culls were regular in the first years after the millennium and when you are qualified for few other professions you're going to do pretty much anything to stay employed – even if it means throwing away the best years of your life. Fear of an alternative becomes especially profound once you've got used to a particular lifestyle and the status afforded by 'doing something in the City'. Massive mortgages, high-maintenance wives (and ex-wives) and expensive school fees can all lead to you overextending yourself and making you a slave to the rat race. Money can also protect you from some of the more scary aspects of life on this planet. As one banker said to me: 'Life is a shit sandwich. The more bread you got, the less shit you eat.'

6. Greed: Sometimes it's simply the love of the dollar that explains it all. I discussed with my colleagues many times how much cash you can comfortably retire on. In my mid-twenties we agreed on a figure of £2.5 million but over time I noticed many of my peers surpass that figure and then start inventing new, higher targets. The attractive gold-diggers became ever choosier as Londoners' wealth grew and constant stories about our peers' stupendous salaries drove us to seek more and more cash. Pathetic.

7. The family: I don't mean working for the benefit of the family, though I'm sure that happens occasionally in the City. Oh no, I'm talking about the thousands of Cityboys who found family life such a chore that anything, including writing tedious research notes that no one would read or talking gibberish to uninterested fund managers, was preferable. Dreadful wives, who were already resentful of the fact that they never saw their husbands, and irritating spoiled children can be a big incentive to stay at work.

Indeed, work can be used to punish them because it's hard for them to complain when it's the long hours that paid for their eight-bedroom pad in Sevenoaks. One colleague, with four children, referred to his hours in the office as 'his time off' and many seemed not to take their full holiday allocation, which always struck me as utter madness. Interestingly, brokers in their forties on their first divorce were also incentivised to stay at work because it was more pleasant than eating another takeaway pizza in a cold, desolate flat watching *EastEnders* on their own.

Frankly, if Neil was answering a questionnaire aimed at discovering why he worked so goddam hard he probably would have ticked the box that said 'all of the above' and that is why he was truly the ultimate stockbroker. He was forever marketing across the world, writing in-depth think pieces and visiting companies to get the inside angle.

Hence, it should come as no surprise that Neil was one of the first Cityboys to own what I believe to be the most evil invention over the last century – the BlackBerry, or 'CrackBerry' as certain wags soon dubbed it. Granted, nuclear weapons, the Uzi 9mm machinegun and mustard gas are also unpleasant innovations, but I think more damage will be done to society from this seemingly innocuous device than all those put together. Well, perhaps that's a slight exaggeration . . .

I think it was late 2002 that Neil waltzed into the office grinning like the Cheshire Cat showing off his latest gizmo but within a year every joker in town seemed to have one. I point blank refused to be issued with such an insidious invention and am proud to report that by the end of 2003 I was the only analyst at Megashite without one. Why would I want to be able to see work-related nonsense sent to my office email address no matter where I was in the world? I can think of few things worse. What made the sinister device even more irritating was the effect it had on salesmen's behaviour when they accompanied me to client presentations. It was when I was on a one-day marketing trip to Edinburgh-based clients in 2003 that I snapped: 'Touch that thing again and you're gonna need surgery to remove it from your arse.'

I have to admit that the force of my own words surprised me somewhat but not half as much as the salesman that they were directed at or the client I was in the process of presenting to. However, it was nothing the little tosser didn't deserve, such was his inability to stop fiddling with his BlackBerry while I was doing my damndest to interest the bored-looking pension-fund manager in my dull sector.

It was during the fourth presentation to Scottish clients that I lost it. The junior salesman accompanying me had spent every meeting checking and responding to his emails on his BlackBerry. I must say, I probably overplayed my hand somewhat and the look of shock on the salesman's face was so extreme it was as if I had just asked him if I could perform the 'Cincinnati Bow-Tie' with his sister. A muffled 'sorry' was all that I received in reply but it had the desired effect and subsequently the surgeons at the local hospital were able to breathe a sigh of relief as they narrowly avoided having to undertake a particularly tricky operation.

I still don't know which malicious no-life loser invented the addictive 'CrackBerry' but if I ever catch him, the pasting he's going to receive will make him think that a brain tumour was a birthday present. By 2004 every front-office worker in an investment bank had one of these horrific inventions and because they acted as our mobile phone too, most of us took them everywhere with us at all times. The sheer evil genius of this means that no matter where stockbrokers are they receive work-related emails continually. Hence, holidays are rarely truly relaxing as we neglect life-affirming things like romancing our better halves or playing with our kids to focus on wearisome work-related horseshit. I firmly believe that this dreadful invention will cause more divorces and neglected childhoods than any other recent technical innovation.

Cityboys often work sixty- or seventy-hour weeks. To think that some sadistic zit-faced spod derived a way to make them work even harder and, effectively, never be out of the office, still makes me crazy as hell. Most City workers are sleepwalking to death anyway and the BlackBerry just gave them another excuse to avoid sucking the marrow out of life because they can convince themselves that they need to work 24/7 because that's what all their competitors are doing. What a bunch of tit-wanks!

Easy, tiger . . . there's another rant . . . sorry about that! Anyway, Neil absolutely loved his BlackBerry and was only ever off it when he didn't need it because he was in front of his computer. He had his own reasons (seven, to be precise) that made him determined to make our team the best but I had one very specific reason: Hugo Bentley. Just when I was beginning to feel slightly less obsessed by his smug demeanour, and everything he represented, our paths crossed again.

Fittingly, I next met Hugo at the Extel awards ceremony in the City Guildhall in June 2002. There were perhaps twenty round tables each seating ten analysts crammed into the large church-like hall. The mediocre food was only matched by the mediocrity of the speech that was given by some minor politician following the lunch. We all sat there praying for his tiresome discourse to finish so that we could find out how well we had done in the survey, but unfortunately we had to endure some piss-poor jokes about John Maynard Keynes before we could discover our fate.

I should probably admit that my coke habit by that stage was beginning to get a bit silly. I was actually coming out of the cubicles while the speaker was droning on, having just refreshed my nostrils, when I bumped into the twat who, perhaps even unbeknown to him, was dictating my life.

'Hello, Steve, just powdering your nose, were you?' Hugo

asked with a quizzical sneer, while straightening his tie in the mirror.

'If you're trying to insinuate I was taking cocaine, you must be off your fucking head. I suspect that says more about your sordid little life than it does about mine,' I said, lying through my gnashing, gritted teeth.

'Well, anyway, how do you think your little team are going to fare today?'

'We won't beat you this time but we will whup your sorry arse either next year or the one after that . . . and Hugo, don't forget that when it comes to the bet we've got until 2004's survey to show you who's boss.'

'Oh, you poor delusional idiot! Do you really think you and your silly little team are ever going to beat me? You can't polish a turd, old boy!'

'Fuck off back to whatever shitty little rock you crawled out from under and prepare for defeat.'

'My boy, I learned what I needed to about you all those years ago during that game of golf. When it comes to the big shots you choke. You can't handle the pressure. You're a loser and always will be. Christ, you're such a choker you'd find a bone in a chicken breast!'

And with that, he left the toilet with a self-satisfied grin on his stupid, fat face. I was so angry that I had to go back to the cubicle and snort another line of Charlie just to calm me down . . . but, funnily enough, it didn't have the desired effect. I marched stiffly back to my seat and sat at the table fuming impatiently . . .

'And the number-one-rated team in the utilities sector is . . . Mighty Yankbank with Hugo Bentley gaining the most individual votes.'

Hugo approached the podium with a brisk, confident step as if there was never any doubt that it was his team that was going to win. He shook the politician's hand, grabbed the little plastic, translucent, obelisk-shaped award, and uttered a confident 'thank you' into the mike. I knew those boys would win but I wanted to see where we stood in relation to them and so, as quickly as possible, grabbed one of the books detailing the allocation of the sector votes and left the building.

The pan-European utilities sector:

1. Mighty Yankbank – 27.2%
2. Merde Bank – 24.4%
3. Megashite – 21.1%

OK, so we were catching these pinheads slowly but surely and I personally was voted the sixth-highest-rated analyst in the sector. As far as I was concerned, we were going to beat them – probably next year but, if not then, definitely the year after that. It was simply a question of when, not if. Hugo was pretending that he wasn't worried but I could virtually smell his fear. Everything was coming together nicely. I just needed to make sure that I stayed focussed and did not allow anything to distract me.

It was about then that she turned up.

7

THE FLOOZIE

A wet dream made human. The essence of sex. The strongest lustful urge personified. Jane Carter was all these things and more. There aren't many women in investment banking. There are even fewer beautiful women. A single glance from Jane had the power to remind you just how wonderful life could be. She was Charlotte Rampling, Julie Christie, Kristin Scott Thomas. She was an English Jessica Rabbit but had the added benefit of not being a cartoon character. She was passionate yet in control, outrageously sexual yet demure, vulnerable yet strong. She had an air of melancholy that was so magnetic that I just wanted to look after her the first time I met her . . . but I also wanted her to look after me too. She was clearly very intelligent and knew all about how to play men, which differentiated the successful female brokers from the also-rans. She had studied economics at Edinburgh University and was a year younger than me. Perhaps most importantly, she had a fantastic rack and the kind of arse I'd happily eat breakfast off.

When she joined our bank as a saleswoman in August 2002, having done the same job for three years at a Swiss firm, and I was introduced to her I could barely look her in the eye. She had long, thick auburn hair, perfect china-doll skin, an exquisite angular nose and the most captivating green feline eyes I'd ever seen. I blushed so fiercely at our first meeting that everyone around us felt embarrassed and began self-consciously talking amongst themselves. When we went through the motions of discussing mutual clients and stock recommendations all other sounds seemed to be blocked out and I had a kind of out-of-body experience. I heard no sounds but her lovely, smooth voice and occasionally my own voice, though I have no idea what I was saying. It was as if I was in a strange dream. A part of me wanted her to leave since what was happening was a little scary but I also wanted to stare at her stunning face for the rest of my life. She didn't just 'have me at hello', she had me before she opened her mouth.

Before I go any further I should probably mention the fact that I'd actually fallen in love with a wonderful girl about eight months before Jane waltzed into my life. I had met Claire at a house party in Notting Hill Gate and we had connected instantaneously. I think I charmed her with my oft-repeated and very pathetic 'I'd like to get something straight between you and me' line and before you could say 'rushing into it' she was living at my house in Shepherd's Bush. Despite her disapproval of my growing rapport with 'the white lady' we had started what can only be described as a great relationship. We had fun; we shared the same sense of humour; we made love constantly and we had such a visceral, animal connection that it really did feel like I'd met my soulmate. It felt so very right. It felt like everything was going to progress smoothly towards a loving, gentle, kind and, dare I say it, adult existence together. It was the first time both of us had fallen in love and that is something that can never, ever be repeated. I was so very happy and so was Claire. Of course, it didn't take me long to fuck everything up.

'Rule number one: you don't get caught.' That's what David Flynn told me when we discussed the pros and cons of having an office affair over a few pints early in my City career. He had preceded this by saying that it generally ain't wise to 'dip your nib in the company ink'. Dear old Tony had piped up at that point and added his particularly charming tuppence worth, 'Yeah, you shouldn't piss on your own chips, son.' Still, the reality is that City affairs are commonplace because City types work such preposterously long hours and have so little time to spend their vast fortunes that they sometimes feel as if they are just pissing their lives away. I suppose there's nothing like a cheeky shag to remind us all that we're not just career-orientated robots waiting for the Grim Reaper.

Anyway, I managed to adhere to my gurus' wise words for about six years . . . that is, until I met Jane. Still, rules are, after all, meant to be broken. The problem is that there's a very good reason why having extra-curricular activities at an investment bank is not the sharpest move around. Office affairs often end in tears and when that happens it could be goodnight Vienna for your career. If the chick you end up making the beast with two backs with happens to be a proper bunny boiler then your chances of keeping your job may become akin to Gary Glitter's chances of becoming a primary school teacher. Investment banks are so paranoid (or maybe that's just me) about sexual harassment cases that if the lady you have shenanigans with feels like it you could end up kissing your career goodbye.

It was at a leaving drinks in November 2002 at some hideous brokers' bar in Canary Wharf that the crime was committed. These leaving drinks were two a penny around that period of the year as many banks, including Megashite, reacted to the dodgy markets by clearing out the under-achievers (or, more correctly, those who had failed to brown-nose the right people). This period was chosen because it was just before bonus time and this meant that the bank would get the benefit of the hard work of those it was about to sack for the cheapest possible price. This ruse also ensured that fewer people shared the bonus pool and 2002 and

2003 were not good years for bankers, so any trick that increased the amount that the high-achievers received was deemed acceptable. It was certainly a cruel trick but if you survived it you were ultimately the beneficiary and so we attended leaving drinks with mixed emotions knowing that the departures of these losers – sorry, I mean leavers – boded well for our own remuneration. Of course, I wasn't shitting myself like many of my colleagues as we approached the year end since my bonus was guaranteed. There was no chance of me being called into a little room by the head of research and being given the 'I'm sorry, it's not working out' speech when even my bonus in lieu of 2003 was in the bag.

There were actually so many departures during those two years that the losers/leavers used to gang together and have joint leaving drinks. This was probably done partly because the £500 or so expense incurred due to the City tradition which required leavers to pay suddenly seemed a little more onerous as you faced the possible prospect of unemployment. These leaving dos would be a little uncomfortable and, often, fewer people attended them than a person's popularity would merit. I used to think it was because people didn't want to be associated with the kind of buffoons who couldn't manage to retain their jobs. It was certainly true that once you ceased to be deemed successful, and hence unlikely to benefit the careers of your colleagues, some tosspots out there treated you like you'd just contracted a particularly heinous infestation of crabs.

Anyway, there was a pool table in this specific bar and Jane challenged me to a game. We had had only limited contact since she had joined the firm. I had gingerly approached her a couple of times on the trading floor to discuss a particular client or a stock idea and had consistently blushed and found myself tongue-tied. I had come to the conclusion that this goddess assumed I was an inbred retard with a speech impediment who had a permanent case of scarlet fever. What is even worse is that I associated throbbing and meeting Jane to such an extent that I inevitably did so when she was approaching me or, indeed, merely mentioned by a colleague. It was a vicious circle that resulted in me trying every excuse possible to avoid communicating with her in any way since I consistently made a total tit of myself. I certainly had no idea that she even remotely fancied me. Frankly, I thought that she was so far out of my league that unless I won the lottery, had plastic surgery to look like Brad Pitt and had Samuel L. Jackson give me a crash course in how to be cool, 'giving her the good news' would remain a faraway dream. How wrong I was.

We played pool and, emboldened by a few pints of the devil's urine, I actually managed to flirt with her over the game. I was also playing pool damned well (since I was at the top of the alcohol bell curve that dictates the quality of my game) and, despite her being a reasonable player was essentially 'taking her back to school'. During the second game, I started show-boating à la Tom Cruise in *The Colour of Money*. We're talking shots behind the back, shots taken while gazing at her eyes and even, I'm afraid to say, the old spinning the cue like a majorette's baton trick. Essentially I was acting like a total cock and getting increasingly arseholed to boot. Hence I was a little surprised when Jane suggested we go out for a cigarette, dismissing our fellow revellers by saying 'too many freaks, not enough circuses'. I was even more surprised when, before you could say 'lawsuit', she was taking me down an alley and was all over me like a bad rash, your honour.

I couldn't fucking believe it! I felt like the cat that had got the cream. She must actually find my playground banter vaguely amusing, I thought . . . or she's mistaken me for someone else! Or she's really pissed. Or she's a nympho. Anyway, whatever the reason, I wasn't going to let this one get away. So, when during our passionate snog, I spied an unoccupied cab cruise by, I flagged it down and told her that we should go back to hers. Much to my stupefied amazement she agreed and I virtually shoved her into the taxi to make sure she didn't have time to change her mind. I was so excited that anyone within about fifty feet who checked out my trouser area would have assumed that I had taken up the ancient art of canoe-smuggling.

It was during the cab drive to her flat in Chelsea that I suddenly remembered a small but arguably important fact that I had conveniently forgotten: I actually had a lovely girlfriend waiting patiently for me back at the ranch – someone I might actually want to marry. BUT THIS WAS JANE CARTER! It was way too late to backtrack now – in the country of the blind drunk, the one-eyed trouser snake is king. The little head was most definitely telling the big head what to do. Before I knew it we were entering her flat and tearing our clothes off with gay abandon. We were naked by the time we reached the top of the stairs and . . . let's just say, it was a lot of fun.

I think that the novelist Jay McInerney summed it up best when he said that there are 'two kinds of men – those who cheated, and those who felt guilty afterwards'. I was most definitely the latter and I was already getting the heebie-jeebies as we smoked our post-coital cigarette. Mr McInerney also understood why stupid men like me jeopardise fantastic, loving relationships for the sake of a quick bunk-up. He knows that we libidinous, cretinous men have four basic requirements: 'shelter, food, pussy and strange pussy' (which I take to mean that of strangers rather than unusually constructed ones). It's a crying shame that our animal instincts can make us do things that are so clearly detrimental to our long-term happiness.

Anyway, I had to get out of Jane's flat asap, but wanted to do so in such a way that it didn't give the game away or make her realise I had a doris. As I was struggling to think up a cunning excuse why I had to kip *chez moi*, Jane simplified things for me: 'Well, darling, that was lovely. We should definitely have a rematch at some point. But you should probably head back to your girlfriend now.'

God's teeth! She knew about Claire. And she wanted another piece of the action in the future. Things were really shaping up here . . . though perhaps less so for Claire than for my incontinent libido. Before you could say 'pathetic, cheating cocksucker' I was out the door like a rat up a drainpipe. I came home and my poor, beautiful girlfriend suspected nothing – even when I took the unusual step of having a midnight shower.

And so our affair developed. It turns out Jane was also a fan of Uncle Charlie and our encounters became more and more sordid, involving champagne, cocaine and hotels at lunchtime. In the good old days, David Flynn had informed me, you used to be able to rent rooms at the Great Eastern Hotel by Liverpool Street station by the hour, but, unfortunately for my wallet, that was no longer the case by 2002. Jane liked the thrill of booking in as Mr and Mrs Smith and I could handle the £300-a-night charge that I was forced to endure, even if it was for just a few minutes – sorry, of course I mean hours – of fun. I was fabricating business trips to avoid making my dear girlfriend suspect anything was going on, but the guilt was tearing me up. I am not the best liar in the world, unless I'm talking to a policeman or a client, and I even began to blush when Claire questioned me. She would innocently ask me normal questions such as, 'How was Edinburgh?' and I would turn scarlet and glance up and to the right. Such was her trust and love for me that even this dead giveaway of my mendacity was ignored.

Things took a turn for the even more sordid when Jane suggested we go to a sex party in Chelsea in early 2003 run by a company called Passion. It was on a Saturday, but as luck would have it, Claire was with her parents in Devon that weekend. I had never done this kind of thing before but have always lived by the old rule that 'you should try everything once, apart from incest and Scottish folk dancing'. Amazingly, I had to send Jane a digital photo of myself by email, since this particular organisation was quite choosy about who participated in their fun and games. Even more amazingly, despite using the suited photograph from the company intranet which made me look like a self-satisfied Nazi with a crystal meth habit, 'the panel' deemed me sufficiently attractive to join in the fun for the paltry sum of seventy-five pounds.

The day arrived and I felt nervous and uneasy. There weren't just butterflies in my stomach, there were full-on giant moths flying around left, right and centre. Jane and I met up at a bar just around the corner from the penthouse apartment in Chelsea Harbour which was being used to house the party. I had come dressed in black tie as Jane had instructed. Jane arrived looking absolutely delicious in a sexy, short red Yves St Laurent dress. She had a dangerously beautiful set of pins and wasn't afraid to use them.

Before we met that evening I'd already had a few sherberts to calm my poor nerves and had been to the toilet several times for nonbiological reasons. My nerves and the bugle were making me sweat profusely and so a clearly concerned Jane felt obliged to give me a little pep talk designed to calm me down and stop me making a total arse of myself:

'Listen, don't get yourself in a state and stop doing so much coke. I've been to quite a few of these parties – in fact, I'm on their "Gold List", which means I get invited every time they have one. It's all very simple. It's either couples or single women who come so there are always more women than men. We'll arrive and stand around in a room drinking champagne for an hour or two. You should take this opportunity to talk to the ladies you're attracted to. Most of the people who come to these things are in their thirties. In fact, the overforties are strictly *verboten*. There's a very high proportion of Eurotrash and you'll find that a fair amount of people have flown in from all over the world just to come to this party. It is the women who are in control and many of them will seek out other women for some girl-on-girl action – that's why a lot of them are here. Anyway, at around eleven or so someone will announce that the fun should begin and then we'll all split off into what are called the play rooms where, hopefully, you can get in amongst it. Some just shag one specific girl with their partner, some participate in mass orgies and others just watch. Some women are simply there for the multiple partners. Most of the participants are regular attendees. Don't act like a perve, don't ever be forceful, and just relax and enjoy. I'd quite like to see you bone someone else and I'm sure you'd like to see me "getting the good news", as you so sweetly put it.'

Well, actually, no! I hadn't really thought about the fact that I'd almost certainly be watching my mistress get porked by a bunch of sweaty, swarthy Continentals. It wasn't that I was in love with her, but there was something other than just pure sex to our relationship. Well, at least I was fairly sure there was something else, though I couldn't for the life of me put my finger on it. Anyway, I was getting seriously cold feet but knew that I'd look like a right tosser if I bailed out now. So, after downing my pint, I slammed it on the bar melodramatically and said with mock courage, 'Come on, let's go! It's time for you to get rogered by a bunch of dagos.'

We entered the voluminous penthouse suite and our coats were taken by an attractive lady. As soon as we walked into the main room I, or more accurately, Jane, was scoped out by pretty much everyone and the conversation dropped notably as the men, and women, took in her breathtaking beauty. It could have just been me, but I couldn't help but feel that my tanned potential playmates were wondering what the hell such a delectable lady was doing with a two-bit loser like me. I was feeling self-conscious and quickly walked towards the table that acted as a bar. As I grabbed a couple of glasses of champers for me and Jane, I felt a tap on the shoulder.

'All right, mate, how's it going? What you doing here? Well, I know what you're doing here, you old sex pest. Fancy that! I ain't seen you at one of these before. Are you with that gorgeous redhead? Christ almighty – you are beginning to impress me, my son.'

It was fucking Tony Player. I couldn't believe it. I hadn't seen him for a year or so. The last thing that I wanted was to watch my former trader shag my lover – or anyone, for that matter. What the hell was I doing here? As I struggled to say something that would give the impression that the situation was normal, Tony helped break the uncomfortable silence.

'Looking at your bird, I reckon you're really beginning to get your shit together. She is raw with a capital R. I think I'm gonna go and talk to her right now.'

'Er . . . Tony,' I said, desperate to try and prevent the hideous vision I had of my former trader getting intimate with my mistress materialising, 'isn't that Claude from Banque Inutile's mining team over there in the corner?'

'Mate, if you look carefully you'll see that many of the punters here are Cityboys. Great networking opportunity, actually. Difficult not to get commission off someone you've seen shag your missus, d'you know what I mean? Of course, it's the only reason I come to these filthy events!' laughed Tony.

'Yeah, I can see how that works. Um . . . I'm just going to have a quick slash.'

The evening progressed exactly as Jane had described and before I knew it was I was naked as the day I was born lying down on a huge bed with a bunch of well-educated nude perverts. However, there was a problem. The problem was, to put it gently, that I was not rising to the occasion. I couldn't believe it but the coke, booze and my nerves were preventing me from delivering the goods. Not only that but the chisel had resulted in my genitals shrinking to an extremely disappointing degree. I'm a grower not a shower at the best of times (and have been heard to claim to incredulous friends that 'acorns do into great oak trees grow') but, frankly, the influence of cocaine had resulted in me resembling a twelve-year-old boy . . . at best. Desperately, I tried to get myself excited by going for gold with a specific brunette whom I had been chatting to over drinks, but it was like trying to force an oyster into a penny slot and she quickly gave up on me, saying to the nearest excited male loud enough for me to hear, 'Ohhh, a hard man is good to find.' I couldn't help but feel that my 'colleagues' were avoiding eye contact with me, such was my obvious uselessness. I had also lost Jane and was feeling very, very alienated. I don't know if it was my imagination but at one point I even thought I heard a football fan on the street below singing, 'You couldn't score in a brothel.'

Before my humiliation could go any further I put my boxers on, retrieved my dinner jacket, got dressed and tried to find the door out. In my drunken drugged-up confusion I entered a room I hadn't seen before. Within it I could just about make out about nine naked bodies writhing around in the semi-darkness. I stared with a drunken leer on my face and suddenly recognised Jane's unmistakable auburn hair at one end of the bed. She was on her hands and knees being taken from behind by some sweaty, lanky streak of piss who was grunting like a farmyard animal. There was something strangely familiar about him . . . oh no, oh my God, it can't be . . . oh dear Lord, what have I done to deserve this?

It was Hugo. Of course it was. I felt sick to the stomach instantly and almost retched. That perverted little fuck was actually reaching the point of no return at the exact moment I poked my head around the door. I caught his eye and he caught mine just as he let loose a gluttonous roar of approval – a primitive war-cry of unbridled ecstasy. He smiled at me with an animal look of satisfaction and theatrically wiped some dribble from his frothing mouth with his forearm. I wanted to jump in and hit him around the face and neck with a pink vibrator that was lying around on the floor but I knew that kind of behaviour was strictly frowned upon at these types of events (or, in fact, most events, truth be told).

I continued to stare in utter disbelief at the scene I beheld and slowly and surely began to realise that my paranoid imagination was simply playing tricks on my little drug-addled brain. It wasn't actually Hugo but some other gangly, inbred arse-wipe. I quietly closed the door and did everything in my power to erase from my memory banks the hideous lustful grimace that I'd seen on that horrible man's smug, sweaty face. But it was no good. I knew that that stomach-churning image would haunt me for the rest of my days. I staggered off into the cruel, cold winter night feeling fit only for the undertaker.

After my dismal performance at the party my relationship with Jane deteriorated. I never told her that I'd seen her in action, nor about my paranoid hallucination. The last time we shagged happened around February 2002 and was completely unplanned – following yet another leaving do. It was what we used to call a 'mid-week sports special' and we were able to use my home because Claire happened to be at her mother's that night. Being unplanned and somewhat drunk meant that Jane had to go back to the office stinking of booze, in the same clothes she wore the day before and to undergo the dreaded 'walk of shame'.

We all know that 'sex is the breakfast of champions' but if you're a woman at an investment bank it is a meal that may just repeat on you. Frankly, the 'walk of shame' from the lifts, through the massive open-plan trading floor to your desk, makes anything on *The Weakest Link* seem like a pleasant stroll in the park. The reaction of the male salesmen whose desks surrounded Jane's revealed once again the similarities between stockbrokers and primary school children. What began as the odd knowing wink and titter soon reached a crescendo of whispering and pointing until at last some wag blurted, 'Good night then, was it Jane?' Apparently, at that point everyone within about thirty feet cracked up and Jane's face went so puce that if

Dulux had been there they could have named a new colour in her honour; perhaps 'Scarlet Lady'.

The difference between how a man and woman are treated by their peers in these scenarios reminds us all of just how sexist investment banking remains. On quite a few occasions throughout my career I was required to go into the office in the same clothes due to an unplanned indiscretion. In that fortunate circumstance I would describe my passage from lift to desk as the 'march of pride'. Instead of an attempt to hide my misdemeanour, my chin would be held high and I would, on occasion, receive high-fives from all my seated colleagues as I passed them on the way to my desk. On one occasion, when it was known that I had gone out with a minor celebrity, my 'swagger of success' received a spontaneous standing ovation from my male colleagues and I responded with a theatrical bow complete with fluttering hand motion.

It seems to me that despite some advances, when it comes to investment banking a man who shags around is a stud, while a woman who 'puts it about' is a slapper. Female brokers especially have a pressure on them to not appear to be floozies because that image hardly goes hand in hand with being a respected professional. This kind of sexism used to always really, really annoy me . . . not because I was a particularly militant feminist but because it encouraged my female peers into living artificially chaste lives and that was always irritating when I was a single cad-about-town.

On the afternoon of that fateful day, a colleague came up to me and recanted the story of Jane's humiliating entrance on to the trading floor. I was bemused by his reconstruction and wanted to play a little game aimed at making me feel like a Don Juan. Needless to say it backfired badly.

'I wonder what lucky bastard was porking her last night,' I said, hoping for some ego-stroking comments from my colleague about how stunningly pretty Jane was.

'Lucky bastard? Hardly, mate. She's the office bike. Christ, she is a knob jockey of the old school. She's had more pricks in her than a pub dartboard. I'm telling you, I know about nine people here who've boned her. She tried it on with me once – saying something naff like "there's a party in my pants tonight and you're invited". What a total slag! She knows I'm married but apparently she likes men with wives or girlfriends so they don't get attached and she can pork others without complication. Word on the street is she may even have the gift that just keeps giving . . . you know what I mean – herpes.'

If my esteemed colleague had been concentrating he would have seen the colour drain out of my face. If he had listened carefully he would have heard my pathetic ego explode into a thousand pieces. I hastily made my excuses and stumbled into the toilet and, helped by my debilitating hangover, was promptly sick. So her sophisticated act was just that – a fucking act. I was a prime pork penis for having fallen for it and now I might have contracted a particularly despicable (and incurable) STD since we had been a little bit sloppy when it came to using condoms. Shit, I might even have given something to Claire. I was sick again. And again.

The thing is, with hindsight, I suspect that my dear colleague was just winding me up. I reckon that he knew that it was me who had been with Jane that night and took the opportunity to make me feel as shit as possible. This is the kind of gag that Cityboys will play on each other all day every day. Still, at that moment in my life this thought was not of comfort – especially when I was sitting in the Jeffries Wing of St Mary's Hospital surrounded by fellow degenerates waiting for the results of my STD test. Thankfully, I was clear. Unfortunately, Jane did leave me with a different type of present, which had even more far-reaching implications.

'What the fuck is this?' screamed Claire, holding my mobile phone in her hands. I was taking a bath reading the Sunday newspaper colour supplements, recovering from a weekend of excess when I was asked this somewhat aggressive question.

Oh Christ! She'd been reading my text messages. Oh fuck, I hadn't deleted Jane's last text message which related to our final 'mid-week sports special'. Oh shit. OH FUCK! Jane's last text had been somewhat unambiguous about the nature of our relationship.

'Steve, every time you fuck me it gets better. We should do another sex party together too but this time DO LESS COKE! Jane xxx.'

Now, I'm no lawyer but I would say that she done me up like a kipper, officer. There was no bullshit on earth that could get me out of this one. I was busted on three different counts: infidelity, drugs and participation at an orgy. You couldn't make it up. I didn't know what to say.

But I didn't even need to say anything. My face gave away the game to such an extent that Claire, without hesitation, threw my mobile at my head with such force that it shattered on impact with the wall behind me. I felt shards of plastic hit my face.

Needless to say, Claire and I split up and I immediately entered a pit of such despair that even just functioning was a trial. For many months, my first thought every single morning when I woke up would be, 'Fuck, it wasn't a dream. I'm no longer with Claire.' I could have transitory moments of happiness but I was always dragged back into the mire of depression by a memory or an association. I would pass a pub in which we had had a romantic drink and would burst into uncontrollable tears. I would hear someone mention a film and then remember that I had seen it with Claire and start welling up. Every time I found something of hers that she'd left in my house, perhaps an earring or a scarf, I would ponder it, look up and envisage her beautiful face again. I would sit for hours in the bath listening to Magic FM play song after song about heartache and loss. I renamed the station Tragic FM and kept punishing myself by listening to the same old depressing songs every day. It was a kind of therapy but it was also self-indulgent torture. Life just seemed so hideously meaningless and the future looked so depressingly bleak. Love is everything; anything else is just tittle-tattle. That one text sent me on such a downward spiral that it would almost cost me my life. But I get ahead of myself – lots of things, some of them even good, happened first.

Apparently, 'It is a truth universally acknowledged, that a single man in possession of a good fortune, must be in want of a wife.' Well, that might well have been true in Jane Austen's day but this was the noughties and I was at the top of my game. I didn't look like Quasimodo, could just about string a vaguely amusing sentence together and had a few bob – which, as far as I could see, meant you could get action most weekends in the Sodom and Gomorrah that is London. Admittedly, I was so guilt-ridden and depressed that I had just blown an almost-perfect relationship because of my pathetic inability to keep it in my pants that I wanted to top myself. But I decided to take the slightly more fun option and do what any sensible newly single rich young man would do – I upped my alcohol and drug intake and went a-hunting gold-diggers.

Gold-diggers are an occupational hazard if you're a premiership footballer or a successful Cityboy. I remember reading about a survey conducted by the National Savings and Investments in 2006 that found that forty-five per cent of the British women they polled said a healthy bank balance was more significant than physical attractiveness in a potential partner. Of course, most Cityboys wouldn't have it any other way since we're at the top of the tree when it comes to earning wedge. This was especially true for the ugly bleeders in the office. Indeed, there is little doubt that brokers unfortunate enough to have a face like a bulldog licking piss off a nettle are often the most ambitious. This correlation suggests a tacit acceptance by pug-ugly Cityboys that the only way to attract 'hardbody chicks' is to flash the cash.

I'd like to pretend that this equation meant that I never felt the need to work hard but I wouldn't be fooling anyone as my Hugo-obsession towards the end of my career drove my desire to win.

The City thrives on greed and the premise that money can get you anything. Call me old fashioned, but I think the Beatles may have had a point when they claimed that money can't buy you love. Unfortunately, many young single Cityboys don't subscribe to this view and are more than happy to settle for a bit of random slap and tickle with girls who ain't after them for their intelligent conversation. Interaction with the opposite sex has convinced them that cash is necessary to get any high-quality action and so they work their arses off knowing that a Ferrari and a Rolex are going to attract a certain breed of perma-tanned high-maintenance chick like flies to shit – which is an analogy with more than just a passing relevance.

So in some ways it seemed to me that things hadn't really changed so much since Jane Austen's time and why would they? Given the choice between working my arse off to break through glass ceilings and climb greasy poles or marrying some rich dude who's going to guarantee you financial security for the rest of your life even if the relationship falters, I know which one I'd choose. If you are an attractive woman, because looks are a prerequisite for most superficial Cityboys, then it seems an entirely logical decision. Of course, love is what it's all about but some women can probably pretend to themselves that they can choose who they fall in love with. It's a long shot but it might just work.

One set of women who really do seem to subscribe to this view are a certain breed of New York women. I imagine their ambitious mothers give them *Pride and Prejudice* as soon as they can read. I once went on a blind date at the New York branch of Nobu with a Manhattan lady. About ten minutes after I arrived the waiter showed what looked like a sassy, power-dressing New York gal to my table. Things looked like they were really beginning to shape up . . . and then she opened her mouth.

About five minutes into our 'meeting', because it certainly wasn't a date that's for sure, I was cursing the name of my colleague whose sick and twisted mind had somehow imagined that I could possibly have got on with this extraordinary harridan. In a moment of weakness and in the absence of alternatives I had agreed to this blind date but it soon proved to be a truly horrific waste of time. I suppose I should have heeded the warning signs. My mate had managed to persuade me to participate in the 'date' by saying that I was perfect for the lady in question since, and I quote, 'She liked her men like she liked her cream: thick and rich.' I had assumed he was joking – he wasn't.

What happened on our 'date' can best be described as a cultural clash of the titans. Her opening gambit was to tell me that 'all life is negotiation' and within two minutes of the conversation I knew that I'd rather eat broken glass than continue this nonsense. What was clear from the word go was that I was not on a date but, rather, was being interviewed for the possible role of husband – a job I soon realised was only marginally better than cleaning the England rugby team's soiled jock straps with my tongue. Questions were fired at me regarding my job, my promotion prospects, whether I owned my house, etc. and all attempts at fun took a back seat while this investigation continued. I, of course, was just interested in a quick bunk-up. As soon as was humanly possible I made my excuses and left.

I can understand why single women in their mid-thirties who lead busy lives can't be arsed to beat around the bush when assessing men, but subtlety is still needed when stalking potential prey. My New York experience showed me that while London might have its share of gold-diggers they were truly uncommitted amateurs relative to their New York-based sisters.

But I also found out around this time of singledom madness that we Cityboys also elicit a very different kind of response from a separate group of women which is equally extreme and even less enjoyable. It was shortly after breaking up with Claire that my painter friend Jim persuaded me to go to an art gallery opening in Shoreditch and this is where I encountered the most intense anti-broker prejudice that I've ever had the displeasure to experience.

The scene I surveyed in the cramped gallery, while nursing a warm glass of Chardonnay, was a bit of an eye-opener. There were none of the hundred-pound hair styles, designer clothes or orange tans that I was getting used to following my split from Claire. Instead, it looked like most attendees had either got dressed in the dark or were having an unspoken bet to see who could look the most preposterous. Feeling extremely out of place in my Ozwald Boateng bespoke suit I still strove to interact with these bohemian types.

I'm sad to report that, apart from those involved in selling the art, who clearly smelled my money, I wasn't flavour of the month in Shoreditch. Within minutes of my arrival I was being harangued by a trio of girls who looked like they'd just walked off a programme called *When Goths Go Bad*. These ladies seemed to blame me personally for global poverty, animal experimentation, the Iraq war and, worst of all, 'phallocentric social structures', whatever they are. I tried to protest that I was a left-wing hippy but any credibility that that claim used to have didn't stand up to close scrutiny any more. I worked in the City, wore pinstripe suits, drove a Porsche and had taken to hanging out with other single Cityboys, buying champagne for random gold-diggers in a pathetic attempt to get laid. Shit, they might have had a point! I was turning into the sort of arsehole I would have mocked relentlessly five years ago.

My encounter with the ugly sisters made me realise very soon that I was on the receiving end of a form of prejudice based entirely on my career choice. The very fact that I worked in the City and was not involved in the art world meant to these jokers that I was a money-obsessed sexist philistine. While this, of course, was basically totally correct at that stage in my life it still seemed a little harsh. I stopped the girls mid-character assassination, saying I needed to get another glass of wine if I was to take any more abuse, and promptly ducked out of the gallery. I hailed a taxi and on the way home pondered the lonely plight of the average Cityboy. On the one hand, there seemed to be loads of women interested in us purely for our cash while, at the same time, there were numerous others out there who wouldn't piss on us if we were on fire, such were their prejudices. Things were dreadfully depressing.

It wasn't just me getting a bit down in the dumps at the beginning of 2003. The markets had been in a piss-poor state for close to three years and a combination of job cuts and shitty bonuses were sending everyone on a bit of a downer. There was a lot of talk from some of my colleagues about going off and doing something useful with their lives though, of course, no one actually had the balls to do it. Hardly a month went by without another huge one-day fall in the stock market and each time it happened my unfortunate colleagues without guaranteed bonuses would sigh and wonder why they bothered working all the hours God sends if they weren't even going to get rewarded properly. People stopped banging on about how massive their bonuses were going to be and just concentrated on brown-nosing so that they could keep their jobs. Although times were a bit moody for these pampered popinjays, with hindsight, it wasn't the kind of hardship that warranted any sympathy. What they were complaining about was getting £150,000–250,000 bonuses on top of their £100,000-plus basic salaries rather than the £400,000-plus of the 'good old days'. In 2007 the average British salary was £24,000 and ninety per cent of the population earned under £46,000. Indeed, the Discovery Channel tells me that around a third of the world lives below the poverty line.

Anyway, every time the numbers on our Reuters screens turned blood red signifying that share prices were falling, the reaction from my colleagues was always amusing to behold and gave a real insight into their differing personalities.

On the trading floor the old hands always tried to present an image of 'seen it all before' nonchalance. Sounding about as convincing as Corporal Jones from *Dad's Army*, they tended to go around telling those few people who bothered to pay them any attention 'Don't panic!' while clearly not taking their own advice. If they dared to bore us with reminiscences about the 'big one' in 1987 some of us cockier, younger brokers would shut them up by interrupting them with impersonations of Uncle Albert's tedious 'during the war . . .' tirades from the sitcom *Only Fools and Horses*. The grads in the office tended to have an air of nervous excitement as if some wag had just turned the fire alarm on during the headmaster's speech. They might not be quite as excited if they knew how many juniors lost their jobs in the immediate aftermath of the '87 crash. The 'last in, first out' policy tends to rear its ugly head when the bad times roll in since it's the big deal-makers (the so-called 'rainmakers') who the bank really don't want to lose. The mid-thirties brokers with young families and huge mortgages have a look of genuine concern on their faces as they realise that if this 'anomaly' turns into a 'correction' (the polite term for a 'crash') then this year's bonus ain't gonna be too hot and that means the villa in Tuscany is going to remain a pipe dream for at least another year. Everyone knows that investment banks' profits have a high correlation with the performance of the markets and so any downturn tends to be about as welcome as Benny Hill at a feminists' convention.

The common feeling we all share is one of total powerlessness. We stare at our Reuters screens like rabbits in the headlights and are immediately transformed from masters of the universe into impotent muppets. It's as if the big swinging dicks have just entered freezing water and shrunk to such an extent that their gender has become unclear. This is one of the reasons

I used to quite like these events: they'd remind the City's arrogant braying buffoons of the concept of humility – a concept most of them have barely ever heard of and one, at that stage in my life, that I was beginning to forget.

Of course, the mother of all recent 'corrections' was Black Monday on 19 October 1987 (though the 1929 Stock Market Crash might claim to be the original bad boy). It's worth discussing it briefly because it still holds an important place in every broker's heart – well, at least those over the age of forty.

I believe it was the great German philosopher Georg Wilhelm Friedrich Hegel who said almost two hundred years ago that 'history teaches us that history teaches us nothing' and if he were still philosophising today and he analysed 'Black Monday' he wouldn't change his view at all. Despite the passing of two decades no one really understands what the hell happened on 19 October 1987, with 'experts' blaming things as diverse as programme trading, the UK hurricane, shares' overvaluation and a lack of liquidity. As far as I can make out the only worthwhile lessons that Black Monday taught us were the following:

1. Never trust 'the experts'. Essentially, no one predicted 'Black Monday'. Frankly, if all the so-called stock market experts were laid end to end, I'd be in favour of it.
2. The stock market is a lottery and can be as irrational as my mad auntie Beryl when she's been on the sherry all day. Some superstitious people refuse to invest in October after the 1929 and 1987 crashes . . . and certain stock market analysts claim that this tendency helps mean that shares tend to underperform over that month.
3. Herd mentality rules. Human behaviour dictates stock markets and humans can panic. Several clichéd City phrases such as 'the trend is your friend' and 'never catch a falling knife' promote so-called momentum trading. Bucking the trend is generally about as wise as putting

your knackers in the care of a scissors-wielding lunatic.

4. Never believe people when they say 'it's different this time' and if they mention 'a new paradigm' of endless prosperity, reach for your gun. Boom and bust cycles will keep happening provided people like one specific ex-girlfriend of mine covet new Jimmy Choos despite not being able to afford them without her (or rather my) plastic friend.

If I had my way, I'd never make predictions, especially ones about the future. Unfortunately, that's what Cityboys are paid to do day in day out. Since it appears that analysts can't even work out why certain major events happened in the past what chance do they have of forecasting the future? History shows us that most analysts couldn't predict a snowstorm in Alaska. This helps explain why only one in seven US research analyst recommendations were negative in February 2000 – a month before a three-year bear market that saw stocks halve in value. Quite simply, important price drivers such as the oil price, interest rates and currency fluctuations are so imponderable that most predictions are about as prescient as Alexander Graham Bell's forecast that 'one day every major city in America will have a telephone' (and he invented the effing thing).

Just before bonus time, which at Megashite was in January, I was called into a little room by the head of research. Chuck Johnson was a Johnson in every sense of the word. He was loud, aggressive and seemed to have taken a Ph.D. at Harvard in being obnoxious, overbearing and boorish (a course that seems to be very popular at American investment banks). Basically, Chuck was your classic Yank stockbroker. When his secretary called me in because Chuck 'would like a quick chat' my heart started racing. I assumed I was about to be kicked out for taking drugs, fiddling expenses or not adhering properly to the numerous post-Enron compliance rules – all of which, of course, I was totally guilty of. I had calmly said 'I'll be right over' but, in fact, was once again frantically searching my brain trying to discern what I was about to be nicked for.

'Steve, we have a problem.' It may have just been me but he seemed purposely to be trying to imitate the classic 'Houston, we have a problem' line from the film *Apollo Thirteen*. With hindsight, it probably was just me.

'Oh yeah . . . you've got a problem?' I said, a little falter in my voice giving the game away that I was scared shitless. By this stage, of course, my paranoia had gone into overdrive and I was searching my mind for any possible wrongdoing I had committed. I became convinced that the compliance boys had found me out for one of two things. I may have been slightly selective in my disclosure to certain key clients about a conversation I'd had with a certain finance director that had suggested that his company's profits were going to be well over five per cent above consensus estimates. Maybe compliance could argue that I was guilty of insider trading (and the FD guilty of 'selective disclosure'). I may also have given some of my favourite clients overly strong hints that I was about to publish a note downgrading my recommendation on a specific water stock. Because I was, for some peculiar reason, now a reasonably well-respected analyst my changes of opinion on specific stocks could actually move the market. Stock prices would generally move down around two to four per cent on the day I moved from a Buy to Sell recommendation and vice versa. What I may have inadvertently done was called 'front-running' and, again, it was strictly *verboten*. Most analysts tend to give hints to clients that they're beginning to question a specific recommendation without telling them a note is about to be published but perhaps I had been too blatant. Since we analysts are in daily contact with quite a few of our clients it would be almost impossible not to show the evolution of an opinion as share prices move up and down. All the client had to do was pick up the hint and then act on it – again, it would usually be hedge fund clients rather than investors from conventional funds, who tended to be a little longer-term in their thinking (and occasionally honest to boot).

'Yes, I'm afraid we do,' he said, looking me straight in the eyes.

God's teeth, stop dragging this out! Just shoot me in the head now, you fucking wanker!

'You can't have not noticed that Megashite's been really suffering recently. Our 2002 profits were down twenty-five per cent year on year and down sixty per cent relative to 1999. There's been a dearth of IPOs, volumes on the market have been terrible and Sarbanes-Oxley's pushing our costs up. When we report full-year results in February the Street is going to crucify our share price. I'm afraid the whole bank need to make some cutbacks and I've been given a remit to take out $40 million from research's cost base. Each team may have to make a sacrifice or two, I'm afraid.'

OK. So that's it. I'm gonna get my final guaranteed bonus and then be told to piss off. It seemed strange to me that he was telling me this now since logic would dictate that he should only do so once I'd received my bonus to ensure that I worked hard right up to my final day. All I could think was that Hugo had won. Just as I was on the point of overtaking that dick-splash, fate had decreed that I was going to be kicked out. My mission was a failure. I must have looked forlorn because Chuck then said: 'Oh no, we don't want to lose you, Steve', almost chuckling with glee at the discomfort he had caused me. I actually think he may have been fucking with me for his own sick pleasure. His ambiguous preamble was probably a power game designed to shit me up just to remind me that he was the boss.

'No, no, Steve. We like you. But we're not so sure about Neil. We know he works damn hard but he doesn't cover that many stocks. We could search around other teams to try and make further cuts but he is the most expensive person on your team and, by the way, if he were to go you would be the logical choice to be team leader. You've got great client relationships and the traders and salesmen all think you're damn good.'

Whoa! I'd gone from facing imminent dismissal to being potentially offered the role of team leader. You couldn't make it up! My ambitious, nasty side told me to immediately accept the proposition and all the added kudos and, more importantly, cash that being promoted would bring. However, two things gave me pause. First of all, Neil was genuinely a really nice guy with a wife and kids who had never done anything to piss me off. He overlooked my tendency to contract 'Colombian flu' most Mondays. In fact, he never questioned my post-weekend 'illnesses' and even took to naming them 'dodgy prawn' days since I tended to use the excuse that I'd eaten a dubious prawn curry on Sunday. He knew it was bullshit and used to joke that I should consider using a different curry house or at least go for chicken next time. He also stood up for me when aggressive salesmen, traders or corporate financiers hassled me. I liked Neil. Secondly, Neil did actually bring something to the party. He was a damn good team leader, had a reasonable client list and wrote incisive think pieces on the sector. My chances of whupping Hugo this year or next were higher with Neil than without him . . . but the money I'd get as team leader! The power! I'd almost certainly be made a managing director. I'd get perks like travelling first class when I went abroad. I'd get respect. My peers in the sector would know I was Johnny Bigballs. I'd lead the team with an iron fist in a velvet glove. I'd rule!

'Yeah. I hate to say it, but I think you've got a point. He works his arse off but he's not vital to our success. However, if I'm made team leader I'd insist on being nominated to be a managing director this summer and I do want my name on one of those full-page *FT* announcements that our bank so loves doing. I'd also insist on a pay review in six months' time and, of course, would expect my future bonuses to reflect my increased workload and responsibility.'

Chuck looked at me with a degree of astonishment. He was clearly impressed about just how hideously Machiavellian I could be. I almost swelled with pride at my disgusting ambition. I felt like Darth Vader talking to the Emperor and getting brownie points for revealing the evil I was capable of. He must have thought that I had a great potential future in this industry!

'OK, Neil goes, then. I agree to all your requests and—'

I interrupted him. 'I hate to say it, but I will need to see your agreement in writing. We all know an oral contract ain't worth the paper it's not written on.' I was getting into this now. The relief at not being sacked coupled with my imminent promotion was going straight to my stupid little head.

'OK. I'll have Penny put together something. I'm gonna sack Neil very soon – probably Friday. We're giving bonuses out next week and this, of course, means he's getting a doughnut' i.e. zero. 'As a sign of my good faith and in recognition of the hard work to come I'm gonna give you an extra hundred grand immediately on top of your guaranteed bonus. You're gonna have to work very hard now. Being a team leader means lots of admin and internal meetings. It also means, if you do your job properly, handsome rewards. But screw it up and I'll tear you a new one. Welcome to the team.'

I tried to justify my actions by remembering the tag line to *The Godfather: Part III* that stated 'Real power can't be given. It must be taken', but almost as soon as I shook his hand my Christian guilt reared its ugly head. Everything had happened so quickly that I felt as if I was in a dream. But in reality, no amount of excuses would change the fact that I had just shafted my boss – a good man who deserved better. Frankly, I could make all the shit justifications known to man, but at the end of the day I was like Heather Mills-McCartney – I didn't have a leg to stand on.

When I look back at my career I would say that it was at that moment that I turned from being a half-decent individual into a fairly repellent Cityboy. Like someone who had been bitten by a zombie, I had been 'on the turn' for some time but now I was undoubtedly one of the living dead. The trip to Ibiza, the purchase of the Boateng suit, the march into cocaine addiction, the rejection of and by my school friends, the affair with The Floozie, the sex party, the end of the only meaningful relationship that I'd ever had, the gold-diggers . . . these were all symptoms of my moral decline and now the process of becoming a Cityboy was virtually complete. The scum always rises to the top. Frankly, I almost welcomed this final stage of my transformation. I had been caught between two stools before – a Porsche-driving pinstriped Cityboy with Christian, left-wing hippy ideals. I now willingly threw away the things that once defined me. I became 'one of them'. My life would be dedicated to making money, snorting beak and boning perma-tanned hardbody chicks . . . and any other meaningful and profound pursuits I could think of. I've never done things in half-measures and would show these Cityboys how to be a proper arsehole. I would be the ultimate Cityboy – MD, team leader and number-one-rated analyst. All would kneel before me and be my minions. Hugo and his idiotic pals would soon set up a religion with me at its head.

What a total cocksucker I became. I had sold my soul to Mammon and lost sight of who I was. That is what the City can do. Reality had once been a friend of mine but I willing rejected her. My old friends had begun to avoid me and even my family began to start telling me to be 'nicer'. I just thought – what has being 'nice' ever achieved? I didn't get where I am today by being 'nice'. Fuck 'nice'. I'm going to be nasty . . . but I'm going to be successful. People around me soon noticed a change in my attitude and saw something in my confident swagger that reflected my enhanced self-belief. I became more dismissive of the secretaries and more mocking of the lowly graduates. I expected, nay demanded, respect and my condescending arrogance permeated most conversations. I would flash money around with contrived nonchalance and get angry at any poor sucker who didn't jump to it when I demanded it. Thinking back on it now makes me cringe and hold my head in my hands.

Anyway, when Neil was called by Penny to go and see Chuck I still had a pang of terrible guilt – knowing that he was just about to face the firing squad.

'Steve, I'm expecting a call from Fidelity at any minute but I've got to see Chuck quickly. So just say I'll be back in five minutes, OK?'

'Yeah, cool. No worries,' I said, studiously avoiding looking him in the eyes as I pretended to be preoccupied with a spreadsheet. The poor deluded fool! He was just about to get the sack and he thought everything was cool and the gang. Mate, you won't give a shit about some cunt from Fidelity in about two and a half minutes!

The next half-hour was not a comfortable one. Eventually, after what seemed an interminable amount of time, Neil returned looking as if someone had just pissed on his grave.

'Steve, come with me. Let's go and have a coffee,' he said like a defeated man.

'What about the Fidelity bloke? I said you'd ring back.'

'FUCK THE FIDELITY BLOKE!' he shouted, red-faced. Now, Neil never ever lost his cool and he never swore. The whole team knew immediately that something was dreadfully wrong. Suddenly, everyone got particularly captivated by whatever they were working on.

Over a skinny latte at the local Starbucks Neil told me about what had just happened. My acting skills had been honed by lying day in, day out to clients and pretending I was horrified by gargantuan bonuses, but this was a tour de force, my finest hour. If Pacino or De Niro had been present they would have been taking notes and telling Stanislavsky where he could shove his pony theories. At one point I saw tears welling in his eyes as he said: 'I've worked my arse off for those tossers and this is how they repay me. And just before bonus time, too. If they think I ain't taking them to court on that one, they've got another thing coming.'

The problem, of course, is that bonuses are entirely discretionary so his chances of forcing some wedge out of Megashite seemed similar to Margaret Beckett's chances of winning Miss World. However, Neil knew that banks did sometimes back down since they wanted to avoid the bad publicity that comes with very visible court cases so he gave it a bash. There was never any court case and I never did find out if he managed to get some cash by threatening legal action. All I cared about was that he never found out what a treacherous little shit I had been. I think I got away with it – at least up until now, anyway.

By June 2003 things were really looking up. OK – I'd lost the love of my life and turned into a completely reprehensible human being. But looking on the bright side, I had overcome my guilt about losing my boss his job and earned £500,000 over the previous year. Also, the markets were beginning to pick up. As soon as the US invasion of Iraq had begun the uncertainty that had been plaguing equities was reduced and markets across the world breathed a huge sigh of relief. 'The Baghdad bounce', as it quickly became known, was made even more impressive when it appeared that the war was to be over in weeks. Baron de Rothschild famously said that you should 'invest when the blood runs in the streets' and anyone who took his advice in March 2003 would have made a packet. Stock markets rose about eighty per cent in the three years following the invasion of Iraq even though the killing dragged on far longer than the official end of the war. While brave soldiers were being blown up by road-side bombs, we Cityboys lay back and reaped the rewards. We were just about to enter a golden age of plenty similar to the late 1990s and I was there at the right place at the right time ready to mint it. I most definitely was on the gravy train and there was no doubt that I was now in the first-class carriage.

The downer in June 2003 was that we didn't beat Hugo's boys in Extel. I was upset but not distraught because the results showed that we were within a whisker of showing those dickheads at Mighty Yankbank who the daddy was and the bet still had one more year to go:

Mighty Yankbank: 25.4%
Megashite: 23.6%
Merde Bank: 21.2%

It seemed clear that Neil's departure had not cost us many votes and that we were going to overtake them next year, and it seemed crystal clear that I was going to receive a tidy sum from Hugo and lay to rest the ghosts that had been haunting me for so many years.

Hugo, of course, tried to goad me on the evening of the results. I had witnessed him once again go up to the podium and receive his award but this time we had had none of our usual acerbic interaction because our paths happened not to cross on the day. Hugo, as was his style, did not let it lie. He called my mobile just as I was bedding down at around eleven.

'Steeeeeve,' he extended my name in a theatrical way, like the snivelling little snake that he was. Judging by his tone, I think he'd had a few sherberts.

'Yes, who is this?' I replied sleepily.

'Oh, it's so close . . . so very close you can almost touch it!' he said with almost maniacal glee.

'Oh, it's fucking you. Fuck off, Hugo, you pathetic little shit.'

'Oh, poor little Stevie! He tries so very, very hard but he just can't quite do it, can he? When will he realise that he's never gonna make it? When will he realise he's a boy and that this is a man's world?'

'Hugo – you really are a loathsome little tit-wank. You're ringing because you're rattled. You know there's only one out-come to this battle and when I take my twenty grand off you next year, you're gonna rue the day that you ever fucked with me.'

'Twenty grand? If you had any cojones, Mr Managing Director, you'd up the stakes. What say you we make it a hundred? Isn't it about time you grew some balls, little man?'

Christ alive! What a tosser! He knew I'd have to accept. This was bigger than both of us. Before I could really think about it I replied: 'OK, motherfucker. A hundred big ones it is. But I want this in writing because I'd trust Harold Shipman with my gran before I'd trust you, you little fuck.'

'So be it. The contract will be with you by the end of the week. Ready your troops for a year of hellish war. To battle and may the best stockbroker win.'

And with that he put the phone down. I did not sleep easy that night. All I could think was that I needed to put every ounce of my being into humiliating that dreadful human being. My life had a purpose and I was going to make sure my team understood how much this battle meant to me. I was going to entertain clients like it was 1999. No Michelin-starred restaurant, major sporting event or pop concert would go unattended. Although there had been serious restrictions on entertainment spend I would use my own money if necessary. I would travel the world talking shit and garnering votes. I would stop mucking around with bleeding spreadsheets. I would hire someone to do the dull, everyday work while I lied, cheated, stole and did whatever was necessary to make sure Hugo's fate was sealed. One of the perks of nicking Neil's job was that I could hire a monkey to come and work for me. I could get myself . . . a graduate trainee.

8

THE GRADUATE

September always had tremendous potential comic value at investment banks because that was usually the month when we had the pleasure of welcoming into our bosom, like lambs to the slaughter, a bunch of ambitious, wet behind the ears graduate trainees. Those of us with a taste for the absurd awaited their arrival as we would a visit by an avant-garde troupe of unintentional comedians. Of the two distinct archetypes, the scared overly deferential buffoon and the preposterous arrogant idiot (who've usually read some book claiming that this is the only way to gain respect in the 'bear pit' that is the City), the latter was always my personal favourite. Little does this poor schmuck know that his attitude will simply condemn him to a series of tried and tested wind-ups that should, if executed correctly, result in a major personality rethink and/or his swift departure. Before things got a bit serious, we used to do something like anonymously putting him on the subscription list for a hard-core gay jazz mag using the office as his favoured address of receipt. Once a poor, unsuspecting grad opened a package containing a DVD of a film called *Shaving Ryan's Privates* much to everyone's hilarity. If that kind of gag fails to moderate a grad's attitude we might use his computer to type into the in-house intranet message system (accessible and visible to the whole bank) the domain name of some dubious website – perhaps www.greasedupchoirboys.com – thus making out he has inadvertently revealed to every co-worker his unusual sexual proclivities.

But towards the end of my career, these fresh-faced ingénues simply reminded burnt-out has-beens like me of the pleasant individuals that we once were and like a bullying older pupil at some dreadful public school I felt obliged to make sure that they faced the same horrors that I had had to endure. My need to mock was fired up as I jealously observed in their young, naïve eyes the optimism that I had once harboured, but had had beaten out of me long ago by the soul-destroying tedium that our job ultimately entailed.

In 2003, my bank's contingent of sixty or so grads generally ticked all the stereotypical boxes: ambitious, white, male, heterosexual Oxbridge graduates who had probably wanted to enter the City since they were about fourteen. Hence most of them had got involved in the 'milk round' at college with all the misplaced enthusiasm of a brainwashed British Soldier about to go 'over the top' during the battle of the Somme. Most of them had already done some City work experience during the college summer holidays when they should have been downing tequila shots at Amnesia in Ibiza (I think that's what I did when twenty . . . though I don't really remember). I used to think that if I had my way any grad who had undertaken such a dreadful misuse of their free time prior to spending thirteen hours a day serving Mammon would be automatically barred. I still remember breezing into the City in 1996 simply because I had nothing better to do and had a brother already in the system. Although nepotism is alive and well, the days of confused, uncertain history graduates entering the City seemed well and truly over by 2003. Now the City insists on the kind of background that invariably produces tedious, production-line robots with all the imagination of a Channel Five documentary.

Benjamin Drip was the archetypal graduate trainee and would serve my purposes excellently. He was a twenty-one year old who had studied economics at Cambridge and managed to come out with a first-class honours degree. He was clearly hideously ambitious and far more sensible than I could ever remember being. From the day he joined our team he worked extremely hard, coming in at 6.45 a.m. and often staying until 8 p.m. and beyond. I once came into the office on a Sunday and found him beavering away at some tedious spreadsheet. If I hadn't been so obsessed with my mission I would have told him there and then to wake up and smell the coffee and stop wasting the best years of his short, little life on meaningless nonsense. Of course, I actually patted him on the back and told him to 'keep up the good work'.

Benjamin was a standard City graduate trainee for several other reasons. For a start, he was white. It has often seemed to me that the heads of recruitment at investment banks choose their graduate trainees utilising the opposite of Henry Ford's dictum that you could choose any colour for your car 'as long as it's black'. The reasons for the domination of the financial services industry by Caucasians are extremely complicated but there can be no doubt that it is a white man's world. Yes, there are a few stockbrokers and fund managers of Asian descent but the number of staff who are black is very low – except, of course, in the canteen or among the toilet cleaners. This fact, unfortunately, gives outsiders the (fairly correct) view that the City is essentially a tight-knit club dedicated to making its racially homogenous members as much cash as humanly possible as quickly as possible. There are exceptions; the former head of Merrill Lynch, Stan O'Neal, was black, but they are few and far between and merely serve to prove the rule. Until this situation is improved it seems unlikely that successful City jobs will appear to be a worthwhile aspiration for our ethnic brothers and sisters (which, of course, they're not).

Benjamin was also male. Over my time in the City more women did enter the ranks on both the buy-side and sell-side but even by 2007 I would estimate that around eighty per cent of front-office investment bankers were male. A class action brought against a German bank in 2006 revealed the shocking statistic that only two per cent of its managing directors were female. Facts like this help explain the long list of recent legal cases brought against City institutions related to the 'culture of sexism' – as mentioned by City trader Katharina Tofeji who took BNP Paribas to court in 2007 (though she lost her case). The vast majority of such cases never even see the light of day and are usually settled out of court by banks keen to avoid the glare of negative publicity and employees keen to avoid protracted legal wranglings. Obviously the City's male domination is partly because those most likely to succeed in the Square Mile are those who exhibit arrogance, aggression and ruthless ambition and these traits are, thank God, less likely to be found in the 'fairer sex'. Interestingly, some have suggested that this fact means that women who do work in finance have to leave their 'femininity' at the door and become mini-Thatchers in order to succeed. In reality, one of Ms Tofeji's complaints was that she was told to 'use her female charms to woo clients' which is a much more accurate reflection of the sexist dynamics that I witnessed at investment banks. Ms Tofeji's solicitor said after she lost her case that 'this judgment is a missed opportunity to deal with the widespread sex discrimination in the City that still persists'.

Every day, I used to see around me female stockbrokers flirting outrageously with their predominantly male clients and doing extremely well partly through this tactic. They would laugh at desperately unfunny jokes for far too long and be overly tactile when taking clients out. Since a good portion of the male clients in the financial services industry are sexually repressed losers it's hardly a surprise that when offered the choice of having lunch with some sassy lady who flatters their ego by pretending to find them attractive or some ugly Neanderthal like me it was what is commonly referred to as a 'no-brainer'. I mean, I had a pair of man boobs to die for back then but that just didn't cut it with the discerning client. Personally, I always felt that we had to use every trick we could find in order to succeed in this hideously competitive industry. That the City's male domination forced certain women to use their feminine charms to woo clients is not only inevitable but, as far as I am concerned, also under-standable. What BNP Paribas was accused of doing was asking a woman to do this which, if true, was not only stupid but about as necessary as my boss asking me to win business by taking clients to strip joints and downing champagne.

These sex discrimination cases are becoming common but I believe that the surprising thing is how few of them there are, since sexism is so clearly rife in the City. Of course, some of the cases are brought by chancers looking to leave their firm with a nice little nest egg and this seems a perfectly rational means of enhancing your remuneration. Banks often settle without actually going to court since they don't want the bad publicity and because they know that unless compliance procedure has been followed absolutely perfectly they probably have broken a few rules. What probably stops certain women is the knowledge that taking legal action may be detrimental to the prospects of other women being employed in the City in the future (especially since they already suffer as a result of concerns about likely pregnancies). I have little doubt that if men had the option of pursuing legal cases designed to make a few million quid towards the end of their careers they'd be at it nonstop. I know I would.

Benjamin was also heterosexual. In fact, much to my bemusement he was thinking of marrying his college sweetheart – at twenty-one, the poor, deluded buffoon! Now, I've never had the slightest problem with our homosexual brothers provided they don't try to ram it down my throat. Still, despite my relative tolerance, I only met three openly gay men during my entire City career – which statistically seems highly improbable. Of course, there could have been loads of closet homosexuals but, if that's the case, then there were a hell of a lot of women pretending to be girlfriends and wives since most people seemed to be hitched. It would, of course, be somewhat understandable if our gay brethren did choose to hide their sexual leaning, such is the macho nature of City culture. More than any other institution that I've ever touched upon (and that even includes the school rugby team and university drinking society) heterosexual credentials were stamped firmly on every conversation. Woe betide some idiot talking about interior design . . . or even worse, feelings. Generally, if you weren't discussing sport, money or birds you were a social pariah. Christ, even I sometimes felt a little effeminate such was the boorish nature of the average chinwag. It got to the point where I wondered whether 'the lady doth protest too much' and I was, in fact, surrounded by a bunch of repressed homosexuals who shrouded their sexuality by only ever banging on about thirty big men wrestling each other in the mud for a funny shaped ball (which would probably give Freud a field day anyway).

The other box that Benjamin ticked was being a nice middle-class Oxbridge graduate. About three months into his tenure I asked him what jobs his university pals were generally getting involved with. Much to my horror he informed me that of his forty friends and acquaintances from Cambridge thirty had entered the City and five were trying to do so! He said that the same was true of Oxford. This was just simply not the case for the people I knew who left Cambridge in 1994. The City was a money machine that was really getting into gear by 2003 and subsequently in the following years it simply sucked up most of the talent that this country, and others, had to offer. Clever scientists who should be solving climate change, smart medical students who should be curing AIDS and outstanding engineers who should be protecting us from rising sea levels are all instead engaged in pointlessly pushing around bits of paper. It is because the City offers rewards that are so massively disproportionate to the rest of UK plc that it seduces from society those gifted individuals who in times gone by would have gone on to become great inventors, scientists and even artists. I have no doubt that the progress of our culture and our society will be all the worse for it.

The arrival of Benjamin was actually a bit of a joy for me because it gave me the opportunity to pass on all the wisdom that I had garnered from David, Tony and my own experience. I began to take him out to Canary Wharf's finest bars (which ain't saying much) and to teach him the lessons that I had been taught. Of course, I neglected to mention ones that might cause me problems like the trick of threatening to leave in order to secure a guaranteed bonus. I had a set routine. I would pop off to the toilets, hoof a load of gak, and then shout at him for hours about how to thrive in the City. He was the perfect coke-companion since he said fuck all and held me, as a thirty-one-year-old managing director at a large US bank, in high esteem. My already out-of-control ego was lapping up every second of his deference. Also, because I was steadily losing my old friends as I turned more and more completely into an egotistical scumbag, I needed someone new to sit there quietly and listen while I explained what an unbelievably successful human being I was: '. . . and another thing. You shouldn't wear shirts with buttons in the collar. That is not the City uniform! Shirts should have no buttons in their collars, they should have no breast pocket and they should have double cuffs. Go and buy three Thomas Pink shirts tomorrow – one in yellow, one in pink and one in blue. And get a pair of traditional humorous City cufflinks, too – taps, dice, light-bulbs, ones that say "VIP" or ones that say "BUY" on one and "SELL" on the other. DON'T FUCK AROUND! This is a serious business. You've got to look the part. No one is going to take advice off some poorly dressed retard who's not wearing wacky cufflinks. Here, here's two hundred quid.' If six years before, dressed in a six-pound suit, I could have heard myself spouting this crap I would have stabbed myself in the neck with a biro.

'. . . and another thing. Make the clients think you love them. Just do that and the rest will follow. They'll forgive you for getting calls wrong or screwing up some analysis. They'll vote for you and where there's votes there's gold, my boy! Pets win prizes, d'you know what I mean?' I don't actually know what I meant by that but if Benjamin didn't either, he didn't let on. He just supped his Diet Coke while his increasingly incoherent boss rabited utter nonsense.

'. . . and another thing. Spreadsheets are a necessary evil but don't get too het up about them. They'll only get you so far. I can't tell you the number of times I've got an FD rat-arsed and he's told me juicy titbits that helped me calculate what the profits will be. Don't you worry too much about working out tax rates and bollocks like that, there are too many imponderables. Just get it off the FD.'

'. . . and another thing. Timing is everything. I tell you, Wall Street really is "littered with the graves of people who were correct too soon," as Gordon Gekko or some other genius so succinctly put it. Some jokers have been saying United Utilities will cut its dividend for years but I tell you now it will probably happen a few years before the 2010 regulatory review. If I'm still around I'll go in all the press around 2007 and make sure everyone thinks that it's my idea and forget about the other losers. It's referred to as taking ownership on an idea, though crueller people might describe it as stealing.'

And so I went on . . . and on . . . and on. Dear old Benjamin sat there probably thinking what a total dick I was but never giving it away. If that was the case he definitely had a future in this industry – I'd been doing that with clients since day one.

The problem was that while I was talking at Benjamin one resounding thought kept hammering away at my tiny little brain: you, Steve, are a fucking dinosaur. Your days are numbered. What's sitting in front of you drinking Diet Coke, not smoking any tabs and probably waiting to go to the gym, is the future of stockbroking. I've always thought that giving up booze and fags didn't make you live longer, it just felt that way but that was not how Benjamin looked at the world. He is a clean, mean broking machine. He is a boring safe pair of hands. He will work diligently and not screw up. He's probably never ever touched drugs and knew more about maths when he was twelve than you do now. He will be efficient and not have 'dodgy prawn' days. He will care about what he does and actually believe that he's doing something worthwhile. He's forgotten more about Excel and PowerPoint than you will ever know. He will do what you do, but do it better. The only thing that you have that he hasn't is a personality.

It was this thought that brought me to my senses: OK, he'd knock up models (financial that is, rather than glamour) quicker than a rabbit gets fucked and produce research notes in minutes but he didn't understand people. He lacked the human touch. Clients would not want to spend four hours over a boozy lunch with him. Clients would not want to go to Las Vegas or Miami on a five-day bender with him. Despite the pernicious influence of the Yank banks and their soul-destroying rules and regulations there are still young men out there who want to have a giggle – even if they are fast becoming a minority as the automatons take over. As long as that is the case degenerates like me have a future – albeit a limited one. You've still got a few years left in you, my son! To paraphrase Daley Thompson: Benjamin and his kind may be younger, stronger and fitter than me but I'll still beat them.

Benjamin actually began to have a positive influence on our team from the word go, which is unusual since most graduates are a total waste of space for the first few months. Indeed, I would say that for their first six months graduates are paid about £40,000 a year to go to Starbucks to get coffees – which, relative to the populace at large, is nice work if you can get it. But Benjamin started getting my models in good order almost as soon as he arrived. He also managed to pass the SFA exam on the first go. If he hadn't he would have been ridiculed remorselessly and never allowed to forget it since it is, without doubt, a total piece of piss. I had told him to do everything in his power to not fuck it up since failure to pass it would condemn him to mockery as long as he worked at Megashite. The SFA qualification is granted if you pass two simple multiple-choice exams that, in my humble opinion, a retarded nine year old wouldn't struggle with. The highly amusing thing is that once you've done it (and have been deemed 'a fit and proper person') you can advise people running pension funds and ISAs about what stocks to buy and sell! My God, after one month at our bank Benjamin could theoretically influence your gran's income! Most banks are now insisting that their graduates take the far harder three-year CFA course though I never bothered wasting my time on such bullshit.

Benjamin even suggested a couple of things that would genuinely help improve my interaction with the clients and, ultimately, my mission to beat Hugo. First of all, he noticed that I kept failing to remember my clients' kids names and so forth. I've always had a sieve-like memory (which was made a shit-load worse by excessive boozing and drug consumption) and this had always plagued me when I was chatting to clients and pretending to be their best mates. So, Benjamin devised a spreadsheet database with all the clients' vital details contained within. This was a fairly obvious thing to do and I knew that some of my competitors had such spreadsheets but I had never got off my fat arse to actually sort it out. The database contained details of most of my major clients' birthdays, their spouse's names, their kids' names, where they lived, what football team they supported, etc. As I was speaking to a client on the phone I would open up the spreadsheet on one of my two screens and nonchalantly ask after little Jonny and Mabel. Then I would console him about how Tottenham got their arse kicked once again at the weekend. Before I went out on a booze-up with a client I'd bone up on his details and impress him by asking after his wife Candida and whether Wolfie was still chasing squirrels. Shit, we even started sending out birthday cards. The clients absolutely loved it, mistakenly thinking that they must have a special relationship with me, when in fact I just had a damn good database with similar details for fifty others!

This was a definite step in the right direction as was revealed by one particularly disastrous client event I organised. In December 2002 I had, as usual, organised a big client Christmas knees-up at a decent restaurant. That year, I had chosen to go to Fergus Henderson's great restaurant St Johns near Smithfield Market. This was a meat-eater's paradise and boasted that it served every part of the animal 'from nose to tail'. I couldn't wait to try it though some people on the team thought it sounded offal. Anyway, the lady I had spoken to at the restaurant persuaded me to opt for the full roast pig, which I did while licking my carnivorous lips. Due to a lack of a client database and my drug-addled little brain I had forgotten that almost half of the sixteen clients attending the lunch would not be able to dine on swine due to being either Jewish, Muslim or vegetarian. Only once we had arrived at the restaurant and my clients looked at the special Christmas menu did it dawn on me that seven were condemned to one choice for starter and one choice for main course – neither of which sounded particularly palatable. Just when I thought it couldn't get any worse, the pig's head was brought to the table on a silver platter and placed between a lovely

Jewish chick and a hard-core veggie chap. I squirmed in my seat and pretended not to notice when a particularly bloodthirsty client leaned over and started sawing into the pig's face, virtually foaming at the mouth as he said, 'The cheek is, of course, by far the most succulent part of the pig.' I held my head in my hands, when some scallywag took my embarrassment to another level by putting a lit fag in the pig's mouth while giggling and nudging the clearly distraught Muslim chap next to him.

The other innovation that my technologically gifted underling brought to the party was an outstanding invention called 'voice push'. He had seen another team at the bank use it and persuaded me to check it out. I cannot describe how truly tedious the job of analyst can be when we do a morning call-round to our client base. Over the course of my career I saw a steady increase in the number of clients leaving their telephone on voice mail. This tendency reached such proportions that I used to sometimes call forty clients in a row on the morning that a company released results and only catch maybe four or five live. There I was, earning half a million pounds a year spending two tedious hours leaving exactly the same fucking message for thirty-five fucking idiots – many of whom would probably delete it without ever listening to it because six other dickheads from other banks had left almost exactly the same message.

This absurd situation was realised by whoever the genius was that invented 'voice push'. Quite simply, I would record the message that I wished to leave using the device and then call my client. On the off chance he or she answered the phone I would talk to them but if their phone went to voice mail I would simply click my mouse and my pre-recorded words of wisdom would be left on their machine leaving me free to call the next poor bastard on my client tick-sheet. It was better than a blast voice mail because they were only suitable very late at night otherwise you risked having a client pick up his phone and hearing some pre-recorded message, which never goes down too well. This wonderful device meant that I could complete my client call-round in about thirty minutes and that I would never leave a duff message because I had pre-recorded a perfect master. It also resulted in the utterly absurd situation of the City being full of machines leaving messages on other machines for people who would probably not bother listening to them. But I didn't care. It lightened my workload and I've always been keen on things that do that.

Benjamin's final cunning plan involved making another database of which institutions actually voted in Extel (as some didn't bother) and the way in which they voted. We had always been a little bit scatter-gun in our approach to the surveys, though we had a reasonable idea about who voted and whether they just extrapolated the vote from the most recent internal broker review. Benjamin found, through interviewing lots of the other analysts on our floor, that he could compile a list of those institutions that voted and those that hated being asked for votes and so forth. Soon we knew exactly which clients we should schmooze and when. We found that certain institutions just used the latest broker review which would mean that we really kissed arse at the relevant time of that internal vote. Or we would be aware that another set of clients would vote when the survey landed on their desk which meant metaphorical blow-jobs would be handed out at around 15 March which is when the paper voting forms for Extel were sent out.

It seemed to me that, with our momentum, Michael's planet-sized brain, my resilient liver and Benjamin's youthful innovations, victory at the June 2004 Extel awards was virtually guaranteed. But I wasn't satisfied with a likely victory. I wanted to make damn sure that Hugo was going to be £100,000 poorer and I was going to be master of the universe. So I arranged a team meeting in December 2003 designed to make sure that we produced some outstanding pieces of research that would blow away the opposition: 'Look, chaps, if I've said it once I've said it a thousand times, we ain't here to sell truth. I just want plausible, innovative stuff that we can vaguely back up and which isn't the same as all the other me-too crap on the Street. And I want price targets that give upside to die for. Any ideas, Michael?'

'The EC are beginning a new market trading CO_2 on 1 January 2005. I believe it will push power prices up and so we should do a big note telling everyone to buy the European generators, especially those with low carbon-intensive plants like nuclear and hydro.'

'Cool. That sounds fine. What about my stocks? Any ideas?' It was quite absurd to be asking another analyst for ideas on my sector, but the team knew me and I'd long ceased pretending to spend much time on UK water.

'Yeah, just say that the signs are that the 2005 regulatory review is going to be really benign and subsequently all the waters are cheap – especially the highly leveraged companies since the appreciation of their equity will be more geared to generous price controls. Why don't you say there'll probably be some M&A from private equity while you're at it?' said Michael.

'Sweet as a nut! That's done, then. Let's get these notes out in January and market them like head cases all over the world.'

And that is exactly what we did. From Tokyo to San Francisco, no client was left alone until they agreed to a meeting which we would use to espouse our new-found high-conviction bullshit.

I opted personally to go to Tokyo since I had never been there and was intrigued by what appeared to be a culture of conformity and weirdness. Broking in Tokyo truly was one of the strangest experiences I've ever had work-wise. My jet lag was so profound that I had no fucking clue what was going on. It really did feel as if I was in a dream for my three days over there – something the film *Lost in Translation* captured brilliantly. But it didn't really matter because the clients I broked to either knew fuck all about the sector or could hardly speak English. Even more amusingly, about ten minutes into my first presentation the client actually fell asleep on me. Now, I know that European utilities ain't exactly scintillating, but this had never happened to me before. I ended up smashing my PowerPoint presentation on his desk and waking him up but it was only another five minutes before his eyes turned redder and started rolling back in his head again. I thought it was a tad rude but the salesman accompanying me told me that this particular client did it quite often, as did certain others. Apparently, it's called 'inemuri', which literally means 'to be asleep while present' and there are strict rules governing who can do it and when. I still think having a kip while someone's supposedly engaging you in a one-on-one presentation is unlikely to be deemed one of the 'acceptable' times.

I was also amused by the ceremony that happened every time you exchanged business cards with a client. The first time I received a business card I just put it straight into my suit jacket's breast pocket. I was later told by a clearly embarrassed salesman that this was a big no-no and that I needed to study the card while holding it by the sides carefully between two extended forefingers and then look up at my client's face and then re-study the card. I followed this procedure from then on.

The final amusing practice was the bowing ceremony that happened after every client presentation. Once we had entered a lift after a meeting my accompanying salesman would begin bowing to the client. The client would then bow back. The salesman would bow lower. The client would bow back slightly lower. The salesman would then bow even lower until his head was at groin level and so on until the lift doors finally closed. At one point I thought the poor little bugger's head would get caught in the rapidly closing lift door. This all looked quite a laugh to me so with an unintentional smirk on my face I started doing it after the next meeting. As soon as the lift doors closed my poor salesman mate explained that a simple handshake would do since I was a foreigner.

Frankly, Tokyo was so alien to me that nearly everything was different. The only thing that was the same was the preponderance of frighteningly tall blond Eastern European strippers in the Tokyo red-light district, Roppongi. As I sat in Roppongi's most famous strip joint surrounded by photos of the world's most well-known male actors who had attended in times gone by, I marvelled at the tiny suited Japanese businessmen getting private dances from pneumatic six-feet tall Helgas wearing four-inch heels. My accompanying salesman informed me in no uncertain terms that these were the Japanese men's favourite strippers. I loved the absurdity of the contrast and paid for my five-foot tall salesman pal to have his own private dance from a chick who was so massive that his face was at the same level as her huge silicon-enhanced breasts even before he sat down.

Apart from Tokyo I also went marketing in Switzerland and Paris where I'm pleased to report the clients all conformed to long-held stereotypes. In Zurich I encountered what can only be described as the most tedious individuals that I've ever met. The Swiss Germans' lack of *joie de vivre* was only rivalled by their fastidiousness. All that was implied by Orson Welles's speech at the end of *The Third Man* about the neutral Swiss's only achievement being the 'invention of the cuckoo clock' rang true. In Paris, I was received with the kind of arrogance that even I, by now a seasoned Cityboy, was unused to. Marketing stocks necessarily requires an assumption that the analyst knows more than the investor receiving the advice and, of course, this is always a major problem when dealing with a Paris-based fund. The only way I was able to prevent numerous arguments from breaking out was through several tried and tested verbal tricks. So, even if the client was making a clearly incorrect assertion I would say: 'I can understand your point of view but would perhaps slightly disagree on just this one small point . . .' If the client persisted in a serious disagreement despite my persuasive arguments I would eventually move on to another subject by saying, 'Well, it takes two to make a market . . .'

Everything was going just hunky dory with the marketing and, like King Arthur's knights, the whole team reconvened back in London in late January 2004 to talk of our victories, having spread the gospel far and wide. We spoke of our successes in distant lands and felt our war campaign had a Napoleonic strategic brilliance that would sweep all the opposition aside. Such was Benjamin's steep learning curve that we even allowed him to call a few small, unimportant clients. He cottoned on extremely quickly about the art of bullshitting those few clients who happened to be annoyingly smart. He naturally understood how to subtly change the subject if a client moved on to areas that he was less knowledgeable about and he quickly learned the golden rule when fibbing to clients: he understood that when a client asks for a specific number, for example what percentage of UK electricity output comes from nuclear sources, and you only have a vague idea about what it is, that you should always make your 'guessestimate' (i.e. lie) a precise number. Never say 'about thirty per cent', say 'thirty-two per cent'; it's much more convincing.

The speed with which Benjamin picked up the meaningless City phrases that I and other senior members of the team spouted also amused me immensely. Within the space of only one morning's client call-round I heard him saying the following inane phrases, all of which are the kind of tired clichés that even an old has-been might baulk at. Since Benjamin picked up most of his banter from me, the banality of his witterings certainly didn't reflect well on the kind of horseshit that I'd been submitting my poor clients to for numerous years:

'The CEO's so incompetent he couldn't hit a cow's arse with a banjo.'

'You've got to fill your boots, they're as cheap as chips. If you snooze you lose.'

'You spoke to the IR guy? Oh, you shouldn't talk to the monkey, you should to talk the organ grinder.'

'You assume they'll call an EGM? You know the old saying . . . assume makes an "ass" of "u" and "me".'

'They're still not cheap even down at this level. Never catch a falling knife . . . believe me, this is a dead cat bounce.'

'No, seriously, with the profit growth that we forecast, this could be a five bagger' i.e. the share price could increase to five times its current value.

'This management team hasn't got a coherent strategy and remember what they say – failing to plan is planning to fail.'

'Buy on the rumour, sell on the fact . . . it's better to travel than to arrive.'

'The trend is your friend but you've got to be in it to win it.'

'Banque Inutile claim United Utilities has a sustainable dividend yield of seven per cent? Frankly, if something sounds too good to be true then it probably is.'

'The FD's never going to stand down. Quitters never win and winners never quit.'

'Why is it going up? Because there are more buyers than sellers.'

Benjamin's contribution to the team was not just his mindless repetition of our pointless gibberish; he really was helping us win. I was happy with the way everything was progressing and things were just about to get even better. It was bonus time and those idiotic Yanks at Megashite decided in their infinite wisdom to give me £650,000. My God! But actually, by this stage I was beginning to believe my own hype. For the first time in my career I concluded that I was probably worth that money. In fact, I was sure there were people out there earning more than me who were not as good. I did the usual mock-horror act when Chuck told me the number but such was my ego that there was an element of genuine outrage in my voice! Anyway, the bottom line was that everything was shaping up nicely; it seemed like nothing could go wrong.

*

'Er, Steve, can I have a quick word please?' Michael looked shifty as he said this. We went into an unused office together – my heart beginning to race. It was the day after the bonus had actually gone into our bank accounts. I'm no Sherlock Holmes but I knew exactly what Michael was going to say.

'Look, Steve, you've probably guessed what I'm about to say. It's been a great ride but it's time to call it a day. I'm going back to being a management consultant. It's been a lot of fun but I've got a young family now and I've secured a deal with Ernst & Young that's going to leave me more time to spend with the wife and kids. I'm sorry, mate, I know how much getting that number one Extel ranking means to you, but I've got to ultimately think about what's best for me and the missus.'

FUCK! Of all the appalling things that he could have said, that was surely the worst. He could have told me that nuclear war was about to break out and that we had four minutes to live and it would have been preferable. He could have told me that I had contracted Ebola and I would have laughed with uncontrollable glee. But to tell me that he was not going to be here to garner votes for Extel meant Hugo was going to win and that was simply unacceptable. Goddam it, I had to think and think fast.

'Listen, Michael, I understand you want to do all that family nonsense. That's all cool with the gang and me, but you can't just piss off now. Not just before our moment of victory. You're on a three-month contract, right? Cool, then I am pleading with you on bended knee that you work up until mid-April helping this team get to number one. That's only another couple of months. Please, please help me. I've got to beat that wanker Hugo if it's the last fucking thing I ever do!' I was literally kneeling on both knees with tears in my eyes when I said this. A passing secretary glanced through the office's glass door, saw me on my knees in front of a standing Michael, and giggled to herself.

'Shit. You really, really want to beat Mighty Yankbank, don't you? I'll tell you what, if you can get Chuck to guarantee me in writing that my unvested equity in Megashite will not be forfeit when I leave then I'll stick around and we'll beat that tosser together.'

'O frabjous day! Callooh! Callay!' I chortled in my joy. I also noticed that my old, trusty pal Michael had become a bit greedy and Machiavellian in his old age. I suppose even the best of us cannot remain unaffected when you're surrounded day in, day out by hideous greed.

Now all that was left for me to do was to entertain clients like I'd never entertained before. I didn't care if they were pointless little muppets with a minor weighting in the survey. I lunched them all and took them to rugby and football games every fucking weekend. If these bastards voted for anyone other than me there would be hell to pay. Shit, I probably spent more cash on some of those fuckers than the commission they gave my bank. When I heard that Hugo was out and about entertaining too and that the whole Mighty Yankbank team were marketing like billy-oh, it just added grist to my mill. By April my liver must have resembled some sort of diseased rotting bag of shit while the inside of my nostrils were so raw that I had a permanent runny nose. My night-time torturers became almost daily visitors as I strove to secure victory. I was killing myself but if it took dying to win then I'd do that. Nothing was going to stop me, not even death!

And so the great day arrived: 9 June 2004. I had not been able to sleep the night before. Hugo had sent a little text message at 10 p.m. saying, 'If not now, then when? If not you, then who, little man?' My reply was slightly less enigmatic and marginally less poetic: 'FUCK OFF.' On the morning of that fateful day I could do no work. All I did was clock watch and the minutes seemed to take hours. At precisely 11.55 a.m. Michael and I took the DLR from Canary Wharf to Bank and then walked solemnly to the Guildhall on Gresham Street. We sat ourselves down at a round table right at the front of the hall by the podium with eight other analysts from Megashite and tried to eat the gruel that was served up. My stomach was so tense that I simply could not consume the insipid prawn cocktail nor the rubbery chicken Kiev. We had to endure some piss-poor speech by some venture capitalist complaining about there being too many regulations in the City. My arse, I thought, we've got too few barriers to wrong-doing. However, in stark contrast to the previous times when I'd considered this a negative issue that needed to be addressed I now thought that 'light' regulation was probably a good thing. That's because lax regulation was helping London to overtake New York as the financial capital of the world and that process, in turn, was helping to line my silk pockets with untold wonga. When the speech finished I saw Hugo go to the toilets and I followed him in. He was at one of the urinals when I opened the door: 'How do you feel, Hugo? The only thing smaller than what you currently hold in your hand will be your pathetic ego once you've lost to me.'

'Silly boy. I look forward to taking your money off you and buying myself another Ferrari . . . you're such a loser you'll never miss an opportunity to miss an opportunity!'

He laughed as he said this, pushed me out of his way, and went back into the main hall.

His confidence was intimidating. Did he know the result already somehow? Suddenly feeling slightly uneasy I followed him back and sat myself down at my table.

Finally, it came around to the presentation of the awards. My big moment was coming and my stomach was doing loop the loops. I had been glancing over at Hugo's table every few minutes and feeling terribly envious of his relaxed demeanour and roaring head-back guffaws. Since the awards were being handed out by sector in alphabetical order we utilities boys would be the very last to hear our result. I couldn't help but feel that this was inevitable – that somehow God had decreed it such. As I heard the lucky winners being named for every other sector in the market my mind drifted off to when all this had begun. To my public humiliation at the Balmoral. To a game of golf in Scotland. To a sewage treatment works outside Edinburgh. I suddenly realised that that experience had been driving me for six years and that my life had been dictated by somebody else. I understood that I had lost myself during the journey. But it didn't matter. I was going to reach closure now. Everything was going to be OK. I was going to prove to myself and everyone else that I was a winner, that I was a great man, that I was a hero.

'. . . and finally, the winner for best-ranked utilities team is . . .'

I could barely watch, such was my hideous nervousness. I gripped the bottom of my chair until my knuckles went white. Even calm old Michael next to me looked unbelievably tense. There were people on other tables talking amongst themselves. I shushed them. How dare they make a noise at my moment of triumph?

'. . . and this is by the narrowest margin ever recorded by Extel . . .'

Just get on with it you fucking idiot.

'Mighty Yankbank with Hugo Bentley ranked as the number-one-rated analyst. We should make a special mention for Megashite who missed out by just 0.1 per cent, and Steve Jones who was the second-highest-ranked individual analyst. This is the eighth time in a row that these guys have been the top-ranked utilities team. They also get the overall award for receiving the most amount of votes across all sectors in the market. So please, put your hands together for Hugo Bentley and the Mighty Yankbank utilities team.'

I felt as if I had died. Nothing has ever felt as bad before or after that terrible day. My insides turned to liquid. I desperately tried to hold the tears back, but I couldn't do it. I sat there with my head in my hands, sobbing like a little girl in front of two hundred of my esteemed peers. I was never going to live this down. Michael put his arm around me which didn't really help things. Somehow my supposed moment of glory was turning into the biggest humiliation that I, or anyone else, had ever experienced.

Hugo calmly strode up to the podium, which was just in front of my table, with the kind of cheesy grin on his face that would have been the envy of Tony Blair. This time, instead of walking off after his usual curt 'thank you', he chose to rub my nose in it.

'This is a great honour. Thank you very much. We at Mighty Yankbank take these awards pretty seriously . . . though perhaps not as much as some people,' he said, looking directly at me, with a huge triumphant grin on his face.

The whole hall erupted into laughter and I went a shade of red that was so bright that, if it had been seen on television, millions would have turned the colour setting down assuming that it was artificially intense. And with that Hugo left the podium clutching his award and laughing hysterically at his own hilarious gag. As he passed my table he stopped, patted me on the back and whispered in my ear, 'I'll see you outside now. Bring your fucking chequebook.'

Once the uncontrollable sobbing had subsided and most people had left, I put my jacket on and dragged myself towards the exit. I had spent the previous ten minutes with my head in my hands cursing the gods, my parents, fate, destiny, Hugo, Michael – anyone or anything that I could blame for the unbearably deep hurt that I felt. Before I got up I wrote a cheque out to Hugo Bentley for 'one hundred thousand pounds only'. I emerged into the sunlight blinking. Outside, Hugo was leaning against a pillar, with one leg crossed over the other looking as cool as a cucumber. I reluctantly ambled towards him holding the cheque out with outstretched hand.

'Thank you for that,' Hugo said, calmly folding the cheque up and placing it in his breast pocket. I turned to leave, unable to speak or think.

'Before you go I want you to understand something. You hate me, but, my poor friend, you've become worse than me. You take this job more seriously than I do. To me it's just a way of making money but you're obsessed. Look at yourself with your bespoke suit and your £300 shoes. I hear from our client base that you used to be left-wing and a bit of a hippy traveller. You don't know who you are any more and that's why you lost. Just because you are a character doesn't mean you have character, little man.'

And with that, he spun around and high-tailed out of there. I just stood there staring at the ground. I knew that he was right. I knew that I was a straw man. I knew that my personality had become so corrupted by anger and bullshit that there was no space left for the good things in me. I immediately walked to Bank tube station and took a train homeward. I walked out at Shepherd's Bush, got on my scooter, which was parked just outside, and drove as fast as I possibly could towards the river. I passed my old school, Latymer Upper, and soon arrived at Hammersmith Bridge. I parked and walked along it until I reached its middle. I then stopped, folded my arms, rested my chin on the balustrade, and stared westward.

I don't know how long I stayed there and I don't really know what I was doing. I'm not sure if I ever really seriously considered jumping. I do remember thinking about it and at that precise moment I heard the cox of a Latymer boat passing underneath shouting encouragement to his rowers: 'Come on, guys! Let's get serious. One pull at a time. We'll get there in the end.'

That's right. We'll get there in the end, I thought, and slowly walked back to my scooter.

Five minutes later I was doing about forty mph along King Street. Suddenly, without warning, I awoke lying on my back, staring at the ceiling of an ambulance. My hands were bloodied and bandaged, my trousers were ripped badly around my right knee and my bottom lip felt massively swollen. A copper was trying to force a breathalyser into my mouth. So that's why I was suddenly conscious, I remember thinking. My good old survival instinct was kicking in. I'd nervously drunk at least a bottle of white wine at the Extel lunch and was over the limit. On seeing the policeman and realising that I could get nicked I had effectively woken myself out of the dream that I was having. Apparently, although I was out cold for about thirty seconds after my head hit the tarmac, I had been having a quite normal conversation with the ambulance men since the crash, though I remember none of it. I immediately pretended to be unable to blow properly complaining that my lip was too mashed. After two further failed attempts the paramedic in charge said, 'For God's sake, this man is hurt. We need to take him to hospital right now.' It only took twenty minutes to get to Charing Cross Hospital but it was almost forty minutes before the next breath test was done. When the results came out borderline but negative I thanked the Lord. However, when I looked at my right knee and saw right down to the knee cap I was slightly less inclined to thank the great stockbroker in the sky.

I think those three days I spent in hospital may have saved my life. I was definitely on the point of having some kind of nervous breakdown, for I had become a monster. I had fucked up the best relationship I might ever have. I had betrayed my boss – a perfectly good man. I had become obsessed by beating some arsehole whom I should have just simply ignored. I had lost most of my old friends and all of my old ideals. I had severely disappointed my lovely, loving family. I had become obsessed by pointless horseshit like money and status. I hadn't given a thought about anyone other than me for months, if not years. I had developed the kind of coke habit that Pete Doherty would deem excessive. The City had chewed me up and spat me out. I had become someone the old me would have crossed the street to avoid.

It took meeting people so much more unfortunate than myself in my eight-man hospital ward to make me realise just how twisted my world view had become and what an ungrateful bastard I was. In my trauma ward there was an unfortunate Polish bloke who didn't have a pot to piss in and who had just broken his back in some building accident. The poor cunt was never going to walk again and no one ever visited him. He couldn't speak a word of the Queen's English, yet he still somehow managed to break a smile and keep some semblance of positivity. What right did I have to feel sorry for myself when I'd be walking fine in two months? As I sat in my hospital bed contemplating the selfish, greedy idiot I had become I decided that the only solution to my problems was to give up my Cityboy world and become a 'civilian' again. I realised that the process of becoming a 'big swinging dick' by definition necessitates one becoming a dick and that I most definitely had made that transition. I needed to leave the City and rediscover the good things in life and maybe even try and do the world some good. My scooter crash was an epiphany and I would emerge from it, like a phoenix from the flames, a new man . . . or rather my old self.

Of course, most of us Cityboys talk about retiring or moving on to something more creative or worthwhile at thirty-five or forty, but very few of us actually do so. We're constantly trapped by a lack of alternatives and the vast amounts of wedge those nasty bosses keep throwing at us at the end of each year. We're like old bank robbers who stay on to do 'just one last job' but never actually give up because we're addicted to the buzz, the money, the lifestyle. It is a commonplace tragedy that we Cityboys throw away the best years of our lives and destroy our health while creating fantasies about what we'll do once we retire. Before you know it you're forty-five with two divorces under your belt and obliged to keep working in that terrible industry for little Tarquin and Henrietta's school fees and the ex-wives' alimony.

Funnily enough, it was a conversation on my last day in hospital with my left-wing father, who, I thought, would fully support my decision to quit, that stymied my determination to leave the City. He came and sat by my bedside and asked me how I was. As soon as I mentioned my plan to leave for pastures new he grimaced slightly and in a calm, measured way explained why I should reconsider.

'Listen, Steve, you're thirty-one now and earning over half a million pounds a year. Unless you've got football skills that I'm unaware of, no other job will give you that kind of a salary. If you leave now, you'll have to start another career at the bottom of the ladder probably earning less than a tenth of what you currently earn and competing with people ten years younger than you. Do you really have the energy to do that? Won't you find that morbidly depressing? Why don't you do another three or four years in the City and then leave knowing you've saved enough to give yourself options? Then you could give something back to society. I don't agree with the disproportionate cash that people in the City earn and nor am I a big fan of the system that they both represent and exploit. I particularly hate the negative impact that Cityboys' conspicuous consumption has on other Londoners but the revolution isn't going to happen any time soon. You're in that system now . . . use it for a bit and then use what you've learned and the cash you've earned to do something good.'

'But Dad, the City really does change you. I've lost sight of everything you or Mum hold dear. I look at the things I've done over the last years and I really don't like what I see . . . what I've become.'

'Nonsense. You may have got a little caught up in the whole thing for a few years, and I won't pretend that the whole family weren't concerned, but I think you're back now. Do three more years and set yourself up for life. Then think about what you really want to do. In the meantime, sell the Porsche, give some money to charity, keep your head down and keep your nose clean.'

I still don't know to this day whether my father's last piece of advice was a subtle acknowledgement that he was aware of my cocaine addiction or whether it was just a turn of phrase. After we hugged and he left I pondered his advice. He was right, of course. I didn't have any alternative ideas about what I'd do with my life. To leave then would have been pretty damn foolish on many levels. I was at the top of my game and the job was just getting easier and easier. The hard work I'd already done meant I knew my sector like the back of my hand and seven years of eating foie gras and watching Kylie and Madonna gyrate around had resulted in numerous strong client relationships. I would take my foot off the pedal and treat the job as a source of income – nothing more, nothing less. I'd hand in my resignation in 2007 or 2008 having hopefully spent the time up to then reconsidering my options and formulating a new life plan. Maybe in the meantime I'd attack the system from within by dishing the dirt via an anonymous column and eventually, perhaps, a book . . .

I hobbled back into work on crutches three weeks after the accident and was welcomed back like a wounded soldier. While convalescing at home I had begun the long and arduous process of recovering my marbles and was just about sufficiently together to go through the motions at work. My secretary had arranged for a card to be signed by most of the people in the office (very few of whom I actually knew) which, together with the regular stream of colleagues who came to my desk to ask how I was, almost made me feel liked. The crying incident was never mentioned again though I have no doubt that most of my colleagues were aware of it. I slowly settled back into the routine of a stockbroker's life but now I lacked the callous ambition and ruthless determination that had both made me a damn fine broker and a total prick. Michael was no longer there to help and that would certainly impact the team but my previous misplaced goal to be a number-one-rated god had been replaced by a simple wish to earn some cash and then get the fuck out.

And, I suppose, I should thank God that I decided to stay. The good times really did roll in the City between 2004 and 2007 and, despite my team falling down the rankings somewhat, I (and pretty much every other Cityboy out there) made disgustingly good money. The commodity bubble helped ensure that the utilities sector outperformed for another three years and we sat back and reaped the rewards of a trend that pushed up the utility sector's commission levels and had nothing to do with our 'brilliance'.

The only recent downer was the fallout related to the subprime crisis and the related credit crunch. There can be little doubt that the multi-billion-dollar write-offs from the major banks, the run on 'Northern Rock' (the first run on a British bank since 1866) and the fall of several banking chief executives really are perfect examples of 'chickens coming home to roost'. The banks' attempts to make profits by granting loans to American trailer trash who couldn't afford them reminds us that short-term unbridled greed is alive and well and living in Wall Street. We may find out soon that the actions of a few greedy bankers have helped result in a major recession that causes untold misery as businesses fail and jobs are lost across the world. The recent fall of the major American bank Bear Sterns could be the first of many. It makes me feel that the lessons of the Enron debacle have all been conveniently forgotten, which tends to be the case when short-term profiteering is the order of the day.

Fortunately for me, these problems made my decision to leave the City in early 2008 all the easier. I gave up taking forecasts seriously a long time ago but the next years really look like they're going to be no bed of roses. A combination of sky-high oil prices, the credit crunch and a declining US economy do not bode well for near-term stock market performance and hence bonuses. In fact, I wouldn't be surprised if we had a major stock-market 'correction' in the next two years that resulted in a clear-out of the mid-tier investment banks and many Cityboys involuntarily having to 'reconsider their options'. No bad thing perhaps.

So I spent three and a half more years in the hell-hole that is the City. I kept my head down and did everything I could to prevent myself from turning back into the beast that I had once become. I gave up Class-A drugs and even started going to the odd yoga class. I occasionally bumped into Hugo but our game had been played out and there was no more aggressive, competitive banter. He had won the contest but perhaps I had ultimately won because I was never going to feel the need to play such games again, while Hugo was still embroiled in that pointless, competitive world. Well, I suppose if I keep telling myself that bollocks long enough I might eventually come to believe it! All in all, those last few years were fairly uneventful and I cruised along becoming less and less motivated. Essentially, I retired in 2004 . . . it's just that I forgot to tell my bank.

On 31 January 2008, I calmly walked into the office as if nothing was afoot. At precisely 9.45 a.m. I went to the local Barclays to ensure that my bonus in lieu of 2007 was sitting pretty in my bank account. It was the biggest one I'd ever received. On finding out that all was hunky dory, I returned to the huge phallic tower that housed Megashite, marched into Chuck's office and handed in my letter of resignation. As usual, every trick in the book was thrown at me to persuade me to stay but they gave up reasonably quickly once they'd realised that I was determined to move on to better, though not necessarily bigger, things. My conversation with Chuck was like two alien species interacting; my former boss was completely unable to comprehend why his arguments about money and promotion now meant absolutely nothing to me.

My last day at Megashite was 20 March 2008. The buggers had made me work a few weeks just to smooth the transition to a new leader and so that my Extel votes were not entirely lost. The previous night's leaving drinks had been renamed 'Steve's retirement party' and I spent the entire time hearing from colleagues and clients alike that they wished that they had the balls to do what I was doing. I told them that it was easier for me to leave than stay but that just received dumbfounded looks of miscomprehension.

On my very last day, I packed what remained of my stuff into an old sports bag and bid my team 'adieu'. The looks of intro-spection on my colleagues' faces as I said goodbye suggested that my radical change of direction had forced them to review their own situations – though few seemed likely to give up the comfortable routine that earning big bucks in a high-powered job provided.

Still, there was one person whom I thought I could perhaps influence. He represented the next generation of brokers and if I could just make one individual fully understand the iniquities of the system then that would at least be a start. I decided to take Benjamin out for an early afternoon drink and plead with him not to make the same terrible mistakes that I had made. This time I wasn't popping into the toilets every ten minutes because the days of being a cokehead were well and truly over though I was, perhaps, somewhat overly exuberant, having had quite a few drinks at lunchtime.

'Benjamin, you've got to get out of this place while you can. It's evil. It's disgusting. You still seem like a nice kid even after a few years of this bullshit, but so was I when I joined up and look what happened to me! This system that we're supporting . . . that we're promoting . . . that we're part of . . . it's . . . it's destroying the world. It's destroying people. We're just going to consume more and more and create bigger and bigger disparities in wealth. It can only end in either bloodshed or environmental disaster. Smart people like you and me need to fight on the right side or we're doomed. WE'RE ALL DOOMED! D'YOU HEAR ME?'

On reflection, I may have laid it on a bit thick! But I suppose

I was not really totally out of the woods, even at that point – it has taken a couple of months back in Goa and out of the Square Mile to calm myself down and fully rediscover who I once was.

Of course, Benjamin didn't listen. In fact, he made a rather convincing case that I was being a hypocritical son-of-a-bitch who was only leaving after having reaped the rewards of the system and made my millions. Frankly, I have to admit that I'm still struggling somewhat with this particular accusation . . . though I hope that perhaps in a few years' time I'll have formulated a vaguely persuasive counter-argument! I suppose I could mention the fact that I plan to donate a decent proportion of my ill-gotten gains to 'charidee' . . . though, of course, I would never do so publicly since, like all good Radio 1 DJs, I really don't like to talk about that.

Benjamin's still working at Megashite and doing very well for himself. I wouldn't be surprised if he became a team leader somewhere in a few years' time. People have to make their own mistakes, I suppose. They never learn from other people's errors. That's one of the tragedies that dictates the human experience.

EPILOGUE
(The Hippy)

I've calmed down a lot since I first started writing this book. Two months spent mostly on a beach in Goa will tend to have that effect. There is a word used out here that is supposed to best sum up the locals' attitude to life: '*susegad*'. This apparently derives from the Portuguese word '*socegado*' and means, according to the *Lonely Planet* guide, 'relax and enjoy life while you can'. I couldn't possibly agree more! It has definitely rubbed off on me and I reckon most of us in the West could all do with a little injection of it. It's this perspective on life combined with the sun, the sea and a fat Enfield motorbike that have helped me slowly but surely rediscover the better aspects of my clearly corruptible personality. I've begun to process those crazy years in that crazy job. I actually feel stronger than ever before – I suppose once you've temporarily lost your mind nothing can ever really touch you again.

I've also moderated my views somewhat. I now recognise that the City is the only industry that our God-forsaken little country has got left and that it brings in shedloads of tax revenue for hospitals and schools. I also don't think Cityboys and the City are evil per se. They're mainly just a symptom of an economic

297

system that will, if left unmoderated, inevitably create an extremely unhealthy and violent society while destroying the environment through global warming and pollution. Still, politicians and the City regulators have got to do more to ensure that the worst abuses that I witnessed, such as insider trading, tax avoidance and false rumour spreading, are clamped down upon. If this does not occur a corrupt and socially poisonous place will just become more so – leading to ever-greater resentment and dissatisfaction from those standing outside the Square Mile with their metaphorical begging bowls, envying our opulence and begrudging us our boundless greed.

Of course, only a wholesale change to the overall system will make society genuinely healthier and fairer but unfortunately this will almost certainly remain just a pipe-dream despite ever-worsening imbalances. Still, small improvements can have a positive impact. I don't believe the tired, old arguments that moderately higher top-end UK tax rates or tighter regulation of the City will result in Frankfurt or Paris becoming the new financial centres of Europe (although ill-conceived dramatic changes could have this unwanted outcome). The reality is that the Square Mile is much more resilient than the doom-mongers like to claim and is, in fact, currently thriving better than ever before. However, moderate reforms will only slightly improve the situation and hence it really is up to the individual Cityboy to make a difference. If enough Cityboys across the world moderate their conspicuous consumption, pay all their taxes and give some of their ill-gotten gains to charity then perhaps society can evolve into a more pleasant place without the catalyst of violent insurrection or environmental disaster.

Shakespeare hit the nail on the head when he pointed out that we humans are primitive beasts but are also angels who are 'noble in reason . . . infinite in faculty'. We have the capacity to do wonderful, altruistic things but are also subject to our base, animal urges. This is perfectly reflected by the Internet. Humans created this most amazing invention and then we initially used it mainly to beat off to porn with. We're just chimps whose brains' frontal lobe mutated about two and a half million years ago, granting us both consciousness and a hideous awareness of our own mortality. As well as inventing gods and preoccupations to maintain our sanity, we invented the wheel, weapons, and eventually stock markets to sell our products in. That we can be greedy, selfish swines should come as no surprise. The City merely facilitates that process and does it in such an extreme and conspicuous way that all those around us feel that they're working in McJobs and find it near impossible not to become resentful and dissatisfied. What we Cityboys need to do is to acknowledge the negative impact our endless selfish greed has on society and try to rediscover our more angelic potential.

Unfortunately, for 'non-Cityboys' all the alternative economic systems have been discredited and now *laissez-faire* capitalism rules the globe. It has been forty long, hard years since there was a genuine attempt in the West to create a fairer socio-economic system that allows the majority, and not just the privileged few, to thrive. The attempted revolutions of 1968 may have set the world on a less racist, sexist and homophobic path but they singularly failed to fundamentally change a system that invariably encourages selfishness and a lack of sympathy for our fellow man. We are now all Thatcher's children and view consumption and the accumulation of wealth as the one true path to fulfilment. Likewise, Milton Friedman's view that companies should attempt to do nothing socially beneficial unless it serves to enrich their shareholders seems *de rigueur*. Nearly everybody simply wants to be rich and little else. When our 2.4 billion brothers and sisters in China and India grow wealthier and, understandably, demand their fridges and cars, then the world really will be totally fucked. How the environment can possibly sustain such a vast and growing 'human stain' is imponderable. Society will also suffer because, although regulations may moderate free-market excess somewhat, the gap between the very rich and the poor will simply continue to get wider and wider. Money makes money and capitalism requires growth. Soon, if trends are not reversed, we will live in Aldous Huxley's *Brave New World* with super-rich 'Alphas' living in gated communities and running the show, whilst 'Epsilons' clean our bogs. Since it is mainly white, middle-class people like me who will inevitably be at the top of the heap you may not hear that many complaints from a certain branch of well-educated commentators about the growing inequities in our society and its developing economic apartheid. Of course, such is the elite's self-interest in maintaining the status quo that it will take a truly massive crisis before our leaders consider tangible change to be deemed necessary. We'll need street violence that makes the Poll Tax riots look like a Cub Scouts convention before politicians consider fairer social policies and America won't sign up to Kyoto until New York's under six feet of water.

I genuinely think that the period I witnessed in the City was an extraordinary one. Those were truly exciting times as the markets reeled from the Internet bubble through to 9/11, Enron, the Iraq war (itself the logical result of the capitalist world's insatiable hunger for oil) and the sub-prime crisis. In truth, however, there is rarely a dull period in the City as markets shape, and react to, world-changing events. The problem is that these events have been accelerating at a frightening rate over the last century and look set to really go into overdrive now. If, on the off chance, I manage to live for another few decades, I believe I will see some of the most momentous developments that this planet has ever witnessed. Life, as always, will be cruel but interesting. I imagine that events will become so overwhelming that the only choice we will have will be whether to laugh or cry. I hope to be able to do what I've done all my life, which is to take the former option.

On a more personal note, I have to confess that there is a

small chance that I will regret giving up my lucrative career . . . but, frankly, I doubt it. If there's one thing I've learned it's that money and happiness do not walk hand in hand. The tragedy of the insidious influence that money holds on society is that when you don't have it you can think of little else and this often results in the conclusion, confirmed daily by the mass media, that only cash can bring contentment. Hence relatively poor people can sometimes feel no need to look at other aspects of their lives when assessing why it is that they feel discontented or unfulfilled. The falseness of this conclusion explains why lottery winners are often provided with counselling immediately on winning the jackpot. If you have ascribed your life-long unhappiness to your relative impoverishment and then discover that overnight enrichment fails to bring instant joy it forces you to reflect on what is truly missing from your life. I would argue that a deeper, more spiritual sense of fulfilment based on age-old concepts like love, friendship, 'physicality' and the discovery of ourselves and the world we inhabit may prove more successful – though, of course, what works for me may have little to do with what works for you.

Anyway, one pleasing outcome of this book is that it will well and truly burn all my bridges. I can't imagine any City firm wanting to hire me after I've just spent several hundred pages revealing what a bunch of corrupt, greedy motherfuckers my former peers are while detailing my pharmaceutical excess. If, in a moment of weakness, I seek to rejoin my profitable career, I somehow suspect I won't be welcome.

The other potential pleasing upshot of writing this book is that I may now be deemed an 'artist'. This has long been an aspiration – not because of the kudos that such a title bestows. No, rather it's the fact that, as far as I can see, 'artists' get away with blue murder. Infidelity can be explained away because 'normal social conventions don't apply to artists' while drunken, boorish behaviour is acceptable because the perpetrator is 'awfully creative, don't you know'. Being an 'artist' sounds like a get-out-of-jail-free card and my analytical ability is still sufficiently lucid for me to want a piece of that action.

Artists also seem to work fairly good hours which is more than could be said for the average Cityboy, who slaves away for up to seventy hours a week. Despite the high pay, I find this use of one's precious time breathtakingly extraordinary. What's even worse is that discussions with pals in 'normal' relatively underpaid office jobs suggest that the general populace has also got the work-life balance horribly wrong. We Brits work longer and harder than pretty much everyone else in Europe and, undoubtedly, many of us live to work rather than work to live. Unfortunately, when I travel on the tube I don't see many cheerful people and most surveys suggest that the majority of workers aren't happy in their jobs. If you take it as read that life is remarkably short, that it is not a dress rehearsal and that you may get run over by a bus tomorrow, I find it truly amazing that so many people choose to engage such a high proportion of their time doing things they simply don't enjoy when they should be 'gathering ye rose buds' while they may. While a need to pay the rent and put food in children's mouths may explain this phenomenon for much of the population we Cityboys never have that excuse since anyone remotely successful should be able to call it a day before forty unless, that is, they've developed a serious Charlie habit or have spent all their cash on slow horses and fast women.

Of course, the reason most Cityboys keep accumulating more and more wealth even though they could retire is greed and its bed-fellow, materialism. These two hideous vices walk side by side with what became my own personal bugbear – competitiveness. I truly believe that competitiveness in all its forms is fucking up this beautiful planet. My battle against Hugo was just the manifestation of this particularly pernicious human trait. The need for a bigger motor, a fitter bird or even more nuclear warheads, will either destroy the world slowly as CO_2 levels keep rising or destroy it real quickly when some wanker presses the button. I've spent three years trying to exorcise the evil of competitiveness out of my system but it ain't easy. It seems such a powerful ingrained force, especially in men, that overcoming it may take a lifetime. Amusingly, I've recently met hippies out here who are competitive with each other over how little they have and how cheaply they're living! This is a more environmentally friendly twist on conventional competitiveness but is still pretty pathetic since their actions are being dictated by a similarly childish need to impress those around them (and there is nothing more uncool than trying to be cool). It just happens to be that in Goa it is how little you claim to have that supposedly gains the respect of your peers – the mirror image of what happens in the City and the West in general. Of course, it is my awareness that all forms of competitiveness derive from feelings of inadequacy and insecurity that serves to make its presence in my personality so very painful. Interestingly, I recently met an old hippy out here who asked me what I was 'seeking'. When I told him 'I want peace of mind', he giggled slightly and, without hesitation, said, 'I – ego, want – desire . . . lose these and you shall have peace of mind.' I've tried to start that process but I reckon that losing the two things that have run my life, and the lives of most of the other jokers living on this sorry planet, may take a little bit of time!

Anyway, this book is the first step in my attempt to do 'something good'. The battle has not yet been won by the forces of darkness. There is hope. I have met so many young people out here who are aware of the need to do something positive that I, against my better instincts, actually feel vaguely optimistic. I am no longer convinced that the light at the end of the tunnel is, in fact, a fast-approaching train. We genuinely can make a difference.

Frankly, I'm not sure what I'm going to do next but I do

know this: although the trends for humankind do not look positive, standing on the sidelines is simply no longer an option. I'm now ready to rejoin the 'real world'. I know that whatever I do choose to do will not involve fucking people over or destroying this beautiful rock we inhabit. That much is absolutely certain.

It may sound unbelievably trite but all that my journey has shown me so far is that love is everything – love for ourselves, for each other and for this planet. Love is what adds meaning to life and what makes life worth living. Everything else is just tittle tattle.

ACKNOWLEDGEMENTS

Big thanks (and apologies) to Toby, Nick, Angus, Jim, Razzall, Jerome, Uppy and Warren – all of whom have unwittingly been providing me with most of the gags in this book for many years. I want to thank all my ex-colleagues and clients from the City for providing the raw material for this book. I'm sorry if I make you out to be a bunch of tossers when quite a few of you are actually decent folk (but I had a point to make . . .). I won't mention any names because most of you are still making millions and you may be tainted by association, but you know who you are.

Major thanks to Piers Blofeld (crazy name, crazy guy) at Headline who first approached me with a view to writing this book and Ross Hulbert who publicised it like a demon. Thanks too to Martin Deeson and my agent Lizzy Kremer at David Higham Associates, as well as the lovely folk at *thelondonpaper* (especially Bridget, Stefan and Lisa) who gave me the opportunity in my 'City boy' column to get a lot of things off my chest that could otherwise have resulted in a major nervous breakdown.

Finally, I must offer my most sincere thanks to my wonderful parents, brothers, uncles and aunts who made me the man I am today. I've asked you not to read this book . . . but if you do please rest assured that all the bits about sex and drugs had nothing to do with me, honest.

If you have any thoughts regarding this book please contact me on cityboy69@hotmail.co.uk.